D0187663

Exploring Lincoln

The North's Civil War

Andrew L. Slap, series editor

A LINCOLN FORUM BOOK

Exploring Lincoln

Great Historians Reappraise Our Greatest President

EDITED BY

Harold Holzer, Craig L. Symonds,

AND

Frank J. Williams

FORDHAM UNIVERSITY PRESS
New York • 2015

Frontispiece: Abraham Lincoln, ca. 1863, photograph by Lewis E. Walker, Washington, D.C. (Library of Congress)

Copyright © 2015 Fordham University Press

Library of Congress Cataloging-in-Publication Data

Exploring Lincoln : great historians reappraise our greatest president / edited by Harold Holzer, Craig L. Symonds, and Frank J. Williams. — First edition.
          pages cm. — (The North's Civil War)
     Includes bibliographical references and index.
       ISBN 978-0-8232-6562-6 (cloth : alk. paper) —
       ISBN 978-0-8232-6563-3 (pbk. : alk. paper)
 1. Lincoln, Abraham, 1809–1865—Influence.   2. United States—Politics and government—1861–1865.   3. Political leadership—United States—History—19th century.   4. Presidents—United States—Biography.
 I. Holzer, Harold, editor, author.   II. Symonds, Craig L., editor, author.
          III. Williams, Frank J., editor, author.
                    E457.E96   2015
                   973.7092—dc23
                    2014033578

Printed in the United States of America

17 16 15   5 4 3 2 1

First edition

Contents

Introduction

Harold Holzer, Craig L. Symonds, and Frank J. Williams

HE IS BOTH UBIQUITOUS AND ENIGMATIC. HE IS AS FAMILIAR as the penny and the five-dollar bill: at once instantly recognizable—yet he is elusive as a chimera. The historical Lincoln, the literary Lincoln, even the cinematic Lincoln, have all proved both fascinating and irresistible. Though some sixteen thousand books have been written about him and more than a dozen major motion pictures (including one depicting him as a vampire hunter) have been released, there is always more to say, new aspects of his life to consider, new facets of his persona to explore.

The Lincoln Forum, a national organization with more than one thousand members, meets in Gettysburg each fall on the anniversary of Lincoln's most famous speech, to provide (as its name suggests) a public forum for these considerations. This volume offers a selection of sixteen of the papers that have been presented at this annual meeting over the past three years. They are arranged more or less chronologically, beginning with a reconsideration of Lincoln's 1860 campaign, by William C. Harris, and ending with an essay about the psychological demons of his wife Mary Todd Lincoln, by Jason Emerson. Yet the purpose of this volume is not to provide yet another biography of the sixteenth president or even a history of his presidency. It is, rather, to shine a light on particular aspects of Lincoln and his sadly abbreviated presidency in the hope that these essays will provoke new thinking, new scholarship, and new understanding.

Several of the essays deal with Lincoln as a commander-in-chief. This is hardly surprising considering that his entire presidency was dominated by the most traumatic war in our nation's history. John Marszalek looks at the tool Lincoln was handed upon the outbreak of war. The prewar army (ever after called the Old Army) was a small constabulary force located almost exclusively on the western plains or the coastal forts. This had to be converted into a tool for fighting and winning a continental struggle along a thousand-mile front. John Waugh examines Lincoln's difficult, even maddening, relationship with McClellan, who commanded this new mass army from the summer of 1861 to the fall of 1862. William C. "Jack" Davis offers a thoughtful look at Lincoln's counterpart, Jefferson Davis, to illuminate Davis's relationship with his principal general, Robert E. Lee. One can only imagine how different events might have been if Lincoln had had Lee to command his armies and Davis had been saddled (no pun intended) with McClellan. Craig Symonds looks at how Lincoln sought to manage the men who ran the Union Navy.

Other essays in this volume deal with Lincoln as a political animal. Despite the nineteenth-century hagiography that sought to elevate Lincoln into a demigod above mere politics, recent scholarship has demonstrated conclusively that Lincoln was an active politician, that he cared about politics, even at the local level, and that he was ever sensitive to the influence of other events on the political balance of power. William C. Harris profiles Lincoln's role in the election of 1860 that made him president. Seward's biographer, Walter Stahr, explores Lincoln's relationship with the man some called "the Premier" of the administration, and Harold Holzer explores Lincoln's curious and sometimes fraught relationship with politics in Seward's New York.

Of all the issues Lincoln had to deal with as president, surely the most important, and the most difficult, was the slavery question. Lincoln hated slavery. Nevertheless, politician that he was, he knew that if he moved too fast against it he might alienate both the War Democrats in the North and the border states, and he was convinced that he needed both on his side to save the Union. On the other hand, if he moved too slowly, he might miss a priceless opportunity. How Lincoln used his sensitivity as well as his political skill to balance these pressures is the subject of three superb essays by Eric Foner, Amanda Foreman, and Richard Striner.

Other issues in this volume range over a wide spectrum. Frank Williams combs through Lincoln's law cases to assess him as a bench judge. Michael J. Kline offers a reconsideration of the so-called Baltimore Plot: Was there, in fact, a credible threat to the president-elect in Baltimore as he made his way to Washington? John Stauffer offers a fascinating look at the origins and cultural significance of Julia Ward Howe's "Battle Hymn of the Republic," and Barnet Schecter investigates the origin and the effects of the New York City draft riots in July 1863 after the Battle of Gettysburg. Finally, Catherine Clinton offers a thoughtful analysis of how the more than seven hundred thousand deaths during the war gave new meaning to mourning in nineteenth-century America.

The editors hope that readers of this volume will be inspired to read more not only about Lincoln but also to read Lincoln himself, for there is no better window into understanding America's greatest president than a careful reading of his own written work.

Lincoln's Role in the 1860 Presidential Campaign

William C. Harris

MAY 18, 1860, WAS ONE OF THE LONGEST DAYS IN THE LIFE OF
Abraham Lincoln. On that day, Lincoln waited at Springfield for
telegraphic reports from Chicago, where delegates to the national
Republican convention would be nominating the party's candidate
for president in the fall election. William H. Seward was the front-
runner for the nomination, but Lincoln and his friends at the Chicago convention understood that the New York senator's reputation
for radicalism on the slavery issue and his public opposition to the
Know Nothings (or Nativists) had made him vulnerable. Illinois
Republicans, as well as many Republicans elsewhere, believed that
Seward could not win critical lower Northern states like Indiana.
Republicans had lost the 1856 election when they failed to carry
most of these states, states that they must win in 1860 to be successful. The upper Northern states appeared safe for the Republicans
even with Seward as the nominee. Lincoln had become popular
among lower North and western Republicans after his remarkable
but unsuccessful senatorial campaign against Stephen A. Douglas in
1858. By the time of the national convention in May, he was in a position to win the nomination if Seward faltered. In addition to Lincoln,

there were several candidates who hoped to win if the balloting became extended. These included Senator Simon Cameron of Pennsylvania, Governor Salmon P. Chase of Ohio, and Edward Bates of Missouri, all of whom, like Seward, had political liabilities. Lincoln, as well as others, concluded that the first ballot would be the critical test. Seward needed to win a majority on this ballot; otherwise, his delegate support was expected to crumble.

The day before the balloting, the Republican convention had adopted a platform that would be acceptable to the lower North and one that Lincoln himself could have written. Of the seventeen planks, only five referred directly to slavery. The platform proclaimed the party's opposition to the expansion of slavery but reaffirmed its commitment to the "inviolate" rights of the states, and it denounced John Brown–type raids into any American community. The platform avoided any mention of the Fugitive Slave Act, which upper North radicals and abolitionists wanted repealed. It also ignored the question of slavery in the District of Columbia. Though we cannot know for certain, Lincoln's managers, led by Judge David Davis, made no promises of office to win delegate support for the nomination. Lincoln instructed them only to promise that if elected he would deal fairly with all Republicans in the distribution of offices. Along with the *Chicago Press and Tribune*, which the delegates at the convention read, Lincoln's lieutenants hammered home the point that Lincoln could win both the upper North and the lower North—and thus the election.

At Springfield, on the morning of the balloting, Lincoln seemed nervous, fidgety—"intensely excited" to his friends.[1] To relieve the tension, Lincoln told stories and played a game of "ball" with several friends. The rules of the game are obscure, but it was not baseball, as legend has it. Later, when he received a telegram reporting that Seward had not received a majority on the first ballot, Lincoln appeared pleased and expressed the view that the New York senator could not win the nomination. The balloting stood: Seward, 173; Lincoln, 102; Cameron, 50; Chase, 49; Bates, 48; and the remainder among seven favorite sons. A successful candidate needed 233 votes to win. The next telegraphic dispatch revealed that on the second ballot Lincoln had closed the gap on Seward to three votes. Lincoln knew then that the news of his nomination would soon come. The last telegram of the morning brought the news that he had won on the third ballot. After spending a few moments in accepting congratulations, Lincoln looked toward home and declared: "Well, gentlemen, there is a little woman at our house who is probably more interested in this dispatch than I am; if you will excuse me I will take the dispatch up and let her see it."[2]

In Congress, the reaction of Republicans and Democrats to the decision at Chicago dramatically revealed how they saw Lincoln's prospects in the election. Republicans, even among some Seward supporters, cheered the results. The Illinois congressman Elihu B. Washburne reported to Lincoln: "The countenances of our republicans were lighted up with joy, and all felt that a nomination had been made which would ensure success. The locofocos [Democrats] who had puckered up their mouths for Seward" earlier when a false report circulated that he had won, "now could not even laugh out of the other corner," Washburne told Lincoln. Democrats had been confident that they could beat Seward. "Many of [the locofocos] were frank enough to admit that . . . there was no use talking, the nomination was a strong one," he said. In the euphoria of the moment, the Republican senators Lyman Trumbull and Benjamin F. Wade sanguinely declared that Lincoln's election was a fixed fact.[3]

Republicans throughout the North celebrated the nomination, despite that some did not know Lincoln's first name. The *New York Times* announced "Abram Lincoln" as the Republican candidate for president.[4] Outside of the party, some Northerners apparently had never heard of Lincoln. Sidney George Fisher, a prominent Philadelphia conservative and writer on constitutional issues, cryptically noted in his diary that the Republicans "had nominated a Mr. Lincoln for President. I never heard of him before."[5]

Northern Democrats, as expected, derided Lincoln's candidacy. Typical of the Democratic response was the *Boston Post's* comment that "the Chicago sectional Convention—a thorough geographic body—has crowned its work by nominating a mere local politician," and, this editor asked, when had "Abraham Lincoln shown ability to warrant this distinction over his competitors?" The *Buffalo Daily Courier* gave its opinion that Republican vice-presidential candidate Hannibal Hamlin was "a man of much higher order of ability than Mr. Lincoln," who was "lacking in culture."[6]

At the other political extreme, abolitionists seemed more upset with the conservative Republican platform, which played down the slavery issue, than the party's nomination of Lincoln.[7] However, Wendell Phillips, the silver-tongued abolitionist orator, harshly criticized the Republican choice of Lincoln. Phillips characterized Lincoln as a "county court advocate" and a "huckster in politics" whose only recommendation for the nomination was that "his past is a blank."[8] Southerners dismissed Lincoln as just another "Black Republican" no different from Seward and Chase.

Republican confidence in victory soared when the Democrats made their final split at Baltimore on June 18. The Northern branch, as expected, nominated Stephen A. Douglas, and the Southern branch selected Vice President John C. Breckinridge as its candidate for president. Lincoln now cautiously believed that he would win the election. Upon the advice of prominent Republicans and following his own political instincts, Lincoln decided not to make any campaign speeches or write public letters seeking voter support. He wrote an Ohio friend that "in my present position . . . by the lessons of the past, and the united voice of all discreet friends, I am neither [to] write or speak a word for the public."[9] Lincoln concluded that public statements on the issues would be used against him, jeopardizing his favored position in the election.

Historically, presidential campaigns were carried on at the state and local level by a vast array of party activists, including newspaper editors. The Republican campaign of 1860 was no exception. Douglas, on the other hand, broke tradition and launched a stump-speaking canvass that even took him into the hostile South. Republicans took a page from old Whig campaign tactics reminiscent of the "Log Cabin and Hard Cider" campaign of 1840 that swept the Whigs to power. They organized "Wide Awake Clubs," built Indian-styled wigwams, raised flagpoles, displayed Lincoln fence rails, exploded fireworks, fired cannons (presumably without the shot), and held torchlight parades in hundreds of villages, towns, and cities in the North. Lincoln's "Rail Splitter" image, while not decisive in his nomination at Chicago, carried an important symbol of democracy and opportunity for all classes in the West and for farmers and working-men in eastern states. The evangelical-type rallies culminated in stirring speeches by Republican politicians. The speakers highlighted the charges of corruption against President Buchanan and the Democrats. At the same time, especially in the West, they virtually ignored their party's antislavery position. Republican stump speakers and newspapers denied the Douglas claim that Lincoln and their party were sectional and a threat to the Union.

The main Democratic charge against Lincoln was that his antislavery policy would destroy the Union and would culminate in black equality. Democrats made no distinction between Lincoln's conservative, no-slavery-expansionist policy and the abolitionists' militant attack on slavery in the South. With no appreciable success, Democrats also revived the old false charge, particularly in Illinois, that Lincoln in opposing the Mexican-American War had failed to vote for supplies for the troops in Mexico. Earlier, Lincoln in his 1858 campaign for the Senate had responded to the charge by researching the printed congressional records and demonstrating that he had always voted to support the troops in the field. Still, his hometown Democratic newspaper professed to "leave it to Mr. Lincoln and his abolition, disunion black republican presses and stump speakers to excuse or palliate . . . his treasonable resolutions, speeches, and votes" on the Mexican War "as best as they may."[10]

Though Lincoln did not campaign, he played an active role in the Republican strategy. Given the use of an office in the state capitol, Lincoln, with funds raised by his friends, hired a young German American, John G. Nicolay, to serve as his secretary. Nicolay, who brought some order to the office, arranged for the publication of two biographies of Lincoln, and answered numerous requests for information, usually by a form letter that Lincoln himself had prepared. The letter said that he would "write nothing upon any point of political doctrine."[11] Freed from much of the correspondence, Lincoln received visitors daily from all walks of life and from all areas, even an occasional Southerner. Many came in groups and pressed into the crowded room to scrutinize and shake hands with "Old Abe." In these meetings with the people, Lincoln revealed little about himself or his plans. He reminisced, told stories, and listened to his visitors in a successful effort to avoid discussing political affairs. Nicolay wrote at the time that visitors "nearly always expressed hope that he would not be so unfortunate as were [Presidents] Harrison & Taylor, to be killed off by the cares of the Presidency—or as is sometimes hinted by foul means."[12] One visitor, former Governor Charles S. Morehead of Kentucky, who had served with Lincoln in Congress as a Whig but now opposed him, disliked "Old Abe's" endless jokes and anecdotes.[13]

Lincoln gave special attention to political leaders and journalists who came to Springfield to see him. His meetings with them often included long discussions about the course of the campaign, followed by invitations to dinner. No visit proved more important than that of Thurlow Weed, Senator Seward's crafty alter ego and editor of the *Albany Evening News*. Invited to Springfield by Judge David Davis and Leonard Swett soon after the Chicago convention, Weed held the key to the extent of support Seward's disappointed eastern friends would give Lincoln in the campaign. The "Rail Splitter" and the "Wizard of the Lobby" met for five hours. The meeting went extremely well. Weed made no demands except for a vague request of fair play by Lincoln, which was agreed to. Lincoln later expressed surprise to his friends that Weed "showed no signs whatever of the intriguer," as his reputation would have it. "He asked for nothing," Lincoln told his friends, "and said N.Y. was safe, without condition." On his part, Weed left Springfield pleased with Lincoln and promised to throw his influence behind him in the East. Weed proved as good as his word. He worked diligently for Lincoln's success and kept him informed of the course of the campaign in the East. Weed even persuaded Seward to shake off his disappointment at losing the nomination—Seward had even threatened to quit politics—and take to the stump on behalf of the party and its candidate. Weed and Seward did not want to be left at the station after Lincoln won the election and political plums and influence were dispensed.[14]

The major Republican newspapers in the East, including Horace Greeley's *New York Tribune*, which had never really warmed to Lincoln, lined up behind the party's candidate. James Gordon Bennett, the imperious, self-styled independent proprietor of the *New York Herald*, at first seemed sympathetic to Lincoln. But he soon turned against him. He feared that Southern secession would follow Lincoln's election and bring disaster to New York's financial interests. In the end, he supported Douglas. The *Herald*, however, dispatched a "special correspondent" to Springfield to send back reports on the "Rail Splitter." The correspondent was cordially received at the Lincoln home, and he provided largely sympathetic reports to the newspaper. Lincoln departed from his policy to remain publicly silent on political issues and reaffirmed to the *Herald* reporter his intention not to touch slavery where it existed; his position, he insisted, was simply to prevent slavery's spread into the territories and thus put it en route to ultimate extinction. According to the reporter, Lincoln "spoke of slavery as an institution that did not meet the universal sanction of the Southern people," but "they were obliged [publicly] to sustain slavery, although they secretly abhorred the institution."[15]

If the correspondent reported him correctly, Lincoln in fact had a false understanding of white Southern opinion on slavery. Such thinking could have contributed to his view that "the people of the South," as he wrote a friend on August 15, "have too much good sense, and good temper to attempt to ruin the government" if he became president.[16] As their private letters and diaries clearly reveal, white Southerners overwhelmingly supported the institution. They bitterly resented Northern antislavery agitation, despite its conservative form as expressed by Lincoln and the Republican party's Chicago platform. They viewed the Republicans as a threat to their social and economic system, to race control, and to the security of their communities, especially after John Brown's October 1859 raid at Harpers Ferry.

Despite his early confidence in victory, Lincoln soon worried that the anti-Republican forces would gang up on his party and fuse their electoral votes in the battleground states of the lower North and even in New York. Because of this concern, and without leaving Springfield, Lincoln became increasingly involved in the campaign. By late summer Lincoln and the Republicans faced serious fusion threats in Indiana and Pennsylvania, states critical to the party's success in November. Both states were scheduled for gubernatorial elections on October 9. The results in these two elections, contemporaries sensed, could foretell the outcome of the presidential election in November. The main question was whether the Know Nothings would fuse with the Douglas Democrats to defeat the Republicans in the October elections and then repeat the strategy in the November election. The Know Nothings had voted for former Whig President Millard Fillmore, the American party presidential candidate in 1856. Complicating the problem for Lincoln and the Republicans was the presidential candidacy of John Bell, whose Constitutional Union party expected to attract Know Nothings and conservative Whigs to their standard as the alternative to the sectional Republican party. Such an eventuality could provide Douglas with the margin of victory in the key states.

Lincoln therefore wisely focused his attention on Indiana and Pennsylvania. On September 20 he wrote New York Governor Edwin D. Morgan, chairman of the national Republican committee, that "the whole surplus energy of the party throughout the nation, should be bent upon" the campaign in those two states. Lincoln told Morgan that "no thing will do us so much good in *Illinois*" or elsewhere "as the carrying of *Indiana* [and Pennsylvania] in the October election."[17]

Indiana was staunchly conservative on the slavery issue, more so than Pennsylvania. The Know Nothings, though a minority, had an effective organization that could rally the faithful to support fusion with their traditional foes, the Democrats, as the lesser of evils in the fall elections. The Douglas forces thus could carry both the October and November elections in Indiana. Fortunately for Lincoln and the Republicans, they had an important ally in Richard W. Thompson, the leader of Indiana's Know Nothings whose hatred of the Douglas Democrats exceeded his ultraconservative position on slavery. Thompson, an old Whig, particularly favored Lincoln, whom he had served with in Congress and who had not publicly attacked the Know Nothings. Early in the campaign, Lincoln learned of Thompson's sympathetic leaning, opened a friendly correspondence with him, and dispatched John Nicolay to meet secretly with him at Terre Haute. His instructions to Nicolay were simple: "Tell him my motto is 'Fairness to all,' but commit me to nothing."[18] The meeting went well, and Thompson promised to work to prevent an anti-Republican fusion in the state. Encouraged by Thompson's response, Lincoln in late July wrote Caleb B. Smith, a Republican leader in Indiana, that "from present appearances we might succeed" in November "without Indiana, but *with* it, failure is scarcely possible."[19]

Despite Thompson's goodwill toward Lincoln and his efforts to prevent fusion in his state, great pressure was brought by prominent Kentuckians with Whig antecedents to persuade Indiana Know Nothings that only Douglas's success in the election could prevent disunion. In an August 2 address at Louisville, which anti-Republican newspapers in Indiana printed, Senator John J. Crittenden argued that "Mr. Lincoln may be a very worthy, upright and honest man." But if elected president, "he must be governed by the political influence and voice of his party," a purely antislavery and sectional party that threatened the South. Such antislavery doctrines, Crittenden declared, "must make every man south feel uneasy in his condition and in his property."[20]

Many Indiana Know Nothings who were mildly antislavery resented the interference of Kentuckians in their election, despite their old party ties as Whigs. Though their state party endorsed John Bell for president, they rejected fusion with the Democrats and indicated that they favored Lincoln in the fall election.[21] Republicans received an additional boost when Democratic Senator Jesse Bright, a bitter foe of Douglas, announced his support for Henry S. Lane, the Republican candidate for governor. By the time of the October election, it was clear that Lane would win the governorship, thereby resolving one half of the lower Northern state puzzle that was critical to Lincoln's success in November. The other half, Pennsylvania, also had difficult political problems for Lincoln and the Republicans.

In Pennsylvania, the Republican cause became extremely complicated because of factionalism between supporters of Senator Simon Cameron and those of the gubernatorial candidate Andrew G. Curtin. Moreover, influential Philadelphia merchants, fearing that Lincoln's election would induce Southern secession and upset their financial interests in the South, favored John Bell or the fusion of the anti-Republican parties. In addition, many conservative antislavery Know Nothings who had voted for Republican candidates in local elections in 1858 and 1859 objected to the so-called Dutch plank in the Republican platform opposing restrictions on immigrant rights. The Know Nothings wanted restrictions. Lincoln's friends advised him to ignore the Dutch plank lest he lose the relatively large Know Nothing vote in Pennsylvania and elsewhere. He took their advice and remained silent on the issue.[22]

The factionalism in the Pennsylvania Republican party disturbed Lincoln. The situation "pains me," he wrote Leonard Swett, an Illinois associate. Lincoln requested that Swett write Joseph Casey, a Cameron lieutenant, and "suggest to him that great caution and delicacy of action" was necessary to prevent "a dangerous explosion" in the Pennsylvania party that could be disastrous in the fall elections. He also dispatched David Davis to the state to remind Senator Cameron and his friends of the critical need to rally behind Curtin in the October gubernatorial election. After a long visit with the senator on August 4, Davis reported to Lincoln that Cameron agreed that Curtin's election was too important nationally as well as in the state for Pennsylvania Republicans to remain divided. A few days later, Thurlow Weed wrote Lincoln that Cameron promised him that he would work diligently for both Curtin and Lincoln in the campaign, a promise largely kept.[23]

Lincoln also asked Alexander K. McClure, chairman of the Pennsylvania State Republican Committee, to keep him informed of the status of the campaign at the local level. On August 27, Lincoln responded to a McClure report on the campaign by asking, "When you say you are *organizing* every election district, do you mean to include the idea that you are 'canvassing'—'counting noses?'"[24] Lincoln's inquiry reveals the keen interest that he took in local party organization during the 1860 campaign. A New York visitor reported after a meeting with Lincoln: "He sat down beside me on the sofa and commenced talking about political affairs in my own State with a knowledge of details which surprised me."[25]

Factionalism in the Pennsylvania Democratic party increasingly worked to the Republican advantage in the Keystone State. The dominant James Buchanan wing of the party had been at odds with the Douglas faction since the split over the proslavery Lecompton constitution for Kansas in 1858. When the gubernatorial candidate Henry D. Foster refused to indicate a preference for president between Douglas and the Southern Rights candidate John C. Breckinridge, whom President Buchanan favored, Douglas supporters denounced Foster as a pro-secessionist candidate. In Philadelphia, an attempt to fuse the Democratic and Constitutional Union or Bell voters in support of Foster failed because of old political enmities between Democrats and former Whigs. By the first of October, it was clear to Republicans, as in Indiana, that their candidate would win the gubernatorial election. When the telegraph wires announced the results of the October 9 elections in the two states, the *Chicago Press and Tribune* excitedly reported: "The doubts and fears of the nation are dispelled"—it meant those of the Republicans. Senator Douglas cryptically told his secretary, "Mr. Lincoln is the next President. We must try to save the Union."[26]

Lincoln also concluded after the October elections that the burden of the presidency and the impending sectional crisis would soon be his. Lincoln's demeanor became sober and withdrawn, reflecting the anguish within him, though he continued to be congenial to visitors. Doubts that he had expressed in 1859 about his qualifications for the presidency returned to haunt him. On October 25, he earnestly told a visitor: "I declare to you this morning [that] I would rather have a full term in the Senate—a place in which I would feel more consciously able to discharge the duties required, and where there was more chance to make [a] reputation, and less danger of losing it—than four years in the Presidency."[27]

But as that modern American philosopher Yogi Berra once said, "It ain't over 'til it's over." The opposition to Lincoln had one last card to play—in New York. Anti-Republican forces in the Empire State, inspired by James Gordon Bennett's *New York Herald* and encouraged by apprehensive border state conservatives, called for a fusion of the state's Douglas, Breckinridge, and Bell electoral votes.[28] Earlier in the campaign, Lincoln had predicted that "the most extraordinary effort ever made to carry New-York for Douglas" would be made by those attempting to throw the old Millard Fillmore or Know Nothing vote of 1856 to the Little Giant. Though Thurlow Weed and other New York Republicans had assured Lincoln that fusion could not be achieved, late in the campaign they began to fear that it might happen.[29] New York's Republican opponents, though not all of them, agreed to a fusion that would give Douglas a majority on the state's electoral ticket. At last, throwing off their complacency in view of the fusion threat, Weed and state Republicans leaders flooded New York City and other vulnerable places with speakers and Wide Awake activists to counter the fusion movement. Four days before the election, Seward spoke to a huge crowd at the Palace Garden in New York.[30] Though the city gave the fusion ticket a majority of thirty thousand votes, upstate support for Lincoln proved overwhelming, and he easily won the Empire State's thirty-five electoral votes.

Election day, November 6, brought tension mixed with anticipation to Springfield. Republican bands marched through the crowded streets, their music punctuated occasionally by the roar of cannon. When Lincoln left his office to vote, cheers rang out from the crowd; even distributors of Douglas tickets hailed the local hero.[31] About midnight and after most returns had been received, Lincoln crossed the street and entered a large room on the public square where wives and daughters of Springfield Republicans had prepared food and decorations. Hardly had he sat down at the table when a dispatch arrived reporting that he had carried New York and thus the election. His only disappointment was that, though he had won Springfield, he had lost surrounding Sangamon County. Lincoln has the dubious distinction of being the only successful presidential candidate in two elections to fail to win his home county on both occasions.

As is well known, Lincoln won all of the free states, except for New Jersey, where, in a then-peculiar state arrangement, he shared the electoral votes with Douglas. In all, he received 180 electoral votes to seventy-two for Breckinridge, thirty-nine for Bell, and twelve for Douglas. Lincoln won 39 percent of the popular vote, which is still the smallest percentage of any winning presidential candidate, but it is understandable in view of the fact that there were four major candidates. The percentage of Lincoln's Northern popular vote was not overwhelming: 54 percent. For all practical purposes, he was not on the ballot in the fifteen slave states; indeed, it was virtually two elections, one in the South between Breckinridge and Bell and the other in the North between Lincoln and Douglas. A shift of 2 percent in certain areas, the historian Richard N. Current has calculated, would have cost Lincoln a majority of the electoral votes and thrown the election into the House of Representatives.[32] There, with each state having one vote, Lincoln's chances of winning would have been problematic.

This interpretation has been challenged by Professor William E. Gienapp. A shift of voters to Douglas or to an anti-Republican fusion ticket, according to Gienapp, could only have made a difference in New Jersey, California, and Oregon, states without enough electoral votes to make a difference in the election.[33] The likelihood of a successful fusion in the battleground states, including New York, could not have occurred because of the bitter historical antagonisms among the anti-Republican factions. Furthermore, the enthusiasm in which Lincoln activists organized and campaigned in these and other Northern states played an important role in attracting first-time native and immigrant voters to the party, particularly non-Irish voters. In the campaign, Republicans effectively exploited Lincoln's "Rail Splitter," "Honest Abe" image as the symbol of a vibrant, egalitarian, and virtuous America and contrasted it to the oligarchical, corrupt, and decrepit Democratic party. Republicans proved successful in trumpeting the malfeasance in the Buchanan administration and Douglas's demagoguery. They wisely played down the antislavery and sectional nature of their party. Despite his earlier "House Divided" speech, which Douglas Democrats never tired of reminding voters, Lincoln's candidacy on a conservative antislavery platform and his careful attention to the campaign in the key lower North made possible the Republican victory in the election.

The Baltimore Plot—
Fact or Fiction?

Michael J. Kline

AFTER MORE THAN A CENTURY AND A HALF, THE QUESTION remains: was the Baltimore Plot real or not? As most people familiar with Lincoln lore know, the Baltimore Plot was a suspected conspiracy to assassinate president-elect Abraham Lincoln in Baltimore as he traveled through that city on his way to Washington in February 1861. To avoid the threat, Lincoln famously wore a disguise and took a night train from Philadelphia, snuck through Baltimore around 3 AM, and arrived unannounced in Washington around 6 AM on February 23, 1861.

As a lawyer, I have always wondered whether there was sufficient evidence to prove a criminal conspiracy to assassinate Lincoln in Baltimore. Over the years, historians have debated whether or not the plot was real. If so, who was involved? Could the conspiracy have succeeded?

In my research, I have uncovered a great deal of evidence of the plot but no smoking gun. No one was ever charged or convicted of the crime. There is no evidence that after Lincoln arrived in Washington there was any effort to look for the alleged conspirators. In fact, in an interview in December 1864, Lincoln himself denied that any such plot existed: "I did not then, nor do I now believe I should have been assassinated had I gone through Baltimore as first contemplated . . . I could not believe there was a plot to murder me."[1] Neither did one of Lincoln's bodyguards on the trip, Ward Hill Lamon, who wrote years later, in 1872, that he did not believe the plot was real but rather a fabrication of the detective Alan Pinkerton: "In [Pinkerton's] account there is literally nothing to sustain the accusation, and much to rebut it. It is perfectly manifest that there was no conspiracy,—no conspiracy of a hundred, of fifty, of twenty; no definite purpose in the heart of even one man to murder Mr. Lincoln at Baltimore."[2]

Lamon was one of the people who helped sneak Lincoln through Baltimore early on the morning of February 23, 1861. If anyone should know whether the plot was real or not, Lamon would. One of Lincoln's few political allies in hostile Baltimore, Worthington G. Snethen, wrote a scathing letter to Lincoln after his arrival in Washington, suggesting that adequate arrangements had been made in Baltimore for the president elect's safety:

> Carriages were to be provided for the accommodation of the whole Presidential party. . . . [Baltimore's] Mayor Brown had assured . . . myself . . . that he should be present in his official capacity, to receive you, and to accompany you alone, in a private two seat carriage. . . . There was to be no procession whatever. A strong force of police was to be present at the Depot, on your arrival, to prevent the pressure of the crowd around the carriages, when they should drive off under the protection of the Mayor. . . . No request was made by any of your friends for the presence of the Police.[3]

Any effort to prove that the Baltimore Plot was real, as a legal matter, needs effectively to rebut such recollections and claims. And the most convincing evidence we have supports the existence of a plot.

One important piece of evidence involves Baltimore's past history, which demonstrates a city prone to mob violence and political unrest. In the law, evidence of habit is admissible in a criminal case. The record shows that Baltimore citizens did habitually commit acts of violence as part of the political process. In fact, just four years before, President-elect James Buchanan had been threatened by a mob when he passed through Baltimore in a carriage on his way to Washington. "For nearly an hour roughs hooted and hissed him, stoned his carriage, and pelted with brickbats his guard of honor." As a result, Buchanan skipped dinner in Baltimore and left quickly for Washington. But hooligans from Baltimore followed Buchanan all the way to the capital and that night reportedly congregated near the National Hotel and "fired revolvers, terrifying the citizenry."[4]

Just a few days before the 1860 election, Worthington Snethen had written Lincoln advising that Baltimore mobs had attacked a group of Baltimore Republicans peaceably assembled. The mob broke up two Republican meetings with violent interference, reportedly with the tacit approval of the Baltimore police, and then attacked a "Wide Awake" march. Wrote Snethen: "Our people behaved nobly in the Wide Awake procession. There were some 300 of them. They walked their whole distance amid showers of eggs, brick-bats, and injurious epithets from the mob."[5] Both Buchanan's treatment and the more recent attack on Baltimore Republicans suggest that Lincoln might have received more of the same had he gone through Baltimore.

In fact, Lincoln was warned about Baltimore even before he left Springfield, Illinois. Congressman Elihu Washburn wrote Lincoln on January 10, 1861: "I believe Va. and Maryland are both rotten to the core. We have had one of our friends from N.Y. . . . in Baltimore, sounding matters there, and he gives most unfavorable reports."[6] In all likelihood, Washburn's reference to "friends from N.Y." meant New York City detectives scouting out the city. New York's chief of police, John Kennedy, had sent several of his detectives to Baltimore in early January 1861 at the urging of Lincoln's friends to investigate matters there.

A more telling warning in January 1861 came to Lincoln from Captain George Hazzard, who wrote to criticize both Baltimore and its chief of police, George P. Kane. Hazzard, who had lived in Baltimore for a time, referred to Kane as "a violent democrat," adding: "I am constrained to state that I have but little confidence in Col. Kane's abilities and less in the integrity of his character. Independent of this there are men in that city who, I candidly believe, would glory in being hanged for having stabbed a 'black republican president.'"[7] Hazzard also accused all of Baltimore's most wealthy and influential citizens of being secessionists and went on to recommend three alternatives for Lincoln in getting through Baltimore:

1. Go publicly through the city. Hazzard felt that it would take an army of fifty thousand men and weeks of preparation to make a perfectly safe passage through what Hazzard referred to as "a hostile city as large as Baltimore."
2. Avoid Baltimore. Hazzard proposed two possible ways to do this: by taking more southerly rail routes or by taking a war steamer from Philadelphia to Washington.
3. Pass through Baltimore incognito. He recommended that Lincoln could do this by leaving Philadelphia privately and unannounced with only a few friends and take a sleeping car at night all the way through to Washington. He recommended that a false mustache, an old slouched hat, and a long cloak or overcoat for concealment could be provided by a friend while Lincoln was in New York City.[8]

None of these alternatives was very practical. Assembling an army of fifty thousand men would take time and be seen as an act of war. Avoiding Baltimore or sneaking through in a disguise would have been seen as cowardly and would have defeated Lincoln's purpose of making a public show on his way to Washington, "to see and be seen." As a practical matter, however, almost any route Lincoln chose for getting to Washington would either take him through a potentially hostile Virginia or directly through Baltimore. Lincoln had particularly good reasons to avoid Virginia. Writing from Fort Leavenworth, Kansas, on October 20, 1860, Major David Hunter had sent the following warning: "On a recent visit to the east, I met a lass of high character, who had been spending part of the summer among her friends and relatives in Virginia. She informed me that a number of young men in Virginia had bound themselves, by oaths the most solemn, to cause your assassination, should you be elected."[9]

Then, in December, the editor Horace Greeley warned Lincoln about taking the most direct route to Washington, through Virginia, saying, "your life is not safe, and it is your simple duty to be very careful of exposing it. I doubt whether you ought to go to Washington via Wheeling and the B&O Railroad unless you go with a very strong force."[10] One of the options for Lincoln was to go through Baltimore via Harrisburg on the Northern Central Railroad. The other was to travel through Philadelphia, on the Philadelphia, Wilmington, and Baltimore Railroad. That railroad's president was Samuel Morse Felton.

In January 1861, Felton had received a visit from a prominent philanthropist, Dorothea Dix, who had spent time in the South. Dix reported to Felton that

> there was then an extensive and organized conspiracy through the South to seize upon Washington, with its archives and records, and then declare the Southern Confederacy de facto the Government of the United States. At the same time they were to cut off all means of communication between Washington and the North, East, and West, and thus prevent the transportation of troops to wrest the Capital from the hands of the insurgents. Mr. Lincoln's inauguration was thus to be prevented, or his life was to fall a sacrifice. In fact, she said, troops were then drilling on the line of our own road. . . . The men drilled were to obey the commands of their

leaders, and the leaders were banded together to capture Washington.[11]

Felton initially took this information to Baltimore's chief of police, Marshal George Kane. According to Felton, "He [Kane] scouted the idea that there was any such thing on foot; said he had thoroughly investigated the whole matter, and there was not the slightest foundation for such rumors. I then determined to have nothing more to do with Marshal Kane."[12] Instead, Felton went to the Chicago detective Alan Pinkerton. At Felton's request, on or about February 3, 1861, Pinkerton and five of his best operatives arrived in Baltimore. They included Timothy Webster, two additional men operating under the aliases Harry W. Davies and Charles D. C. Williams, and two women, Kate Warne and Hattie Lawton.[13]

Pinkerton and his agents immediately set up shop posing as secessionists from various Southern cities and began to work their way into the confidence of suspected Baltimore secessionists. Each of these agents began writing daily reports detailing the information they were learning through their clandestine operations. These reports Lamon derided as "neither edifying or useful: they prove nothing but the baseness of the vocation which gave them their existence."[14] In fact, from a legal standpoint, the Pinkerton reports are quite probative.

First, they were written contemporaneously, with the events faithfully written and dated on the day in which they took place or perhaps the next day. The contemporaneous nature of the reports makes them more credible than accounts like Lamon's, written years later.

Second, the reports provide specific details as to the time, place, and manner of the alleged conspiracy. They reveal events that can be independently verified, such as the Select Committee of Five hearings, conducted by Congress in early February to investigate rumors of secessionist plots to capture Washington. Several of the plotter's names are given in Pinkerton's reports, and locations of various meetings are specified. Intricate details are given that tend to rebut a charge of fabrication.

Third and most significant, the essential elements of the reports' claim to a conspiracy to assassinate Lincoln are corroborated by accounts of others not affiliated with Alan Pinkerton. And these accounts merit further exploration as well.

By the time Lincoln boarded his inaugural train in Springfield on February 11, 1861, Pinkerton and his agents had already been stationed in Baltimore for over a week. But Lincoln had been receiving reports of rumors and actual death threats for weeks, even without Pinkerton's reports. In his farewell address to the people of Springfield, Lincoln hinted that he might not ever return: "I now leave, not knowing when, or whether ever, I may return, with a task before me greater than that which rested upon Washington."[15]

Eleven days later, in a speech given in Philadelphia on the morning of February 22, 1861, the day before he was to travel to Baltimore and just hours after learning of the Baltimore Plot from Alan Pinkerton, Lincoln directly alluded to the possibility of his own assassination: "But, if this country cannot be saved without giving up that principle [that all men are created equal]—I was about to say I would rather be assassinated on this spot than surrender it. . . . I have said nothing but what I am willing to live by, and, in the pleasure of Almighty God, die by."[16]

Clearly, the possibility of his own death was on Lincoln's mind. The above comments were given only a few hours after Lincoln met in his Philadelphia hotel room with Alan Pinkerton, who shared with the president-elect the facts he and his agents had uncovered.

One such fact was Pinkerton's identification of one Cypriano Ferrandini as one of the ringleaders of the conspiracy. On the evening of February 15, 1861, Pinkerton met Ferrandini at Barr's Saloon in Baltimore. Ferrandini worked as the head barber in the basement of Barnum's Hotel, reputedly a secessionist hangout. In his report written that date, Pinkerton recounted the following:

Ferrandina [*sic*] said that never, never shall Lincoln be President—His life (Ferrandina) was of no consequence—he was willing to give it for Lincoln's—he would sell it for that Abolitionist's, and as Orsini had given his life for Italy, so was he (Ferrandina) ready to die for his country, and the rights of the South, and, said Ferrandina . . . "we shall all die together, we shall show the North that we fear them not—every Captain . . . will on that day prove himself a hero. The first shot fired, the main Traitor (Lincoln) dead, and all Maryland will be with us, and the South shall be free, and the North must then be ours . . . If I alone must do it, I shall—Lincoln shall die in this city."[17]

Ferrandini's reference is to Felice Orsini, an Italian radical who had attempted to assassinate Napoleon III a few years before and was executed for it. The Orsini reference is interesting because it tends to give Pinkerton's account an extra bit of credibility—it is simply too specific to be an invented detail. It seems more likely that Ferrandini, an Italian (or Corsican) immigrant, would be familiar with and hold his fellow countryman Orsini in high esteem. The Ferrandini statement is also what in the law is termed "an admission against interest." Such statements are deemed sufficiently probative that they are an exception to the hearsay rule and can be admitted to prove guilt.

On Election Day 1860, Lincoln had received only a little over one thousand votes in Baltimore, about 3 percent of the total cast. He never received any invitation from Baltimore officials to visit the city on his way to Washington, in contrast with the other major cities on the route. Pinkerton reported that while operating at Barnum's Hotel in Baltimore, he overheard a conversation involving Marshal Kane from which he determined that Kane would be providing no police escort for Lincoln, unlike other cities on the route:

From the familiar manner of Marshall Kane and many of
the rabid Secessionates [sic], there could be no doubt but
that they were aware that Kane was not giving an Escort. . . .
It was impossible for Marshall Kane not to know that there
would be a necessity for an Escort for Mr. Lincoln on his
arrival in Baltimore, and, that if with this knowledge Marshall Kane failed to give a Police Escort, then I should from
this time out doubt the loyalty of the Baltimore Police.[18]

There is also evidence that the plotters had spies following Lincoln as his train headed toward Washington, reporting on his movements to conspirators in Baltimore. George Stearns, an employee of
Samuel Felton's PW&B Railroad, recalled that "[The Baltimore plot-
ters] had spies following Mr. Lincoln and were in constant communication with these parties in Baltimore giving them information of
Mr. Lincoln's movements."[19] This corroborates a similar statement
recorded by one of Pinkerton's operatives. On February 23, 1861, the
Pinkerton man Harry W. Davies reported that the suspected Baltimore plotter Otis K. Hillard, with whom he had been in contact for
the past week or two, claimed that "they had men on the lookout [for
Lincoln] all the time."[20] On February 12, 1861, Davies recorded
another interesting conversation he had with Hillard:

[Hillard] then asked me if I had seen a statement of Lincoln's route to Washington City—I replied that I had—Hillard said, "By the By, that reminds me that I must go and see
a certain party in the morning the first thing." I asked him
what about—He replied "about Lincoln's route, I want to see
about the Telegraph in Philadelphia and New York and have
some arrangement made about Telegraphing." I remarked
"how do you mean?" Hillard said "Suppose that some of
Lincoln's friends would arrange so that the Telegraph messages should be miscarried, we would have some signs to
Telegraph by: for instance supposing, that we should Tele-

graph to a certain point 'all up at 7,' that would mean that Lincoln would be at such a point at 7 o'clock."[21]

From this account, we can surmise that the conspirators had cohorts shadowing Lincoln at least in New York and Philadelphia, and perhaps other cities, and were developing a crude code for reporting his movements. This same Otis K. Hillard made the following offer to the Pinkerton operative Harry W. Davies on February 19, 1861: "Give me an article of agreement that you will give my Mother Five Hundred Dollars, and I will kill Lincoln between here and Havre-de-Grace," and then exclaimed in the language of Brutus, "Not that I love Lincoln less, but my Country more!"[22]

It became well known, through published reports, that Lincoln's train was to pass through Baltimore at 12:30 pm on February 23, 1861. As previously indicated, the train would approach from one of two places, Harrisburg on the Northern Central Line or Philadelphia on Samuel Felton's PW&B Railroad. Final reports indicated he would arrive from Harrisburg at the Calvert Street Station, which is where the Baltimore crowd waited for him on February 23, 1861. The president-elect's railroad cars would then be pulled by a team of horses across town and placed on tracks at the southbound depot. The fact that most American cities—Baltimore included—had no connecting stations added to the danger of exposure and vulnerability. That morning, Otis K. Hillard boasted to the Pinkerton operative Harry W. Davies that he was to have the first shot at Lincoln:

> Hillard afterwards told me that all those men standing there were National Volunteers, and that they stood in that position on the side of the hill so as that when the carriage containing Lincoln should come up the hill they could rush en-mass upon it, and around it, when Lincoln was to be slain—they reasoning that with such a dense crowd around the carriage, it would be impossible for any outsider to tell

who did the deed. In connection with this Hillard said that from his position he would have the first shot.[23]

The National Volunteers were a paramilitary group of several thousand men that had allegedly taken an oath to assassinate Lincoln. Corroborating evidence that their plot was real comes from sources other than the Pinkerton reports. On February 7, 1861, George Stearns, one of the PW&B Railroad's employees, wrote the following letter to Maryland Governor Thomas H. Hicks:

> Dear Sir: On Sunday last a man who said he was from Baltimore called on our Bridge tender at Back River and informed him an attempt would be made by parties from Baltimore and other places to burn the Bridge just before the train should pass, which should have Mr. Lincoln on Board and in the excitement to assassinate him. The man who imparted this information will not give his name. He was an old gentleman very respectable in his appearance. He said he was a friend to the R Road and did not wish to see its property destroyed if it could be protected. Very Respectfully Your Obt Servant George Stearns[24]

Lincoln, of course, was a lawyer, and he knew the power of corroborative evidence. On the night of February 22, 1861, soon after learning of the plot from Alan Pinkerton, Lincoln received a visit from William Seward's son, Frederick. Seward had with him several letters, including the following one written by Col. Charles P. Stone:

> A New York detective officer who has been on duty in Baltimore for three weeks past reports this morning to Col Stone that there is serious danger of violence to and the assassination of Mr. Lincoln in his passage through that city should the time of that passage be known—He states that there are banded rowdies holding secret meetings, and that he has

heard threats of mobbing and violence, and has himself heard men declare that if Mr Lincoln was to be assassinated they would like to be the men—He states further that it is only within the past few days that he has considered there was any danger, but now he deems it imminent—He deems the danger one which the authorities & people in Balt. cannot guard against—All risk might be easily avoided by a change in the travelling arrangements which would bring Mr Lincoln and a portion of his party through Baltimore by a night train without previous notice.[25]

The New York detective who made this report to Col. Stone was David S. Bookstaver. He was totally unaware of Pinkerton's parallel investigation. Whatever doubts Lincoln later expressed, Fred Seward recalled that this corroborative account convinced the president-elect that the plot was real. Lincoln himself would later recount to the historian Benson J. Lossing that once he concluded that Fred Seward's report was prepared independently of Pinkerton's investigation, he was convinced the threat was genuine. As Lincoln recalled: "I met Frederick Seward. We went to my room together, when he told me that he had been sent, at the instance of his father and General Scott, to inform me that their detectives in Baltimore had discovered a plot there to assassinate me. I now believe such a plot to be in existence."[26] More corroborative evidence came from an anonymous woman in Baltimore who on the morning of February 22, 1861, wrote Lincoln the following:

Dear Sir[:] I think it my duty to inform you that I was advised last night by a gentleman that there existed in Baltimore, a league of ten persons, who had sworn that you should never pass through that city alive—This may be but one of the thousand threats against you that have emanated from some paltry Southerners, but you should know that your friends may be watchful while you are in the place as it was asserted positively to be the fact. God defend and bless you—The prayers of many go with you. A Lady.[27]

Still more corroborative evidence arrived from the Peace Conference delegate Lucius E. Chittenden of Vermont. In his book published in 1891, Chittenden recalled being summoned in February 1861 from Washington to Baltimore under secretive circumstances. He was taken to a private home and introduced to several men from Baltimore who told him they knew positively of a plot to murder Lincoln in Baltimore, claiming to have the names of the individuals involved. The plotters had reportedly rehearsed the crime, whereby they would halt Lincoln's rail car as it was pulled through the streets of Baltimore from one depot to the other, at which point several conspirators would enter the car, stab Lincoln, and hurry to a waiting schooner that would transport them to Mobile, Alabama. To add to the confusion, bombs and hand grenades were to be tossed into the rail cars. Chittenden recalled that he was told: "We know that they are not all hired assassins. There are men among them who believe they are serving their country. One of them is an actor who recites passages from the tragedy of Julius Caesar in their conclaves. They are abundantly supplied with money."[28]

This account is corroborative of the suspect Otis K. Hillard's comment paraphrasing Brutus's "not that I loved Caesar less but Rome more" line in exclaiming "not that I love Lincoln less but my country more!" Yet further corroboration came from newspaper accounts of what Lincoln might have faced had he gone through Baltimore according to the original plan. Pinkerton's reports described the plotter's plan to get up a diversion in the form of a fight and/or egg-throwing incident that would draw any police away from Lincoln and his carriage. On the evening of February 23, 1861, after it was known that Lincoln had slipped through Baltimore, Pinkerton reported a conversation he had with one of the suspected conspirators, James H. Luckett, that day:

He [Luckett] said that . . . they would yet make the attempt to assassinate Lincoln; that if it had not been for the d—d spies somewhere, Lincoln never could have passed through Baltimore; that the men were all ready to have done the job, and were in their places, and would have murdered the d—d Abolitionist had it not been that they were cheated. He said that Captain Ferrandina [*sic*] had had about Twenty picked men with good revolvers and Knives; that their calculation was to get up a row in the crowd with rotten eggs, and brick-bats, and that while the Police (some of whom understood the game) would be attending to this, that Captain Ferrandina and his men should attack the carriage with Lincoln and shoot everyone in it, and trust to mixing up in the crowd to make their escape—but that if any of the members were taken, the others were to rescue him at all cost, and at all hazard.[29]

In fact, a *Philadelphia Inquirer* account of the morning of February 23, 1861, noted: "There were many reckless boys and dissolute young men in the crowd, who had eggs and other missiles in their pockets, which, as is presumed, they designed throwing at somebody."[30] Added the *New York Times*: "A correspondent of the Macon (Ga.) Telegraph, writing from Baltimore, states that Mr. Lincoln would have been egged beyond the shadow of a doubt had he passed through that city according to the programme. The writer speaks of his own knowledge, for he was in the crowd at the depot, heard the threats of those composing it, saw the eggs, and, what is more to the purpose, had nasal proof of their bad quality as they were prematurely crushed in the swaying crowd."[31]

But the president-elect was already safely in Washington. Lincoln's cortege left Harrisburg without him on the morning of February 23, 1861. It traveled to Baltimore on the Northern Central Railroad, arriving at the Calvert Street Station. A reporter for the *Philadelphia Inquirer* described the scene as one of absolute mayhem:

The imperfect arrangements of the railroad company were here brought to a climax when the train stopped. Over ten thousand people were in and around the depot. The officers (either of the railroad or the police) whose duty it was to have kept the mob back, were negligent or unable to be of service. The members of the suite were therefore, jostled and tossed to and fro, utterly without protection. Many of them, finding it impossible to remain with their friends, escaped in such manner as they could, and secured private carriages. It is astonishing that those who managed, or pretended to manage, the depot arrangements should have been so ignorant or incompetent as to have allowed the crowd to enter the space necessary for exit from the cars. This was the most trying ordeal which the party were forced to undergo during the entire trip. . . . The crowd surged and pressed, and as one after another of the suite emerged as best he could from the cars, the shouts and yells become almost deafening. One gentleman was taken for the President elect, and narrowly escaped injury through the anxiety and curiosity of those assembled. Others were forced over a platform several feet in height, and others jammed against the sides of the cars. The cry of "pickpocket" was raised, and provoked a rush, and if possible, additional confusion. And amid this noise, bustle, mob and excitement, the visitors were ushered into the Calvert Street Station of the Northern Central Railway at Baltimore.[32]

These independent reports fully corroborate Pinkerton's account, only missing one key element—Lincoln's assassination—for the simple reason that Lincoln was not with the cortege when it arrived at the Calvert Street Station. Those in attendance had reason to know that Lincoln would not be there, as it had been previously announced that Lincoln had already passed through and was in Washington. Nonetheless, the crowd and conspirators remained in place, hoping the report of Lincoln passing through was merely a "sell."[33]

Yet further corroboration of the dangerous situation came from the Baltimore attorney William Schley, who on February 23 reported to Lincoln:

> A vast crowd was present at the Depot to see you arrive, this morning, but at "Ten" you may judge the disappointment at the announcement of your "passage" through unseen unnoticed and unknown—it fell like a thunder clap upon the community—was denied as a "hoax"—&c. until the truth was made beyond a doubt—A large "police force" was present to preserve the peace, besides your many friends to resist attack—which I now declare was meditated and determined—By your course you have saved bloodshed and a mob.[34]

Final corroboration can be found in a news story published in 1862, identifying William Byrne, also identified by Pinkerton, as one of the ringleaders of the plot (the reference to Wigfall is to Texas Senator Louis T. Wigfall, who remained in Washington during the winter of 1861, gathering intelligence that he shared with the Confederacy):

> For a long time it was believed that an Italian barber of this city was the Orsini who undertook to slay President Lincoln on his journey to the capital in February, 1861, and it is possible he was one of the plotters; but it has come out on a recent trial of a man named Byrne, in Richmond, that he was the captain of the band that was to take the life of Mr. Lincoln. This Byrne used to be a notorious gambler of Baltimore, and emigrated to Richmond shortly after the 19th of April, of bloody memory. He was recently arrested in Jeff. Davis's capital on a charge of keeping a gambling house and of disloyalty to the chief traitor's pretended government. Wigfall testified to Byrne's loyalty to the rebel cause, and gave in evidence that Byrne was the captain of the gang who were to kill Mr. Lincoln, and upon this evidence, it appears,

he was let go. Of course, to be guilty of such an intended crime is a mantle large enough to cover up all other sins against society and the divine law.[35]

In sum, Lincoln's claim that he never believed there was a plot to murder him in Baltimore is contradicted not only by his own statement to Benson J. Lossing but by a mountain of convincing evidence otherwise. But what of Ward Hill Lamon's stubborn insistence that there was no conspiracy—that, rather, the plot was invented by Allan Pinkerton to "shine in the professional way"?

It must be said that Lamon's statement lacks credibility, particularly because it was written after he and Pinkerton had become mortal enemies. After getting Lincoln safely to Washington on February 23, 1861, Lamon was determined to celebrate. Pinkerton witnessed him drinking at Willard's Hotel and talking there with a reporter. Pinkerton had always been adamant that to maintain security, he did not want his or his agents' real names to be published. Concerned that Lamon would reveal his identity to the reporter, Pinkerton motioned to Lamon and privately cautioned him to say no more. But Lamon told Pinkerton that the reporter had already figured out Pinkerton's identity. Pinkerton wrote a scathing report later that day, in which he called Lamon "a brainless egotistical fool." Years later, Lamon got hold of the report and became enraged, writing in the margin that it was "an infamous lie from beginning to end."[36] He and Pinkerton would remain enemies the rest of their lives. Yet in a later memoir, edited by his daughter, Lamon claimed: "It is now an acknowledged fact that there never was a moment from the day he [Lincoln] crossed the Maryland line, up to the time of his assassination, that he was not in danger of death by violence and that his life was spared until the night of the 14th of April 1865, only through the ceaseless and watchful care of the guards thrown around him."[37]

So why were none of the alleged Baltimore plotters ever charged with the crime of conspiracy? Several important reasons may explain this mystery. First, the accused would have had a public trial, and this would have taken place in Baltimore. As a practical matter, there is no way a Baltimore jury would have convicted anyone for such a plot. Putting Baltimore citizens on trial would have further inflamed an already volatile situation in the slave state of Maryland. Second, Lincoln himself might have been called as a witness. This would have been both embarrassing and possibly dangerous for him. Besides, given how he was ridiculed in the press as a coward for passing through the city in disguise, Lincoln likely wanted to let the Baltimore Plot story fade away as quickly as possible.

Pinkerton's operatives, too, would certainly have been called as witnesses. This would have blown their cover, particularly that of Timothy Webster, who continued gathering intelligence from Richmond and Baltimore after Lincoln's arrival in Washington. In addition, a trial would have been impractical. By some accounts, there were thousands of National Volunteers in Baltimore, all of whom had sworn an oath to kill Lincoln. How could all of these conspirators be rounded up and held for trial? And finally, there were more important things for the Lincoln administration to focus on. Seven states had seceded, and more threatened to do so. Fort Sumter would be fired upon just seven weeks later. The Civil War was about to begin.

Perhaps the best evidence of what Lincoln might have faced had he gone through Baltimore in broad daylight derives from the riot that occurred there on April 19, 1861. Earlier that month, in response to a call from Lincoln for seventy-five thousand troops, soldiers from Massachusetts and Pennsylvania headed south from Philadelphia to Washington aboard Samuel Felton's railroad. When the train stopped in Baltimore because of barricades thrown across the tracks, the troops had to disembark and march from the PW&B depot at President Street Station to the B&O depot at Camden Street. Along the way, rioters pelted them with brickbats and rocks, and shots were fired. When the smoke cleared, ten Union soldiers and eleven Baltimoreans lay dead in the street.

The Old Army and
the Seeds of Change

John F. Marszalek

WHEN THE CIVIL WAR ERUPTED AT FORT SUMTER IN APRIL 1861, Americans could hardly believe what was happening. Though conflict had been in the air for a decade, many Northerners thought the South was bluffing, and the South thought, as one Southerner put it, that "You may slap a Yankee in the face, and he'll go off and sue you, but he won't fight."[1] The startling outbreak of war took place in a country that had changed dramatically in only ten years. The cascading crises of bleeding Kansas, Dred Scott, and John Brown were accompanied by changes almost as dramatic in population, industry, and transportation. The army, too, changed in the decade of the 1850s, and it would change more after the war began, though the changes would prove to be impermanent afterward, when the culture of the Old Army reasserted itself.

Many of the changes of the 1850s were measurable. The population of the United States grew from 23,191,876 in 1850 to 31,443,321. Although Vermont gained only 0.33 percent in population, New York gained 25 percent, Illinois a whopping 101 percent, and frontier Texas an astonishing 184 percent. Viewing the sections separately, the South gained 27 percent in population while the North gained 41 percent. In 1860, the nineteen free states, seven territories, and the District of Columbia numbered 19,200,000 people, of whom about 237,000 were free blacks, while the fifteen slave states contained 12,240,000 people, some eight million of whom were white. There were also 250,000 free blacks and around four million slaves.[2]

Other aspects of the change could be measured, too. In 1850, domestic manufacturing, which in those days included fisheries and mines, was valued at $1,019,106,061 and grew by 1860 to be worth $1,900,000,000, an increase of 86 percent. Inventions such as the Wilson machine for sewing, Louis Pasteur's pasteurization, George Pullman's railroad sleeping car, Hamilton Smith's rotary washing machine, the invention of the baby carriage, and Bunsen's gas burner all helped revolutionize life. Manufacturing establishments, most of them small and mostly centered in the North, implemented techno-logical change and cleared the ground for the later revolution in steel. New York and Pennsylvania blazed the trail, with over 22,000 factories in each state. The slave South was far behind, with Virginia (5,385) and North Carolina (3,689) leading the way. Even in the agri-cultural sector, though cotton from the South topped national exports, the Northern states led in the production of both wheat and corn. In 1850, cotton production had stood at 2,445,793 bales, each bale weighing four hundred pounds. As 1860 approached, that amount had grown to 5,196,944, an increase of 110 percent.[3]

As the nation grew in population and productivity, arguments over the future of slavery split it apart. The Compromise of 1850, the publication of *Uncle Tom's Cabin*, the 1854 Kansas-Nebraska Act, the Supreme Court's 1857 Dred Scott decision, the violence surrounding fugitive slaves, and then John Brown's frightening 1859 raid all made the argument over slavery more hysterical. At the same time, other change was also evident. Giuseppe Verdi was com-posing *Rigoletto* and *La Traviata*; P. T. Barnum was touring the "Swedish Nightingale," Jenny Lind; Charles Darwin published his *Origin of the Species* in 1859; and that same year Colonel Drake sank the first oil well in Pennsylvania. Earlier in the 1850s, French

Captain Claude Etienne Minié invented his deadly new projectile: the minie ball.

Through it all, one area of American life seemed solidly and reliably unchanged: the American military. There were only 15,259 enlisted men and 1,098 officers in the Old Army in early 1860. They were organized into nineteen regiments: ten infantry, four artillery, two dragoon, two cavalry, and one of mounted rifles. Breaking it down further, there were 198 company-size units, which manned the seventy-nine frontier posts and fifteen installations along the Atlantic Ocean and the Canadian border. Americans consciously kept the army size down and stationed the force far from population centers, in part because of the long-held national fears of a standing army. Consequently, most of the U.S. Army was stationed on the frontier, across the Mississippi River, guarding the migration of white settlers against the Native American desire to maintain their homes and hunting grounds.[4]

At West Point in New York State, the United States Military Academy, often under attack for being elitist, continued to produce second lieutenants for the Old Army. In 1861 there were some two thousand graduates of West Point living throughout the nation, though only 821 of them were still serving with the regular military. The reason so many left the service was no secret. Service was boring, pay was low, and promotion incredibly slow because it came through the separate regiments, not the army as a whole. An officer could not advance in rank until someone above him in his own regiment died, quit, or was promoted. Consequently, officers could stay at one rank for a very long time. Fifty-year-old captains were not unheard of, and colonels commanding regiments often grew old and decrepit in their offices. At the start of the Mexican War in 1846, when one aged colonel tried to put his regiment through its parade ground paces, he dropped dead from the effort. The officers subordinate to him were sorry to see him die, of course, but they were even happier to contemplate the opening his death created for their own careers.[5] Another reason officers left the service in the 1850s was because civilian life offered lucrative opportunities for the particular skills taught at West Point, especially engineering, canal and railroad building, and manufacturing. These paid better and were more challenging than filling out bureaucratic military forms in out-of-the way army posts.

When the Civil War came, therefore, there were relatively few West Point–trained officers available for service, and, despite myths to the contrary, most of them stayed in the Old Army. The United States Army retained 624 of those then serving and added 122 more of those who had retired but now resumed service. The Confederacy attracted the service of only 197 serving officers and ninety-nine more who came back from retirement. Significantly, some 958 past West Point graduates did not serve in the war at all. These individuals are generally unknown to history, yet their story is worthy of study. Even more fascinating are four West Pointers who initially decided to stay with the Union, then left to join the Confederacy— William T. Magruder and Donald C. Stith from Maryland, Richard K. Meade from Virginia, and Manning M. Kimmel from Missouri.[6]

Though the United States Military Academy remained a chief source of army officers, its culture did not reflect a democratic American ethos. Even after the reforms implemented by Sylvanus Thayer between 1817 and 1833, the academy had its own culture and values. Early in the nation's history, a mythology developed that the colonies had won their independence because during the Revolutionary War the American militia had proven superior to the British regulars. This reverence for the civilian soldiers, combined with a concept of American exceptionalism and anti-Europeanism, fed the national antipathy to a standing army. Consequently in 1790, Congress had authorized an army of only 1,216 men. After all, when needed, the militia would rally to do the real fighting. When the War of 1812 demonstrated the inefficiency of the citizen soldier, the nation slowly moved toward a greater professionalism. Winfield Scott, a genuine hero of the War of 1812, helped institute a variety of reforms. Yet his aristocratic leanings, illustrated by his affection for gaudy uniforms and his emphasis on the importance of an officer being a learned gentlemen, butted against the nation's equalitarian strain.

In spite of all that, by the eve of the Mexican War in 1846, the Old Army had become more professional. For one thing, it was larger, embracing some 8,509 officers and enlisted men. Manuals in military science, like those of Dennis Hart Mahan and his West Point student Henry W. Halleck, gave officers a solid dose of French military thinking. The army now had three branches: infantry, cavalry, and artillery. It also had a functioning though rigid staff system, and it had standardized weaponry and regularized tactics. Success in the Mexican War provided the nation with a dose of confidence, seemingly showing Americans just how powerful their homeland had become.[7] As the noted historian Russell Weigley phrased it: Dennis Hart Mahan, the West Point professor and writer, convinced his students "that the United States should have a good army, and . . . that a good army was a professional one."[8] Though the American public retained its belief in a democratically organized force of volunteers, this was the mindset of the professional American military on the eve of the Civil War.

Another important issue within the army's officer corps during the 1850s was the weakening of nationalism. The sectional arguments over slavery proved more powerful than patriotism in both the Old Army and the nation at large. Northern and Southern West Point cadets frequently jostled and struck each other, and sectional cliques developed. The militia system was out of date and in some places had become little more than a social organization, and now the professionalism of the Old Army was becoming endangered. Technological change affected the army, too. This was especially evident in the adoption of the rifled musket and the minie ball and in the continuing influences from Europe, to which American officers had traveled regularly to learn the latest military advances. A number of civilian reformers such as secretaries of war John C. Calhoun and, in the 1850s, Jefferson Davis all continued to influence the Old Army. But there remained an unanswered question: Was this small professional army and weak militia up to the task of fighting an internal conflict of the magnitude of the American Civil War?

When the war began in 1861, the thirty thousand troops that rushed to Washington constituted the largest collection of soldiers ever seen in the United States. No one could have imagined such a large force even a few years previously. Only two men in the country had ever led an army numbering as many as 14,000 men, and they were both in their seventies: John E. Wool was seventy-seven, and Winfield Scott was seventy-five.[9] Their Mexican War experience was to play little direct role in the war that followed. The historian T. Harry Williams, in his *Lincoln and His Generals*, described the 1861 situation well in the very first paragraph of his classic book: "Armies could be raised and weapons manufactured quickly, but it took time and battles to train generals. And it took time and blunders and bitter experiences to develop a modern command system."[10]

Perhaps the best example of how unprepared the army's leaders were for a civil war is the fact that both sides went into battle without really knowing where they were going. Accurate maps simply did not exist. General Henry Halleck, commanding in the West in 1862, had to use maps he had purchased in a bookstore. Not until 1863 did the Army of the Potomac have reliable maps of the state of Virginia.[11] Even more amazing, no one in the United States Army had devised any serious strategy for fighting the war. Winfield Scott's so-called Anaconda Plan was not a mature operation proposal but rather a response to George B. McClellan's proposal to cross the mountains from Ohio to capture Richmond.[12]

In addition, Abraham Lincoln, who most historians believe became the best strategic mind of the war, was a neophyte about military matters when the war began. Yet, unlike many of his generals who thought they knew it all because they were products of the Old Army (or, as McClellan said: "I can do it all"), Lincoln at least had the humility to question, to admit mistakes, and to improve his insights continually. He was a pragmatist, and this included not only his military thinking but also his selection of the men who were going to lead his armies.[13]

Lincoln had few good choices available. Winfield Scott was already in place as commanding general, and his reputation as the nation's first soldier was well deserved. No one else could match his stature, but in 1861 he was a tired old man, unable to summon the energy to provide the leadership the military needed. When Lincoln reached out to Robert E. Lee, he was approaching an individual whom Old Army officers universally respected. George McClellan's prewar and early wartime records were impressive, but there was no way to know how he might evolve as an army commander. Then, too, because Lincoln was calling out the state militias and volunteers, he needed to choose some men who had the kind of public support that could rally the volunteers—the so-called political generals. Some members of the Old Army deprecated this, but it was obvious that there were too few professionals to officer the huge army being assembled, and Lincoln had little real choice.[14]

Despite some early missteps, Lincoln eventually chose a team of three generals who brought the war to a successful conclusion. All three were West Point graduates and veterans of the Old Army: Ulysses S. Grant, William T. Sherman, and Henry W. Halleck, and all faced enormous criticism during the war. Before 1861, few would have predicted that any of them (with the possible exception of Halleck, and he only because of his academic achievements) had the makings of a great general. On the Confederate side, conversely, Jefferson Davis and Robert E. Lee were considered exemplars of the military craft. Neither Grant nor Sherman had any national reputation at all.

Grant and Sherman both had attended West Point reluctantly and only because the dominant males in their families told them to go. Neither enjoyed his experience there because neither had the spit and polish that the Old Army demanded. Even after graduation, Sherman was bored with every military assignment he had, most of them in the South; Grant was so despairing as a result of his lonely duty at a variety of frontier army posts that he betrayed an inability to hold liquor. Like many West Point graduates, both Grant and Sherman resigned their commissions in the hopes of a more fulfilling civilian life and instead found only failure. The classic scene of Sherman, the failed banker, and Grant, the failed farmer, accidentally running into each other on a St. Louis street in the late 1850s expresses it all. Such men seemed unlikely material to transform the Old Army and lead it to victory in a new kind of war.

Unlike Grant and Sherman, Halleck found success in everything he did in the Old Army and also in civilian life after he left the military. While an army officer, Halleck became secretary of state of the California territory after the Mexican War. He was the driving force in the convention that wrote the constitution for the new state of California. He was also one of the nation's leading land lawyers and the author of several books on how to convert Spanish property claims into American law. At the same time, he managed one of the world's largest quicksilver mines, contributing to the success of the 1849 gold rush. His book on military theory was considered so important that even the new president, Abraham Lincoln, read it to bone up on his military duties. Had Halleck not been in California, far from the scene of action when the war began, he, and not McClellan, might well have been Winfield Scott's replacement. Instead, he was given important command in the West. There he so well orchestrated the early war successes that Lincoln named him commanding general.[15]

Grant, on the other hand, had to battle to get into the service at all, and he would not have made it without political support from the Illinois congressman Elihu Washburne. Similarly, Sherman initially gained his high military position because his father-in-law was Thomas Ewing, a leading Whig politician, and his brother, John Sherman, was a congressman and then senator. Grant earned his place by spending the early war years whipping the rowdy 21st Illinois Regiment into shape, and Sherman had to face the ignominy of being called "insane" in newsprint because of his military failings.

Grant and Sherman got their chance largely because they served in the Western theater, which would prove the decisive theater of the war. Had either been compelled to serve or remain in the East under the glare of high expectations and newspaper impatience, the course of their service would undoubtedly have been far different. After Sherman had served in a subordinate position in the Battle of Bull Run, Lincoln sent him to Kentucky as an assistant to the hero of Fort Sumter, Robert Anderson. Sherman had been promised that he would never have to hold overall command, but when Anderson resigned because of health problems, Sherman found himself in a leadership position. He worried himself sick, convinced that the United States was not taking the conflict seriously enough. He found the soldiers, volunteers not professionals, to be inadequate to the task. He slept too little and smoked and drank too much. He developed a reputation of being an eccentric. In December 1861, a newspaper labeled him "insane," and other newspapers followed suit, in truth paying him back for his harsh treatment of reporters in Kentucky. Don Carlos Buell replaced Sherman in Kentucky in November 1861, and his commanding officer, Henry W. Halleck, gave Sherman a menial job: command of a recruit training facility at Benton Barracks, Missouri. "Crazy" Sherman, many believed, would spend the rest of the war years there, at best.[16]

The second young officer in the West, U. S. Grant, faced his first trial by fire in the small Battle of Belmont on November 7, 1861, on the western bank of the Mississippi River across from Columbus, Kentucky. It was very nearly a disaster. After a good start, his men lost their focus and found themselves facing a successful Confederate counterattack. As they fell back to the steamboats that had brought them to the battlefield, Grant had to gallop his horse up a gangplank to escape capture.

It was just as well that Grant continued to have Washburne to protect him.[17]

Both Grant and Sherman, exemplars of the new kind of officer, had to deal with Halleck, who had been molded by the culture of the Old Army. Halleck looked after Sherman and promoted him as he helped him pull out of his depression, but he was more skeptical of Grant. When Grant went to see Halleck in St. Louis in late January

1862 to discuss an idea he had for breaking Confederate General Albert Sidney Johnston's defense lines at Fort Henry and Fort Donelson, Halleck greeted him disdainfully, cut him off, and dismissed his ideas. Grant did not give up, however, and with the help of Admiral Andrew Foote, Grant was able to convince Halleck that an offensive against the Confederates at Fort Henry and Fort Donelson made sense. Grant and Foote took Fort Henry on February 7, and Grant followed up by taking Fort Donelson on February 15, 1862. The nation was electrified when Grant insisted on unconditional surrender, and it gave Grant his new nickname: "Unconditional Surrender" Grant.[18]

Halleck remained unimpressed with Grant despite these victories. Demonstrating his Old Army mentality, Halleck grew angry at Grant for not sending proper reports and told Grant that the sloppiness of his command after Donelson had attracted attention in Washington and resulted in calls for his dismissal. Halleck complained to McClellan, then the overall Union Army general, that there were rumors that Grant was drinking again, and McClellan gave Halleck permission to fire Grant. Halleck briefly did dismiss him but soon brought him back again at Lincoln's specific request.[19]

When Grant became commander of the Army of the Tennessee, Sherman commanded a division in his army. With the Confederate defense line in Tennessee shattered because of Grant's victory at Fort Donelson and Albert Sidney Johnston's retreat to the railroad center at Corinth, Mississippi, Halleck decided to press forward, using the Old Army strategy of massing his troops against the enemy's smaller numbers. He planned to merge Grant's army with Don Carlos Buell's army, then in Nashville, and with John Pope's army recently victorious at Island Number 10. Halleck himself would leave St. Louis to lead this massed force against Corinth and Johnston's Confederate army there. As a rendezvous, Sherman chose a level plain high above the swollen Tennessee River at Pittsburg Landing and a small country church called Shiloh. There he waited the arrival of Buell, Pope, and Halleck.

To everyone's amazement, Confederate General Albert Sydney Johnston surprised Grant's army at Shiloh on April 6, 1862, before Buell, Pope, and Halleck arrived. The Confederates very nearly drove the Army of the Tennessee into the Tennessee River. After the first day of savage fighting, during which Sherman excelled, Union troops huddled along the banks of the Tennessee River in a driving rain, apparently beaten. Sherman was sure that Grant would order a retreat, and when he met Grant that night, he was about to make that suggestion, then thought better of it. Instead, he said, "Well, Grant, we've had the devil's own day, haven't we?" "Yes," Grant replied, "lick 'em tomorrow, though."[20]

And that was precisely what happened. On the second day, Union troops drove the Confederates off the battlefield and back to Corinth. Grant was impressed with Sherman's battlefield performance at Shiloh, and Sherman was impressed with Grant's no-nonsense determination to overcome all obstacles and win. The bond between the two men, begun at Fort Henry, was solidified at Shiloh. They respected each other for their traditional bravery, determination, and success, and they were also beginning to show indications of a new view toward battle. The assumptions and protocols of the Old Army had proved disappointing, but at Shiloh and afterward, these two men became the public face of the New Army as it emerged in the West.

Their reputations moved into the ascendency. Sherman gained a promotion to major general of volunteers, thanks to Grant's fulsome praise, but reporters attacked Grant for negligence in being surprised on Shiloh's first day. They implied, at least, that Grant had been surprised because he had been drinking. Sherman angrily defended his friend, and soon the reporters were attacking him, too, just as they had earlier in Kentucky.[21] Shiloh was a major Union victory, and it demonstrated the two men's skills, but it also resulted in Grant and Sherman experiencing harsh attacks and seeing their reputations fall significantly.

When Halleck arrived to assume command of the finally combined army on April 11, 1862, he betrayed his Old Army priorities by berating Grant for the sloppiness of the camp at Pittsburg Landing. He issued orders reorganizing the army and took Grant's Army of the Tennessee away from him. Grant's new position as second-in-command of the overall force, while technically correct according to Old Army regulations, effectively put Grant on the sidelines. During the Corinth campaign of May 1862, Halleck simply ignored him. Grant grew so discouraged he considered quitting and going home. Sherman talked him out of it, and Grant stayed. It was obvious, however, that as long as Halleck was around, Grant would not play a major role in the western war effort. Both Grant and Sherman could very well have been lost to the Union military effort in this early part of the war—because of Old Army thinking.

Then matters changed dramatically. Thanks to the successes of his forces in the West—mainly because of Grant—Halleck received orders from Lincoln to come to Washington and assume overall command. Halleck did not think Grant was up to the task of becoming his successor as commander in the West, but he did so anyway, and when he did, New Army thinking supplanted Old Army values. Grant at once began to put that new thinking into practice. Just as he had lobbied hard for the campaign that resulted in the capture of Fort Henry and Fort Donelson, now he proposed to move immediately on Vicksburg. Halleck had wanted to delay such a move to prepare better and had refused to allow Grant to go on the offensive until everything was ready. Nevertheless, as 1862 came to an end, Grant was able to move forward. He soon discovered, however, that another problem stood in the way.[22]

To maintain good relations with an important war Democrat from Illinois, Lincoln appointed Congressman John A. McClernand to command an independent army in order to capture Vicksburg. Grant would have been within his rights to object. Not only was McClernand a political general; his somewhat vague command responsibilities also intruded on those of Grant. Certainly other officers found this appointment curious at best. The very thought of a nonprofessional like McClernand commanding a major expedition put West Pointers into a veritable panic. When Grant enquired about their relative spheres of command, Halleck relayed Lincoln's answer that when the troops McClernand had recruited arrived in Memphis, Grant could use them as he wished. Grant's initial plan to attack Vicksburg was to march his army southward down the length of the state of Mississippi and attack Vicksburg from the east. But McClernand's insertion into the campaign changed that. Grant returned to the line of the Mississippi River and assumed overall command of the unified armies on January 2, 1863. In effect, instead of complaining to the president about his appointment of McClernand, Grant had instead adjusted his plans to ensure that McClernand's force became merely a part of the Union army.[23]

The rise of both Grant and Sherman and the eventual shelving of Halleck illustrate the extent to which New Army values were superseding those of the Old Army. In effect, the United States Army reformed itself in the midst of a civil war. Those reforms were enough to ensure victory, but they were far from complete. The Old Army had been transformed by the forces that fought the Civil War, but it came back to life soon after the war was over, and its spirit lived on into the twentieth century. The postwar army remained stagnant, reveling in its Civil War victory and perceiving change as somehow an insult to the volunteer soldiers who had fought the war. Senator John A. Logan, a Civil War political general, wrote an influential book in which he insisted that it was the volunteer soldier, not the professional West Pointer, who had won the war—a new twist on the old minuteman theme of the years before 1861.[24] Permanent reform did not come until the twentieth century, after the vast majority of the Civil War generation were in their graves. To understand the character of the forces that fought and won the Civil War, the stubborn influence of the Old Army cannot be ignored.

Seward and Lincoln
A Second Look
Walter Stahr

WILLIAM HENRY SEWARD LIVED A LONG AND EVENTFUL LIFE: he was a leading lawyer, a state legislator, the governor of New York, federal senator for twelve years, secretary of state for eight years. This chapter, however, will focus on Seward's relationship with Abraham Lincoln.

Seward met Lincoln for the first time on Friday, September 22, 1848, at a political rally in the Tremont Temple in Boston. Seward was at this time one of the nation's best-known Whigs: former governor, likely to become U.S. senator, often mentioned as a future presidential candidate. Physically, Seward was a small, slight, unimpressive man with reddish hair, a large nose, a weak chin. Abraham Lincoln was, at this time, coming to the end of his first and only term in Congress; he was not running for reelection but out campaigning (like Seward) for the Whig presidential candidate Zachary Taylor.[1]

The audience that evening, as Seward described it in a letter to his wife Frances, were "three thousand Whigs, a most intelligent and respectable body of men." He spoke to them for about "an hour, in an argument severe and dry." After Seward spoke, Lincoln addressed the crowd briefly, in what one paper called a "humorous strain of western eloquence." When he finished, the crowd "gave three cheers for Old Zack, three more for Governor Seward, three more for Mr. Lincoln, and then adjourned."[2]

Some Lincoln biographies state, based on a postwar interview with Seward, that Seward and Lincoln shared a hotel room on the next evening in Worcester, Massachusetts. I wish this were true, for it is a great story, the tall and gangly Lincoln and the short, intense Seward talking late into the night about slavery. But Seward was not in Worcester on that night; he was in Springfield, Massachusetts, addressing a large Whig crowd there. And Lincoln was not in Worcester either; he was on his way home by train to Illinois, probably in Albany by then, or even beyond.[3] As best we know, Seward and Lincoln did not meet for the next twelve years: Seward spent most of this period in Washington, serving in the Senate, and Lincoln was mainly in Springfield, Illinois, working as a lawyer and running for Senate.

Lincoln and Seward did have some indirect communication, however. In 1854, after one of Seward's speeches against the Kansas compromise, Lincoln's law partner William Herndon wrote to Seward that "your friend" Lincoln "thinks your speech most excellent." Herndon wrote Seward again in late 1858, after Seward's famous Rochester speech, the speech in which he called the slavery issue "an irrepressible conflict" and predicted that "the United States must and will, sooner or later, become entirely either a slave-holding nation, or entirely a free-labor nation." Herndon noted, in his letter to Seward, the similarity between Seward's "Irrepressible Conflict" speech and Lincoln's "House Divided" speech. Seward responded to Herndon: "No one can regret more than I do the failure of Mr. Lincoln's election [for the U.S. Senate]. He is just the man we need here, and Illinois just the state for which such a man is wanted."[4]

By early 1860, Seward was the strong favorite to secure the Republican presidential nomination; Lincoln was not thought to have much of a chance. How did Seward fail and Lincoln succeed at the Chicago nominating convention? Let me cite a few points from the Seward side.[5]

First, anti-Catholics: Seward was known as the friend of Catholics and immigrants. As governor, he had fought to reform the New York public schools so that they would serve Catholics as well as Protestants. More recently Seward had opposed and mocked the anti-immigrant Know Nothings. We tend to forget how well Millard Fillmore, the Know Nothing presidential candidate, did in the election of 1856: he won 15 percent of the vote in Illinois, 17 percent in Pennsylvania, and 24 percent in New Jersey. Those who had voted Know Nothing in 1856 had not died or disappeared by 1860; thousands of them had become anti-immigrant Republicans.[6]

Lincoln had written to a friend, in 1855, that he was "not a Know Nothing. . . . How can anyone who abhors the oppression of negroes, be in favor of degrading classes of white people?" But Lincoln's statement was not public in 1860. What *was* public was Seward's long record on these issues. Congressman Thaddeus Stevens declared that "Pennsylvania will never vote for a man who favored the destruction of the common school system of New York to gain the favor of Catholics and foreigners." Not for the first time or the last, the nominating convention opted for the candidate with less of a "track record" on a controversial issue.[7]

Second, corruption: The Republican party prided itself on being the party of clean government, contrasting itself with the corrupt Democratic Buchanan administration. Seward himself was generally viewed as clean, but his best friend and chief advocate was Thurlow Weed, and Weed was viewed as perhaps the most corrupt politician in all of New York. The state legislature had just passed a bill to divide New York City into a "gridiron" for private railroads. The rail companies had bribed legislators, and Weed was viewed as the mastermind behind both the bribery and the bill. Weed's reputation rubbed off on his friend Seward. James Dixon, a Republican senator from Connecticut, otherwise inclined to support Seward, said that he would oppose him because "his administration would be the most corrupt the country has ever witnessed."[8]

Third, Pennsylvania: Everyone knew that, on the convention's first ballot, Pennsylvania would vote for its favorite son, Senator Simon Cameron. But who would it vote for on the second ballot? Lincoln's manager, Judge David Davis, negotiated with Cameron's manager, Joseph Casey, and they reached a deal: if Pennsylvania would support Lincoln on the second and later ballots, Cameron would have a prime place in Lincoln's cabinet. Admittedly, this is controversial, for some believe that Davis honored Lincoln's instruction, "make no contracts that will bind me." But if you go to Harrisburg, to the Dauphin County Historical Society, and look at the letter that Joseph Casey wrote to Simon Cameron on May 24, 1860, you will, I think, agree that there *was* a deal. Casey wrote to Cameron that the Pennsylvania delegation was able "to control & make the nomination. It was only done after everything was arranged carefully and unconditionally in reference to yourself to our satisfaction." Casey contrasted the willingness of Lincoln's men to negotiate with how the Seward men "refused to talk of anything but unconditional nomination."[9]

Seward was at home in Auburn when he received the news that he would not be the nominee. A friend who was with him at the time recorded in his diary that Seward learned the news even before reading the telegram: another friend, running from the telegraph office, shouted out as he approached: "Oh God, it is all gone, gone, gone! Abraham Lincoln has received the nomination!" According to this diary, Seward "was the most composed of the three or four who were present." After initially thinking that he would let Lincoln fend for himself in the campaign, Seward changed his mind and campaigned tirelessly for his former rival Lincoln. Seward spoke in fifteen different states, including hostile states such as Missouri. No man did more to secure the election of Lincoln than Seward.[10]

In the course of his month-long campaign tour of the western states, on October 1, 1860, Seward stopped in Springfield, and Lincoln came to the train station to meet him. Charles Francis Adams Jr. noted the greetings were exchanged "standing in the aisle of the car," with Lincoln "embarrassed" and Seward "constrained." They went out, and Seward made a short speech, promising that New York would give Lincoln a majority of sixty thousand.[11]

During the campaign, Seward rallied the Republican faithful and mocked Democratic concerns about Southern secession. In November 1860, however, as Southern states called secession conventions, Seward changed his tone dramatically. A group of Wide Awakes came to Seward's Auburn house, no doubt expecting some kind of triumphant victory speech. Instead, Seward counseled conciliation. Americans of different political parties "are not, never can be, never must be, enemies, or even adversaries. We are all fellow-citizens, American brethren."[12]

That was Seward's tone throughout the secession winter; he was the leading Senate Republican in the search for compromise. In January 1861, not long after the papers had announced that Seward would be the secretary of state, he gave a much-anticipated Senate speech. In the first section, closely based on Jay's second Federalist letter, Seward reviewed the reasons why the United States was stronger as a single nation than as two or more separate nations. In the second section, he outlined the compromises he was prepared to accept to keep the nation together, including a constitutional amendment to "clarify" that the federal government had no right to interfere with slavery in the states.[13]

Seward continued to seek compromise up to and after Lincoln's inauguration. He disagreed with Lincoln's draft inaugural address, thought it too bellicose; indeed he disagreed so violently that he wrote Lincoln a short note, saying that he would not serve as secretary of state. Lincoln persuaded Seward to remain in the cabinet, in part by changing the address, using and improving Seward's suggested final sentence. Seward's draft read: "The mystic chords which proceeding from so many battle fields and so many patriot graves pass through all the hearts and all the hearths in this broad continent of ours will yet again harmonize in their ancient music when breathed upon by the guardian angel of the nation." Lincoln's revision: "The mystic chords of memory, stretching from every battlefield, and patriot grave, to every living heart and hearthstone, all over this broad land, will yet swell the chorus of the Union, when again touched, as surely they will be, by the better angels of our nature."[14]

Lincoln and Seward also disagreed about Fort Sumter. Seward argued that Lincoln should give up the fort, as a way to conciliate the border states. Indeed, on April 1, Seward wrote Lincoln a note: "We are at the end of a month's administration, and yet without a policy, either domestic or foreign." On the domestic side, he urged Lincoln to "change the question before the public from one upon slavery" to the simple question of "Union or Disunion." The best way to do this, Seward believed, was to surrender Sumter. On the foreign side, Seward suggested that the president should demand explanations of recent actions from the European powers and if necessary convene Congress and ask for a declaration of war upon France and Spain. And he ended by suggesting that perhaps Lincoln should devolve upon someone, one person, perhaps Seward, the "energetic prosecution" of these policies.[15]

Lincoln drafted a response that he apparently never handed to Seward, although he probably shared its contents at a personal meeting. There *was* a domestic policy, he wrote, in his inaugural address, with which Seward had agreed and still agreed, excepting Fort Sumter. As to foreign affairs, he and Seward had cooperated in the past few weeks "in preparing circulars, and instructions to ministers, and the like, all in perfect harmony, without ever a suggestion that we had no foreign policy." And as to the main point, overall control, Lincoln was clear: "I must do it."[16]

These two documents are interesting but not that important. What is more important is that, over the course of the next four years, Lincoln and Seward worked together so closely and so well.

Haven't we all written an e-mail that we regretted? Haven't we all had a disagreement with our manager?

One reason these two documents—Seward's note and Lincoln's draft response—have received so much attention is that they are among the *very few* similar letters between the two men. Lincoln and Seward were together in Washington for almost every day of the four years of the Civil War: they did not need to write each other letters, for they saw each other every day. To be sure, there are many letters and notes from Lincoln to Seward in the *Collected Works of Lincoln*, but they tend to be short: please see this person; let us make this foreign appointment. And an electronic search of the Abraham Lincoln Papers at the Library of Congress reveals more than two hundred documents from Seward to Lincoln, but again they tend to be short and routine. There are also more than two hundred letters from *third parties* to Seward among the Lincoln papers: many of them political reports. But you could read through all of this paper and not find out much about the relationship between the two men, for that relationship was face to face.[17]

One gets a better sense from diaries and memoirs describing the two men together. Gideon Welles complained about how, on important issues, Lincoln only consulted one man: Seward. Ralph Waldo Emerson described visiting the White House on a Sunday morning with Seward, spending time first with the Lincoln boys and then Lincoln himself, chatting about pending foreign policy questions. Edward Dicey, the British journalist, noted a joke Seward told at Lincoln's expense—and in Lincoln's presence: Seward had "always wondered how any man could ever get to be President of the United States with so few vices. The President, you know, I regret to say, neither drinks nor smokes." Frederick Seward recalled how, as the two men "sat together by the fireside, or in the carriage, the conversation between them, however it began, always drifted back into the same channel—the progress of the great national struggle. Both loved humor, and however trite the theme, Lincoln always found some quaint illustration from his western life, and Seward some case in point, from his long public career, that gave it new light."[18]

Lincoln especially relied on Seward in foreign affairs, about which Lincoln confessed, at the outset of his presidency, he knew little. The *Trent* crisis provides a good example both of Seward's foreign policy and his relations with Lincoln.[19] It started, from Seward's perspective, in November 1861, when Seward learned that Charles Wilkes, captain of an American naval ship, had fired across the bow of an unarmed British merchant ship, the *Trent*, bound from Cuba for Britain. Wilkes seized from the *Trent's* deck four Confederate diplomats bound for Europe and steamed with them north to the United States, letting the *Trent* go on its way to Britain.[20]

When Wilkes reached the United States with the four Confederate captives, he was hailed as a hero; the House voted to give him a gold medal. When news reached Britain, however, the United States was denounced, and in late December Seward received the formal British response, demanding that the United States apologize and return the four men to British control.

Lincoln's initial view was that Seward should play for time: that he should suggest to the British that the dispute be resolved by international arbitration. Lincoln even drafted a letter along these lines for Seward to send to the British minister.[21] Seward knew, however, that the British would not accept such an approach. They would view it as mere evasion; they might well declare war against the United States. There are several versions of the discussion between Lincoln and Seward, including an unfamiliar one, by Charles Francis Adams. Seward recalled for Adams that, when he had first read to Lincoln his draft response, explaining why the United States should surrender the four Confederates, Lincoln "declared that he could not agree with it at all, and he then undertook the task of preparing a substitute, to which [Seward] immediately consented. But when the [Lincoln] substitute came and was compared with the [Seward] original, it was at once found so insufficient the President voluntarily aban-

doned it, and acquiesced in [Seward's] draft with a few modifica-
tions."[22]

Seward also spent much of his time with military men and matters. In July 1861, for example, right after the first battle at Manassas,
Lincoln and Seward spent two days together, in Lincoln's carriage,
visiting the Union army camps in and around Washington.

One of Seward's military roles was to help with recruiting. In late
June 1862, the Union was in desperate need of more men, but Lincoln feared that if he called for them, right after McClellan's defeats
near Richmond, there would be a panic. So he sent Seward to New
York City, to see what he could do with the governors. Seward settled
in at his favorite hotel, the Astor House, and spoke with the governors, some in person but most by telegraph. The result of his labors
appeared in the newspapers July 2: a backdated letter from the governors to Lincoln, *offering* him additional troops, and a letter from
Lincoln to the governors, thanking them, and calling upon the states
for an additional force of three hundred thousand men.[23]

The summer of 1862 was also the summer of the debate over
emancipation; there was considerable pressure upon Lincoln to issue
some kind of emancipation decree. Seward was *not* among those
who favored a decree; indeed he wrote to Charles Francis Adams
that "it seems as if the extreme advocates of African slavery and its
most vehement opponents were acting in concert to precipitate a ser-
vile war, the former by making the most desperate attempts to overthrow the federal Union, the latter by demanding an edict of
universal emancipation as a lawful and necessary if not, as they say,
the only legitimate way of saving the Union." For Seward, the right
way to emancipate the slaves was by advancing the armies, freeing
slaves in the process, and by winning the war, which would hasten
the inevitable end. In another letter he wrote that "proclamations are
paper without the support of armies."[24]

On July 13, 1862, Lincoln, Welles, Seward, and Seward's daugh-
ter-in-law Anna shared a carriage while riding out to the funeral of
Secretary of War Edwin M. Stanton's infant son, James. Welles later

recalled that it was during this carriage ride that Lincoln first discussed an emancipation proclamation. Lincoln, according to Welles, declared that "he had given it much thought and had about come to the conclusion that it was a military necessity absolutely essential for the salvation of the Union, that we must free the slaves or be ourselves subdued." Per Welles, Lincoln returned to the subject "two or three times on that ride" and "before separating the President desired us to give the question special and deliberate attention, for he was earnest in the conviction that something must be done."[25]

This carriage ride conversation, I believe, is largely a myth. Yes, there was a carriage ride on that day; we know that from two family letters Welles wrote on the same day. But neither of those letters mention emancipation. One letter includes the phrase, "I hardly knew what to make of it," which some have interpreted as an allusion to emancipation, but the whole letter makes it clear that what surprised Welles was Seward's invitation, not Lincoln's remarks. Most important: how likely is it that Lincoln would discuss such a sensitive political topic in the presence of Anna Seward, not quite an outsider, but not an insider either?[26]

On July 22, at a cabinet meeting, Lincoln read aloud to his colleagues what we know as the draft preliminary Emancipation Proclamation. Seward is usually quoted as saying that he approved of the concept but advised delay. In one version, Seward told Lincoln at this cabinet meeting that "I approve of the proclamation, but I question the expediency of its issue at this juncture. The depression of the public mind, consequent upon our repeated reverses, is so great that I fear the effect of so important a step. It may be viewed as the last measure of an exhausted government, a cry for help, the government stretching forth its hands to Ethiopia, rather than Ethiopia stretching forth her hands to the government."[27]

It is a great quote, but not, I think, what Seward said at this cabinet meeting. The quote comes from a book published after the war by the artist Francis B. Carpenter. Far more reliable are the notes taken by Stanton at the cabinet meeting, on Executive Mansion notepaper. Stanton noted that he and the attorney general were in favor of "immediate promulgation" of the draft proclamation but "Seward against it; argues strongly in favor of cotton and foreign governments. . . . Seward argues—that foreign nations will intervene to prevent abolition of slavery for sake of cotton."[28]

From Stanton's notes and sources such as Seward's foreign correspondence, it seems that Seward's initial stance on the proposed proclamation was *not* "this is a good idea but not the right time." Rather, his initial position was "this is a bad idea, but for God's sake if you are going to do this, do not do it now." Those are rather different.[29]

What exactly were Seward's concerns about "foreign nations and cotton?" Both Britain and France, before the Civil War, imported most of their cotton from the United States; the war interrupted that trade and caused considerable distress among both workers and manufacturers. This distress turned into political pressure, especially in Britain, to recognize the South. There was of course countervailing pressure from abolitionists, who hated slavery and wanted Britain to support the North. But the South's British supporters argued that slavery was a necessary evil in the American South, that only through slavery could it produce the cotton so essential to both nations.[30]

Seward raised these concerns not long after the cabinet meeting, in a letter to his friend John Stuart Motley, the historian who was America's minister to Vienna. (Historians, in the nineteenth century, were considered good foreign representatives.) Seward asked Motley whether he was sure that "under the reductions and pressures which could be applied to some European populations, they would not rise up and resist our attempt to bestow freedom upon the laborers whose capacity to supply cotton and open a market for European fabrics depends, or is thought to depend, on their continuance in bondage?" Motley simplified the question and answered with a resounding no; he believed that a proclamation would strengthen British support for

the United States because it would strengthen the hand of the abolitionists and their allies.[31]

As we know, Lincoln delayed issuing the preliminary proclamation but then announced it on September 22, 1862, not long after the
Union victory at Antietam. Over time, emancipation, and black
troops, would change the war, but not immediately; indeed the Union
troops were crushed at Fredericksburg in December 1862 and then
floundered in the mud in early 1863. It was not until July 1863, with
victories at Vicksburg and at Gettysburg, that the United States really
had something to celebrate, and Seward gave one of his longest and
best speeches of the war, from his doorstep in Lafayette Square.

He stressed that, for him, this was still a war for the Union, not a
war against slavery. "The country shall be saved by the republican
party if it will, by the democratic party if it choose, without slavery if
it is possible, with slavery if it must." He predicted that, one by one,
the rebel states would start to rejoin the Union; they were like the
stars in a great constellation, and the "attraction that brought them
originally together, however weakened, cannot be utterly broken."
But this would not happen on its own: his listeners should be prepared to vote for the Union, fight for the Union, perhaps die for the
Union. His listeners must resolve that "you will not wait for draft or
conscription. Ask not whether the enemy is near or whether he is far
off. Ask only is there still an enemy in arms against the United
States—a domestic one or a foreign one—array yourselves to meet
that enemy."[32]

A few months later, in November 1863, Seward was one of those
on the train with Lincoln from Washington to Gettysburg. After dinner, a crowd went to the Wills house, where Lincoln was staying, and
tried to persuade him to give a speech. When Lincoln said he had no
speech to offer, the crowd went to the adjoining Harper house, where
Seward was staying. Seward had a speech ready; indeed a speech
that he gave to the Associated Press, probably because it was unclear,
till the last minute, whether Lincoln would travel to Gettysburg—so
Seward had prepared to stand in. In his remarks, Seward said that

the war was being fought to establish one simple central principle: that "whatever party, whatever portion of the Union prevails by constitutional suffrage in an election, that party is to be respected and maintained in power until it shall give place, on another trial and another verdict, to a different portion of the people." With this principle established, he concluded, "this government of ours—the freest, the best, the wisest, and the happiest in the world—must be, and so far as we are concerned practically will be, immortal."[33]

At about eleven o'clock that evening, Lincoln left the Wills house, with some papers in his hand, and went to the Harper house, where he spent an hour with Seward. Did they discuss Lincoln's draft speech for the next day? We do not know, but it seems likely; the two men had discussed so many drafts over the years, both Lincoln drafts and Seward drafts. The next morning, according to contemporary newspaper accounts, Lincoln and Seward toured the battlefield by carriage. Seward was at Lincoln's side on the platform during the ceremony; at one point during Everett's two-hour address, Lincoln whispered something into Seward's ear.[34]

During the next year, 1864, Seward spent more and more time on politics. He remained, by and large, at Lincoln's side, including through the month of August, when Lincoln's political advisers, including Weed, told him that he had no chance of winning the election. Seward disagreed, writing to his wife that he was "firm and hopeful." In early September, while Seward was in Auburn for a few days, he learned that Sherman had captured Atlanta. He spoke to a crowd gathered in his garden, not only praising Sherman and his men but attacking the Democrats, whose peace platform would in Seward's view "give up the very object of the war at the ballot box." Moreover, a Democratic victory would lead not just to one division of the nation but to a series of rebellions and secessions, as in the fissile states of South America. How, Seward asked his audience, can we "save our country from this fearful danger?" A voice called out, "vote Lincoln in again!" Seward responded: "You have hit it exactly my friend. We must vote Lincoln in again, and fight him in at the same time."[35]

Seward's work for Lincoln's reelection was not limited to speeches. He was deeply involved, for example, in efforts to get Union votes at the Brooklyn Navy Yard. Many of the thousands who worked there were hostile to the administration, and Seward believed they should be presented with a simple choice: vote Union or lose their jobs. Gideon Welles resisted these efforts, denouncing in his diary the "vicious New York school of politics" that would "compel men to vote." And the *Brooklyn Eagle*, a Democratic paper, complained that "no man who will not vote for Lincoln can get work in the Navy Yard."[36]

Seward was in his hometown of Auburn on Election Day—he believed that it was a duty to vote—but back in Washington as soon as possible. He gave another speech from his doorstep, predicting that the rebellion would soon end, "and within three years you will have to look mighty hard to find a secessionist." The newspapers reported his closing as follows:

> The re-election of the president had placed him beyond the pale of human envy or detraction, as he was above human ambition; all would soon learn to see him, as the speaker and the audience had seen him—a true patriot, benevolent and loyal, honest and faithful. Hereafter all motive of detraction of him would cease to exist, and Abraham Lincoln would claim his place with Washington, Jefferson and Adams, among the benefactors of his country and the human race.[37]

Seward's political work did not end with the 1864 election; he spent much of the month of January 1865 working on the antislavery amendment. It speaks volumes about the relationship between the two men—how much Lincoln trusted Seward—that when Lincoln wanted to get the amendment past the hurdle of the House of Representatives, he turned to Seward. It was not going to be easy: the Republicans did not have the requisite two-thirds majority in the House; it was going to take some votes from Democrats and border state Unionists. But Seward knew how to get things done on Capitol Hill; he knew the members and the lobbyists.[38]

Those who have seen the movie *Lincoln* will remember the scene in which the lobbyists pass cash to a congressman by bumping into him in a bank lobby, dropping dollar bills and helping him collect them. I am not sure it happened that way, but one of the lobbyists wrote to Seward that he was sure of getting the amendment through, explaining: "Money will certainly do it, if patriotism fails."[39]

One afternoon in early April 1865, Seward, two of his children, Frederick and Fanny, and a friend of Fanny, started from his house on a carriage ride. A few blocks from the house, the driver got down to fix a broken door, and the horses bolted. Over the screamed protests of his daughter, Seward foolishly jumped from the carriage, hoping to catch the reins and stop the horses. He fell badly and was taken up from the pavement, unconscious, and carried to his house. When the doctor arrived a few minutes later, he found that Seward had broken an arm, several ribs, and his jaw.[40]

Stanton telegraphed to Lincoln, who was near Richmond, that Seward's life was in danger, that he ought to return to Washington. The next morning, however, after visiting with Seward, Stanton wrote Lincoln that he could remain; it seemed the secretary of state was out of danger.[41] On April 9, when Lincoln returned to Washington, the first thing he did was to visit his friend Seward in his room. "You are back from Richmond?" Seward asked, his voice a mere whisper. "Yes," Lincoln replied, "and I think we are near the end." In order to converse more comfortably, Lincoln stretched himself out on Seward's bed, resting his head on his elbow, near Seward's pillow. Lincoln remained with his friend Seward for about an hour and then left. About an hour later, Stanton woke Seward with the news that Richmond had surrendered. "God be praised!" was Seward's reaction; he then listened as Stanton read to him the details, fresh off the army telegraph.[42]

As we know, John Wilkes Booth and his assassination co-conspirators planned to kill not only Lincoln but Vice President Johnson and

Secretary Seward. Some have suggested that Booth targeted Seward because, by federal law, if both the president and vice president died, the secretary of state would have a critical role. He would not become president—the president pro tempore of the Senate was next in the legal line of succession—but the secretary of state would have the responsibility for organizing an election. A good lawyer would know, however, that in the event of the death of the secretary of state, his assistant, or the chief clerk, would serve as secretary of state. But Booth was an actor, not a lawyer, and it seems unlikely that he considered these legal details. He targeted Seward because he viewed him (as many people did) as the deputy president. Booth wanted to stage a new version of Shakespeare's play, one in which not only the tyrant, Caesar, died, but also the co-tyrant, Seward.[43]

And Booth's colleague, the tall, strong rebel soldier Lewis Powell, almost did kill Seward. He talked his way into the Seward house, saying he had medicine he had to deliver. When he failed to persuade Seward's son Frederick to open the bedroom door, he clubbed Frederick with his pistol, cracking his skull in several places. Powell then burst into Seward's bedroom, brushed aside the screaming Fanny, pressed Seward into the bed with one hand, raised high his knife with the other, and slashed at Seward's neck. He missed the first time, but slashed again and again, cutting open Seward's face and neck.

He failed, however, to sever the key arteries; Fanny's screams brought help from her brother Augustus and an army sergeant Robinson, and they wrestled the assassin off Seward, suffering stab wounds of their own in the process. Once again the doctor arrived, finding the house bathed in blood, but amazingly everyone survived.[44]

It is not quite clear how Seward learned of Lincoln's death; there are various versions. Noah Brooks, in his report of April 20, wrote that Seward had a few days earlier asked to have his bed moved near the window. "His eye caught the stars and stripes at half-mast on the War Department," and Seward told the attending nurse that "the

President is dead." The attendant, who had been instructed not to trouble the patient, "stammered and changed color as he tried to say nay," but Seward persisted. "If he had been alive he would have been the first to call on me." And then Seward "lay in silence, the great tears coursing down his gashed cheeks, and the dreadful truth sinking into his mind."[45]

It may be a myth, but if so it is one that was written down within days of the event and not contradicted by Seward or others, so I am prepared to accept it.

Mourning in America
Death Comes to the Civil War White Houses

Catherine Clinton

WHEN SHE ENTERED THE EXECUTIVE MANSION, HER NEW home, it was with a great deal of trepidation. Her husband's elevation to the presidency had followed years of struggle but was a well-deserved triumph, which she savored. She had served him as a political sounding board, promoted his best speeches and his career in government, and stood by her man—despite family conflicts that gave the couple a bumpy start to their marriage. The conflict between in-laws was but one of many obstacles to the couple's marital happiness, as they had also lost a child, a young son, but the wound of this early tragedy seems to have healed. She had given him other sons, and now, as they moved into this new home with young children, they embarked on a new and significant phase of their lives.

She could not expect to rest on her laurels, as her well-acknowledged skills as a political wife would be tested—as would her husband's talents during 1861. She moved into her new home, brushing aside rumors that she was partial to the enemy because of family connections.[1] The new president would need all her support, and she remained true to his cause, convinced he could lead his nation to victory. Yet it pained her to endure a home constantly besieged by those begging favors, advice, influence—unburdening as well as demanding petitioners—alongside the legitimate interruptions of military men, diplomats, and others to whom a wartime president must administer. She hated to see his face become worn with care, his frame even more gaunt—his health even more precarious in the White House than out of it.

Detractors found her style imperious: she played favorites, matchmaker, and more from her perch at the center of the presidential court, a target for gossip and bad press among jesters and hangers-on. She earned a royalist nickname, repeated behind her back, but tried to maintain regal repose. Despite reports to the contrary, many of her household employees defended her against criticism. Perhaps they were as moved as the nation, because she would lose another child, in the White House—and that is where this story begins . . .

'Tis a tale of two first ladies, as this description could apply to either Varina, the second wife of Confederate President Jefferson Davis, and his first lady in Montgomery and then Richmond, or to Mary, Abraham Lincoln's first and only wife, who followed him from Springfield to Pennsylvania Avenue to serve as his first lady. A larger story of mourning may be interwoven with the deaths of these two symbols of sons lost, and of how mourning became perhaps the most potent ritual of the Civil War era.

The death of a child is something extremely traumatizing—yet something all-too-common in nineteenth-century America. Statistically speaking, most antebellum American mothers could expect to lose a child, primarily during infancy or at least before adulthood. Scholars continue to debate this core factor in nineteenth-century parenthood and its effect on behavior toward children, but these analytical and ideological battles are not germane and suffice to say there is evidence on both sides.

Clearly parents became distraught over children's funerals no matter how common it became. Perhaps this is what drove so many Americans—40 percent according to Richard Carwardine—into the arms of evangelical Christianity during the early decades of the nineteenth century.[2] The world was becoming more networked, more accessible, more modern—yet children kept dying—one in ten infants died before the age of one in midcentury.[3] And childhood mortality reached one in four for America's white parents.

Of the four sons she bore, Varina Davis only had one son live to adulthood, and he predeceased her, dying at twenty-one. One of her daughters died, and one of her daughters survived her—so Varina gave birth to six children yet outlived all but one. Mary Lincoln lost two boys at three and twelve, another son at eighteen, and only her oldest, Robert Todd Lincoln, survived his mother.

Within this climate of dread, fear, and a parade of family loss, American writers in midcentury appealed to sentimentality, with stories, images, and poems about dying children intended to comfort the grieving parent. Mothers especially were exposed to a constant stream of messages about angels being called back to heaven. A verse from the *English Woman's Domestic Magazine* in 1863 reflects this:

On the Death of a Little Child

Immortal bud of mortal birth,
    To thee brief date was given,
The flower that was too fair for earth
    Is called to bloom in Heaven.[4]

People had to find ways to cope with the overwhelming consequences of children's mortality. In 1854 Caroline Howard penned a piece about the death of a child

In the sleep of death, with white hands intertwined
    upon her breast,
And flowers around her pallid, marble face
    that she loved best

So Howard, like many of her sister scribblers, tried to soften the blow of loss by portraying a deceased child as calmly reposed.[5] This might have worked to some effect during the antebellum period, but by the time the Civil War erupted, mothers confronted a very different dynamic.

The maiming and slaughter of hundreds and thousands of sons during the four years of the Civil War imposed an unimaginable burden, ringing down the curtain of reality. Historian Drew Gilpin Faust has told us much about death in midcentury America and about the Civil War's role in reshaping attitudes toward citizenship.[6] In his film on this topic, *Death and the Civil War*, based on Faust's *Republic of Suffering*, the documentarian Ric Burns chronicles key features of the era: the Good Death, the *hors mori*—the hour of death to be witnessed and narrated. Faust describes the sorrow of losing loved ones to die as "strangers in a strange land"—the soldier's lot.

Before 1900 less than 20 percent of Americans died away from home—so the Civil War was the largest and most cataclysmic anomaly for nineteenth-century death. Faust points out General Orders no. 33, dealing with soldiers' burials, includes phrasing "as far as possible" and "when practicable."[7] War imposed crushing expediency, and the times were indeed a-changing. Military leaders were hired and fired to wage war, not to tend to niceties. Union General George Meade complained after Gettysburg: "I cannot delay to pick up the debris of the battlefield."[8] And so at Gettysburg, as it was elsewhere, women might be drafted to pick up the pieces—like the ill-fated Elizabeth Thorn.[9]

Keeping track of the wounded and dead was even more challenging. The Union established centers in Philadelphia, Baltimore, and Louisville to keep count of the more than a million names that were eventually recorded in official battle ledgers.[10] Clara Barton heroically spent a good number of years devoting time and energy to tracking down those soldiers who were lost and abandoned by the system that enlisted them but still sought by families that gave them up.[11] Through her efforts more than twenty thousand soldiers were cleared from the missing list. It was only in 2012 that thanks to the Museum of Civil War Medicine and the GSA the building where

Barton carried out much of her work is being rehabilitated into a historic site.

Families of Civil War soldiers were perpetually confronted by loss and grief and asked to perform duties in the face of deprivation. Ministers encouraged the grief stricken to "vent, or it will break the heart" but also warned of exhibiting any "excess of sorrow." Mourners must not forget the afflictions of others or become "neglectful of responsibilities to others or to personal health."[12] The mourning customs required by Victorian propriety were quite exacting: a mother mourned a child for a year, and a child mourned a parent for a year. Siblings and grandparents were mourned for six months, aunts and uncles for two months, and only a month for first cousins. But a widow was expected to mourn for two and a half years.

A society widow went through several visible stages: Heavy or Deep Mourning was the first stage of Full Mourning, when a woman might cover her face and head in a veil. Then she might uncover her head but still remain in widow's weeds and only appear outside the home in full mourning regalia. Second Mourning would continue for the next twelve months before half-mourning wear would become appropriate—the last six months. Widows would have to wear crape throughout the first two years following a husband's death. Crape is derived from the Latin *crispare* (meaning to curl): Victorian mourning crape was imported originally from Bologna.

A widower, by contrast, was expected to wear black crape on his hat or a black armband for only six months.[13] However, wartime did allow for relaxations, as when Susan Caldwell of Warrenton wanted to wear mourning weeds but was forbidden to do so by her husband in the army, for reasons of economy.[14] Scarcity of cloth as much as impoverished coffers caused adaptations in the South.

In the North, family members found appropriate textiles and suggestions for costumes readily available. Indeed, there had been a boom in mourning wear imported from England, where Queen Victoria's mourning for her husband Albert triggered a rise in the "Black Branch" of the fashion industry. In the States, *Godey's Lady's Book* consistently "featured a half page hand-tinted portrait of a group," and as Drew Gilpin Faust pointed out, at least one of these costumes would be appropriate for mourning—even if it was recommended for half-mourning—"a Leghorn hat trimmed with a black plume."[15]

Bombazine, a cloth with a silk warp, a worsted weft, and a twilled finish, became the basic fabric of widow's weeds. Seamstresses turned the worsted finish outward to make the fabric look dull. Mourning crape, crimped into three-dimensional patterns, was essential, used for trim, draped over skirts, a symbol of loss for Civil War families. In her 1869 edition of *Household Management*, Mrs. Beeton offered advice on the "Renovation of Crape."[16]

Mourning jewelry also became a preoccupation of the fashionable—as *memento mori* ("Remember you must die") gained popularity. Mourning jewelry was required to have a dull finish, like the widow's weeds. This came from the ancient superstition concerning reflected images—turning portraits to the wall, covering mirrors. So women were discouraged from wearing anything but dark, dull finishes—jet or onyx were popular. (It was not until 1893 that the Libbey Company of Ohio would introduce black glass jewelry.)

Flowers and fauna were a favorite décor on this jewelry because of their symbolism—ivy for immortality and myrtle as a sign of love and victory. Forget-me-nots and pansies were used as symbols of remembrance. The mauve shade of the pansy became especially popular when adapted for half-mourning costumes. This era also ushered in the fashion for charms and pieces made of hair.

We know how central hair can be to grief, as the cutting of hair has been associated with mourning. In the Balkans women might cut off their hair and leave it as a sign of respect on the graves of deceased relatives.[17] The use of hair in European *memento mori* jewelry dates back to the seventeenth century. In the early 1800s French prisoners of the Napoleonic War living in the Tunbridge Wells area of Kent were famed for their skills at making decorative hair jewelry.[18] Bracelets, necklaces, earrings, watch chains, and other items became treasured mementos.[19] As *Godey's Lady Book* suggested:

> Hair is at once the most delicate and lasting of our materials and survives us like love. It is so light, so gentle, so escaping from the idea of death, that, with a lock of hair belonging to a child or a friends, we may almost look up to Heaven and compare notes with angelic nature, may almost say: "I have a piece of thee here . . . "[20]

The death of a child was something with which Mary Lincoln was painfully familiar. She had lost her second born, Edward, when he came down with a bad case of diphtheria, and after fifty-two days of suffering, his body gave up the struggle. The boy died a few weeks shy of his fourth birthday.[21] Mary's mother and stepmother had each lost babies—her sister Elizabeth had lost her first born in 1836—but on February 1, 1850, Eddie Lincoln's death was a terrible blow. Lincoln suffered stoically, writing to his brother three weeks after his toddler's funeral with poignant simplicity: "We miss him very much."[22]

While Lincoln mourned with reticent dignity, his wife was consumed with mourning—severe weeping spells and a lack of appetite. Lincoln sought out Dr. James Smith, the cleric who had conducted Eddie's funeral service, to counsel his grieving wife. Smith got Mrs. Lincoln through a difficult period. She penned verse to commemorate her boy's death: "Bright is the home to him now given/for of such is the Kingdom of Heaven."[23] She also officially joined Smith's church in 1852.[24] Lincoln's faith and the meaning of his church attendance remains a subject of lively engagement. Whatever his spiritual proclivities, Abraham Lincoln seems to have had a genuine appreciation of Rev. Smith's pastoral care and enjoyed bracing theological discussions with him.

Burying Eddie might have been one of the hardest things the Lincolns had ever done. For each of them, the death of a loved one represented the return of a dark shadow. The Lincolns did not intend to forget this most treasured boy but clearly wanted to climb out of the deep trench of sorrow—and joyfully greeted the birth of William Wallace Lincoln four days before Christmas in 1850. His safe arrival, so close to the holiday celebration, proved a godsend for the entire family and lifted the gloom. The birth of Willie Lincoln, within ten months of Eddie's death, seemed to signal a renewed commitment to their union.

Mary also regained her footing as a materfamilias, first with Willie and then with her fourth and final child, Thomas Lincoln, born in April 1853. This son was nicknamed Tad—presumably because his very large head at birth had reminded his father of a tadpole. But even after the birth of two more babies, Mary confided to a friend in July 1853 that she did "not feel sufficiently submissive to our loss."[25] The death of Eddie haunted her.

Seven years later, during Lincoln's run for the White House, her sister and brother-in-law, Ann and Clark Smith, lost their ten-year-old son, Clark, to typhoid fever (and they would lose a second son, and his uncle's namesake, Lincoln Smith, in 1862).[26] A family funeral in the middle of jubilant politicking was a sobering reminder of her good fortune with three healthy sons. She longed especially to see her son Robert, who had been sent away to school in the East and had been gone for nearly a year; she confessed to being "*wild* to see him."[27] Mrs. Lincoln was known as an emotional parent who rarely imposed discipline on her younger sons born after the loss of Eddie.

With her husband's election and the move to Washington, as well as an impending war on the horizon, Mary struggled against the odds to keep her husband and family on an even keel. Once in the White House, she tried to keep Sunday for family activities, and her sons enjoyed the egg rolling on the White House lawn that took place on Easter Monday, April 1, 1861. The Lincolns diverted their boys from the serious matters swirling around them.

Even Mrs. Lincoln's talents could not withstand the pressures brought to bear following the attack on Fort Sumter on April 12. As William Stoddard would later suggest, "War has no Sunday, no day of rest, no hour that is sacred above the others."[28] The next month the family was rocked by the passing of Elmer Ellsworth, whose death in Alexandria, Virginia, became a touchstone for the nation embarked on the course of war. The Ellsworth funeral on May 25 signaled the Lincolns' first personal contact with loss, the first son fallen to the enemy.[29] Willie and Tad were somber, but the family was comforted by the arrival of their oldest son Robert, home from Boston on May 27.

The White House was not an easy place for the Lincoln family to maintain equilibrium. Just as the boys were getting used to the loss of their hero, Colonel Ellsworth, another White House favorite, Edward Baker, was killed in action at Ball's Bluff on October 21, 1861, on the field of battle. Baker was an old friend of the Lincolns from Springfield and so esteemed that the Lincolns named their second child after him. The day before his death, Baker breakfasted at the White House. An officer passing the Executive Mansion spied Baker and the president in a pastoral moment: "Mr. Lincoln sat on the ground leaning against a tree, Colonel Baker was lying prone on the ground his head supported by his clasped hands." Baker shook Lincoln's hand when he bid farewell and gave young Willie, playing nearby, a farewell kiss.[30]

Baker's funeral on October 24 was another emotional family ordeal. Mrs. Lincoln wore a dress in a shade of purple to Baker's funeral, instead of the traditional black. This Victorian fashion of wearing purple for mourning was only recently introduced and offended some ladies, which added to the controversy over the first lady's Confederate ties and to her multiple shortcomings, according to detractors. Mary Lincoln became embroiled in layers of scandal; more than just a tiff over the shade of her dress threatened to engulf her.[31]

Mrs. Lincoln confidently suggested the White House substitute large receptions for expensive state dinners because it would be "more in keeping with the institutions of our country."[32] When she first broached the subject, her husband was skeptical, but her arguments won out. One of Lincoln's secretaries, John Nicolay, proclaimed, "La Reine has determined to abrogate dinners."[33] And "La Reine" got her way.

Indeed, the Lincolns were the first residents of the White House to see the potential of making their home a national stage. They introduced the practice of bringing artists and performers into the Executive Mansion to include public performance as part of their official entertaining.[34] Mary decided to throw a very large ball in early February and issued seven hundred invitations, hoping to funnel all these guests into the East Room. Not only the work of such an event but the worries associated with such an enterprise became immediate and acute. The Lincoln secretaries, by this time openly hostile to the first lady, referred to her behind her back as "Hellcat."[35]

Mary ignored Senator Benjamin Wade, who wrote indignantly: "Are the President and Mrs. Lincoln aware that there is a civil war? If they are not, Mr. and Mrs. Wade are, and for that reason decline to participate in dancing and feasting."[36] But feast they did, as heaping plates of partridge, quail, duck, turkey, foie gras, beef, and the president's favorite, oysters, greeted guests, as well as an elegantly appointed, white-gloved Abraham Lincoln, with Mary at his side. A cake in the shape of a fort and elegant spun-sugar desserts amused the throng. The Marine Band played the "Mary Lincoln Polka," composed to honor the first lady. The rooms were not overcrowded because only about five hundred showed up, but the *Washington Star* pronounced it the "most superb affair of its kind ever seen here." Not even Kate Chase's lavish soiree the next evening (with songs by the Hutchinson family singers) could dampen the occasion as a success for the Lincolns. However, dissenters composed a counter ditty, "My Lady President's Ball," which offered mournful verses composed from the perspective of a wounded soldier bemoaning follies at the White House. Satires and lampoons of Mary's reforms appeared in several journals.

The only thing that caused Mrs. Lincoln to think about postponing the event was a "bilious fever" suffered by her eleven-year-old son, Willie. This beloved child, William Wallace Lincoln, represented the dearest hopes of both his parents. He was a studious and affable boy and an especially good example for his brother Tad. A frequent visitor to the White House commented, "his self-possession—aplomb, as the French call it—was extraordinary." His resemblance to his father was common praise, and because of this, it was often assumed he was his father's favorite child.[37]

Mary was deeply fearful when he fell ill.[38] When he didn't improve rapidly, his mother wanted to do away with the scheduled ball. Lincoln prevailed on her to wait and see and called in Dr. Robert Stone, who pronounced that the boy was "in no immediate danger."[39] They were able to set aside fears, to leave Willie in the capable hands of Elizabeth Keckly, Mrs. Lincoln's dressmaker who became an indispensible member of the household.

Elizabeth Keckly served as Mary's dresser on the night of the ball and recalled that when Lincoln first saw his wife in her white satin dress with a long train and a low neckline, he remarked, "Whew! Our cat has a long tail to-night." When this failed to get a response, he went on "Mother, it is my opinion, if some of that tail was nearer the head, it would be in better style." This easy banter demonstrated that they were not in the grip of anxiety, leaving Willie to another's care.[40] Lincoln did veto dancing, and the couple absented themselves to look in on Willie several times during the evening—under watchful eyes, his breathing grew labored.

By the next day Willie's situation deteriorated. The papers reported the boy's dire condition. Over the next few days, Lincoln cancelled a cabinet meeting, and Mary omitted her regular White House levee to stay by Willie's bedside. Intimates shared family stresses over this fortnight, as a cabinet secretary confided to his diary that the president was "nearly worn out with grief and watching."[41] Willie's best friend Bud Taft attended the sickroom, trying to help him rally. The president would find the Taft boy asleep on the floor, fearful to leave Willie's side.[42]

When Tad became sick as well, segregated into another bedroom, Lincoln's official correspondence included a reference to his "domestic affliction."[43] The president was distracted, and his wife sat next to Willie's bed, day after day, trying to erase memories of the sickbed vigil for Eddie a dozen years before. His mother's constant prayers and his father's nightly visits failed to rouse Willie from the permanent slumber into which he drifted. The boy breathed his last on a long grey winter afternoon, dying February 20, around 5 pm. As the light slipped away, so did their boy. The Lincolns were inconsolable.

Keckly washed and dressed the body and watched as the president looked down on his dead child, confessing, "My poor boy, he was too good for this earth. God has called him home. I know that he is much better off in heaven, but then we loved him so. It is hard, hard to have him die."[44] Lincoln sobbed over the small, frail body laid out on the bed. Mrs. Lincoln's grief was volcanic, and she gave into hysteria and convulsions.[45] The president knew his wife wouldn't be up to tending to Tad. Rebecca Pomroy, a nurse working in a Washington hospital, was ordered to the White House.[46] Tad collapsed, and Robert, called home to return from college, struggled to control his grief.

The White House was shaken by the loss of this boy as well. William Stoddard suggested that malaria had felled him; some papers suggested typhoid had killed him.[47] Whatever the cause of death, the loss was a heavy burden for the entire Executive Mansion.

The days following Willie's death were an incredible strain on the president. His wife was too stricken even to get out of bed. News of federal military victories flooded in—the capture of Fort Henry in Tennessee on February 6 and the February 17 surrender of Fort Donelson, with Ulysses S. Grant's famous ultimatum: No terms except unconditional and immediate surrender can be accepted.

Hundred-gun salutes competed with the tolling of bells. Willie was laid out in the Green Room. The family planned a funeral service in the East Room, to be conducted by Dr. Gurley, the pastor of Mrs. Lincoln's New York Presbyterian Church. Mary joined Robert, Tad, and Abraham for a final, private farewell, refusing to subject herself to public ceremony. White House mirrors were covered in crape; bouquets surrounded the body. Members of Congress and the Cabinet, generals and diplomats crowded in to pay their last respects.

Lincoln went with the casket to a vault at Oak Hill Cemetery in Georgetown. The president had his own mourning rituals—locking himself in the Green Room on the Thursday after Willie died. He wanted to be alone to meditate on the one-week anniversary, as well as for several Thursdays thereafter, in the very room where his son's body had lain before being shut into a casket. The president was occasionally called out of meetings by Tad to give him his medicine. He ignored convention and counsel, indulging the boy shamelessly. Perhaps it was a way of putting his mourning over Willie into the background by putting his son Tad in the forefront.

While the two remaining Lincoln sons struggled to help their father cope with their mutual grief, Mary retreated. She took to her bed and drew no practical relief from visiting friends' religious platitudes. Only the trappings of mourning seemed to rouse her.[48] Prescribed rituals were clung to like masts in the stormy seas of grief washing over Americans during these terrible times.

Lincoln feared that his wife might never regain her equilibrium. Keckly recounted Lincoln's taking his wife to the window of the White House and pointing out in the distance St. Elizabeth's, a mental hospital, and warning her she might have to be sent there if she could not recover.[49] Robert Lincoln summoned his aunt, Elizabeth Edwards, who arrived at the White House the day after the funeral. She found her sister shut up in a room, prostrate with grief—and her nephew Tad weeping that he would never see Willie again. By February 25, Tad had improved under Rebecca Pomroy's care, even though he could not yet sit up. Elizabeth Edwards finally persuaded Mary to get out of bed, dress, and attend church services. Elizabeth believed that "my presence here has tended very much to soothe the excessive grief."[50]

Tad could not abide being left alone. He and the president began to spend more time together, as a kind of mutual therapy. The little boy could be found shadowing his father by day, in and out of his father's office all day long. Since Lincoln kept such late hours, Tad also might often be found curled up asleep next to his father's desk of an evening. Many nights the father would carry his son into his own bed, and the two might try to keep the other from nightmares.

As her husband and Tad became closer, Mary let anxieties engulf her, wrapping around like wraiths of fog refusing to lift. But the good counsel of women, like the wife of her husband's secretary of the navy, Mary Jane Welles (who would lose six children) and the nurse Rebecca Pomroy, as well as other spiritual advisors, supported Mary during her healing process.

The family moved out to a cottage at the Soldiers' Home to find a change of scenery. At the cottage, Lincoln and his young son enjoyed being surrounded by boys in uniform. Secretary of War Edwin Stanton, assigned a residence near Lincoln's, rarely spent the night at his Soldiers' Home cottage, sleeping more often at his house on K Street or in his office at the War Department. But Stanton moved his family to the cottage for the summer in 1862.

The Stantons' young son James became ill and took a turn for the worse at the end of June. Ellen Stanton's sickbed vigil created a terrible dilemma for Mary. She had been out at the cottage less than a month when the Stanton boy became ill. A messenger summoned Stanton from the War Department on July 5, insisting "the baby is dying." Mary had come to escape memories of her own son's ordeal, and Lincoln had gone into Virginia to rally the troops. With raw memories engulfing her, Mary packed her bags and took Tad and Robert to New York, arriving on July 9. The very next day the Stanton's child, less than two years old, died of his illness, brought on by smallpox inoculation. This seemed a tragic echo of losing Willie, losing Eddie— too many losses.

Four days after the Stanton's child was laid to rest, Mary came back to the Soldiers' Home with her two sons. During her time in Manhattan, Mrs. Lincoln was swathed from head to toe in black, hidden by her mourning garb when she ventured out. Her only recorded purchases were books by Shakespeare and Scott for the Presidential Library.[51] She visited the Broadway clinic run by the New England Relief Association. Following this stop, she headed for the Park Hospital, where the first lady greeted wounded soldiers, where they "fully appreciated her kindness and womanly sympathy."[52]

Returning to Washington mid-July, she embarked on a program of ministering to soldiers. By summer, nearly eight thousand soldiers in the District of Columbia were sick and wounded, and their care was a critical concern to the women of Washington. Mrs. Lincoln threw herself headlong into this new vocation and solicited one thousand dollars from a Boston merchant, which was donated to the military hospitals.[53] Work became a tonic for her low spirits.

The novelist Ann Stephens accompanied Mary Lincoln during several of these tours of duty, "walking for hours through the wards to say cheering words of hope and encouragement to the wounded and sick; laying fresh flowers on their pillows and offering them delicacies brought from the White House." During their time together the first lady confided to her companion if it were not for these visits, her heart would have been broken by the loss of her child.[54]

During this period Mrs. Lincoln regularly lost control of her emotions. When a woman reporter, Laura Redden, stopped in at the summer cottage in August 1862, Mrs. Lincoln greeted her warmly. But when Mary "burst into a passion of tears," Redden was so moved that she broke protocol and reached out to embrace the distraught first lady. She put her arm around the bereaved mother who "could neither think nor talk of anything but Willie."[55]

Fresh torrents of grief flowed freely when her young half-brother, Alexander Todd, died of wounds received at the Battle of Baton Rouge on August 19. Mrs. Lincoln never publicly acknowledged the deaths of any Confederate relatives but privately mourned "baby Alex," a particular favorite of Mary's. Alex's youthful death, struck down by friendly fire, contributed to her melancholy.

Struggling against her overemotional nature, Mary Lincoln found herself enthralled by an increasingly popular pastime in Civil War America: spirit circles. These were gatherings organized by mediums who practiced spiritualism, communing with those who had "crossed over," talking with the dead. This belief in contact with the dead was one of the fastest-growing movements in nineteenth-century America, accelerated by the mounting Civil War death lists.

The attempt to communicate with the dead proved irresistible to Mary in her weakened state—and indeed to hundreds upon thousands before and especially during the war. The rise of Victorian sentimentality blended nicely with spiritualist philosophy. Abby Sewall explained: "'tis sweet to call to mind the loved of earth who have passed away, and think how soon we shall be like them, free from sorrow and care . . . the thirst for immortality is not implanted in our hearts in vain."[56] Sewall suggested that the church, the state, and medical experts could not provide succor for the "disease of a starved heart."[57] Naturally, many took advantage of these starved hearts.

A few years before the war, Oliver Wendell Holmes reflected on the spiritualist culture wars in the *New York Tribune*: "While some are crying against it as a delusion of the Devil, and some are laughing at it as an hysteric folly, and some are getting angry with it as a mere trick of interested or mischievous persons, Spiritualism is quietly undermining the traditional ideas of the future state which have been and are still accepted."[58] It was a kind of fearful symmetry that the telegraph (along with the concept of electrical forces) premiered in 1848, just when the Fox sisters in upstate New York burst into the headlines. It was no accident that their talent was described as a "spiritual telegraph" that allowed them to communicate with those who "passed over."[59]

Spiritualism caught fire because it coincided with the deepest needs of American women at midcentury. At a time when nearly half the deaths in New York state were children under five, it is no wonder that grieving mothers sought Summerland, the spiritualist name for heaven—with hopes for reconnecting with lost loved ones. Elizabeth Stuart Phelps's *The Gates Ajar* reflected the spiritualist ideal that graveyards must be transformed from doleful stone gardens into a "site designed for the contemplation of happy memories and heavenly reunions."[60] Harriet Beecher Stowe (like her sister Catharine) had a healthy distrust of mediums. Nevertheless, she was obsessed with the idea that she might be able to talk to her dead children. Stowe was not alone: the more than two million Americans subscribing to spiritualist beliefs in 1850 would triple their numbers by the summer of 1862, when Mary Lincoln, like so many American mothers, faced grief over the loss of a child.[61] The Civil War fueled intense interest in spiritualism.

When Mary Lincoln sought out spiritualists in the summer of 1862, she was recklessly needy. Her dabbling in the spirit world, not her good works at the hospital wards, stimulated gossip in 1862. By 1863, Mary Lincoln's association with charlatans continued to tarnish her reputation. The memoirs of the spiritualist Nellie Colburn assert that she knew both the Lincolns from spirit circles in wartime Washington and that Lincoln himself was a spiritualist. Lincoln's presence in the eminently respectable Georgetown parlor of the Laurie family does not indicate much beyond his indulgence of his wife. However, Lincoln did take meetings with spiritualists—even without Mrs. Lincoln present.[62] By contrast, Mrs. Lincoln confessed that her ability to communicate with her dead boys brought great comfort—a longing mirrored in the lives of thousands of mothers across the nation during those dark days.[63]

So in many ways the death of Willie symbolized the tragic loss of a beloved son, any mother's child, and the loss of what might have been. Mary Lincoln's plunge into spiritualism was symptomatic of the era when millions averted their faces from what was, longing for what could never be.

Varina Davis took no such dive with the loss of her beloved "little Joe" in the spring of 1864. Varina was no stranger to mourning, nor was her husband Jefferson. Indeed, she had to undergo the very stressful ordeal of being a nineteen-year-old bride on honeymoon, when her new husband—the thirty-seven-year-old widower Jefferson Davis—took her to the grave of his first wife, who had died ten years earlier.[64]

Varina had difficult relations with her husband's older brother Joseph, who was like a surrogate father to Jefferson. Joseph's family management included moving a widowed sister-in-law and her orphaned children into the Jefferson Davis plantation home, which did not endear him to Varina. Luckily, she escaped Mississippi when her husband entered the House of Representatives shortly after their marriage, following his distinguished military service in the Mexican–American War. In 1847, he became the U.S. senator from Mississippi. Next he was drafted by Franklin Pierce as secretary of war in 1853. Guy Gugliotta's wonderful study of the Civil War era, *Freedom's Cap*, tells the fascinating story of the rebuilding of the Capitol dome, which provides a colorful and compelling narrative of congressional politics during the decade before he Civil War, including some of Davis's more memorable schemes, like the attempt at forming a camel brigade for use in the southwestern desert.

By the 1850s, Varina Davis had become a popular society hostess in Washington. Laura Holloway complimented, "the home of Mrs. Jefferson Davis was much more the gay center of Washington society than was the White House."[65] Davis was in no way trying to supplant the first lady but rather understood that Jane had slipped into deepest mourning. When her husband was elected president in 1852, she had already lost two sons, and on their way to Washington for the inauguration, the Pierces' only remaining child, a son, was killed in a railway accident before his parents' eyes. His bereaved mother spent most of her husband's administration as a recluse, and the Smithsonian today has one of her gowns for half-mourning in its collection, a black silk taffeta skirt with an óverskirt of black tulle embroidered with silver dots.[66]

While Jane Pierce was distracted by her grief, Varina Davis unofficially shouldered some of this first lady's entertaining responsibilities. Davis herself had been a social ingénue at nineteen, when her husband had taken her to the Polk White House. But by the time of her husband's administration, she was a polished and skilled matron; Mrs. Davis made sure every member of the House of Representatives received at least one invitation to a Davis fête during the winter.

The demands of family and society, politics and private concerns provided variety and challenge throughout the 1850s.

In April 1859, the couple faced their own crisis when they welcomed a new son, whom Varina very much wanted to name for her father: William Howell. But Jefferson Davis had other plans and insisted that they name the boy Joseph E. Davis, after his beloved brother, who William Cooper documented, was someone Varina believed was her "nemesis."[67]

The wrangle over the baby's name was debilitating. Varina conceded that her husband had the right to make such decisions but was so sickened by this quarrel that she cried her eyes out. She decamped to Maryland to recover from the birth, being nursed by the daughter of Montgomery Blair. She regretted paying "the highest compliment in a woman's power to a man whose very name was only suggestive to me of injustice and unkindness from my youth up to middle age." She fretted too that the baby looked like a Davis and not a Howell.

Joseph Davis was thrilled with this news of a namesake and did what he could to reward his brother's wife. When Little Joe was just a baby, his uncle offered to pay an all-expense paid trip to Europe for Varina, her three children, and a nurse, to accompany him on the Grand Tour. She stubbornly refused.

Her resentment had not abated by 1861 when on a visit to Richmond, Joseph confessed in private to his sister-in-law that the naming of this child had "obliterated all memories of ill feelings between them." But Varina refused to let bygones be bygones and told Joseph that she "knew how much her husband loved his brother, and that she would require her children be respectful" yet went on to declare, with blunt force, that "I owe you nothing, & perfectly appreciate your hostility to me."[68]

By the time Davis became the Confederate president, the couple were reconciled and operating as a team. Varina had been disturbed by their first home, but now she resided in a three-story Italianate mansion fitted with gas-burning chandeliers (gasoliers) and rich American Rococo Revival furnishings, in the house at Twelfth and Clay in

Richmond, leased by the Confederate government to serve as the Executive Mansion. By the time they moved into their new home, Little Joe was reportedly his father's favorite, climbing on his papa's lap at the dinner table. Nightly, he asked his father to join him in prayers before bed.[69] In December 1861, Varina gave birth to another son, who was named William Howell Davis, in deference to her wishes.

Visitors to the Confederate White House were charmed by the children. Both Joe and Jeff wore Confederate uniforms, and some observers commented that like many young boys, they possessed "unbroken wills." But they were doted on, and by late 1863, as an observer reported, Davis's voice had "a melancholy cadence in it which he is unconscious of as he talks of things as they are now."[70] But the children were a great diversion, and Varina confided that Joseph "was the greatest joy in his [her husband's] life."[71]

So it was the deepest tragedy when Varina Davis had just arrived at her husband's office at the Customs House midday on April 30, 1864, taking her husband his lunch, when a servant showed up to fetch Jefferson and his wife—Joe had fallen off the piazza at the Executive Mansion. Varina later recounted that she had left him playing happily with the other children and their Irish nurse, Catherine. But apparently Joe had wandered off on his own, out onto the balcony, where workmen were doing construction. And whether he was climbing the balustrade or some other scenario, his body was found on the brick courtyard pavement below by his older brother Jeff, who began to wail and went to fetch the nurse. He could not wake his brother up, and Jeff told the neighbor, Mrs. Semmes, who arrived before the boys' parents, that he had prayed that God would wake Joe up. The boy was still alive when Varina and Jefferson found him with a skull injury and two broken legs, but the broken boy expired before the doctor arrived. The doctor who had been fetched for the injured boy tended to his mother instead—prostrate with grief and seven months pregnant at the time.

The boy was brought into the mansion, where Jefferson Davis repeatedly chanted over his son's dead body, "Not mine, Oh, Lord, but thine." The parents, rendered senseless, hovered over the lifeless corpse. When a courier arrived with a dispatch from General Robert E. Lee, requiring a response, Davis sought help from Varina, but they were both unable to rise to the occasion, and the Confederate president confessed, "I must have this one day with my little son."[72] The dispatch was taken to General Cooper to answer. His secretary Burton Harrison made arrangements and tried to minister to the distraught Confederate president.

A witness observed that Davis's face "seemed suddenly ready to burst with unspeakable grief, and then transfixed into a stony rigidity."[73] But Davis refused to rest, and Varina awaited the return of her beloved sister, Margaret, who was away for the day. Their close family friend Mary Chesnut, the wife of former South Carolina Senator James Chesnut Jr., had planned to leave the Confederate capital the next day; she had taken Margaret out on a boat on James River with friends for a picnic and to watch a prisoners' exchange. Many of the details of the family's grief, and the sad funeral that followed the next day, were recorded in Chesnut's diary.

Mrs. Davis sent her carriage to fetch the returning picnickers, who were told by the coachman that Little Joe was dead. Mary Chesnut recorded that on the ride back to the Davis home the "silence [was] broken only by Maggie's hysterical sobs." When the party arrived, the house was lit up in every room, but the mansion was silent. Burton Harrison reported that Davis was up all night pacing.

The Chesnuts postponed their departure to attend the funeral, which was an amazing outpouring of grief. The death of a child was always a sentimental and tragic affair, and the people of Richmond took their opportunity to shower the Davis family with condolences. The death became a public event: nearly a thousand children wound up the hill to Hollywood Cemetery for Joe's burial. While the president and his pregnant wife stood witness, each child dropped a bunch of spring flowers or a green spray on the plot, which became a mass of white flowers. Burton Harrison recalled: "The terrible self-control of Jefferson Davis was even more heartbreaking."[74] Constance Cary (who would become Burton's bride) remarked that Davis looked older than his fifty-five years, and she was haunted by Varina's "mournful, dark eyes."[75] So many of the mourners were struck by the cloaked figure of the first lady burying one child while pregnant with another. Davis's biographer commented, "Richmond had no remembrance of a more moving funeral."[76]

On May 2, Jefferson Davis returned to his office and the business of nation and war.[77] Varina was complimented as well on her brave face: "Mrs. Davis, although she was in mourning, at first for her father, and then for her little son, courageously fulfilled all the social duties of her position."[78] The first lady delivered her seventh and final child, a daughter, on June 27, christened Varina Anne but nicknamed "Piecake" (or just "Pi") by her family. However, to the rest of the country, she symbolized her father's dream and was known as the "Daughter of the Confederacy." She never remembered the balcony from which her brother fell to his death. In September 1864, her father had the workmen tear it down. When he was in prison following the fall of the Confederacy, Jefferson Davis was brought by a doctor a twig from the grave of his son Joe, and "he meditated on . . . that little mound to which was laid so much of my tenderest love and highest hope of earthly things. The promises which find their fulfilment in a in a [sic] better world were mingled with the memories of my buried hope."[79] Davis died in 1889 and was reunited with his son in a gravesite in Richmond in 1893.

Mary Lincoln was unable to make the funeral train trip, with her husband's remains accompanied by Willie's coffin, back to Springfield in 1865. But she was buried at the Oak Ridge cemetery in 1882 with three of her sons and her husband, the martyr president in whose honor she wore black for the remainder of her life.[80] Varina Davis buried six of her seven children and a husband. She would confide to her daughter Margaret, shortly before her own death in 1906: "I'm going to die, don't you wear black. It is bad for your health and will depress your husband."

Abraham Lincoln, Admiral-in-Chief

Craig L. Symonds

IN CONSIDERING THE GENIUS OF ABRAHAM LINCOLN, THE context in which we might use the word "genius" is what the *Oxford English Dictionary* lists as the fourth meaning of that word: "A natural ability or tendency which fits a person for a particular activity." The first meaning of the word, by the way, is "the attendant spirit in classical pagan belief allotted to every person at birth," a definition that makes all of us geniuses. But Lincoln's particular genius, the particular activity for which he was fit, was the ability to see the whole clearly and, more importantly, to manage the people around him in a sympathetic, compassionate, yet realistic way, to move them in the direction that he believed was necessary. His was, as Doris Kearns Goodwin notes in the subtitle of her book, a "political genius."[1]

But we must be careful when we use that phrase. Do we mean that Lincoln was somehow gifted with the intellectual and psychological tools to become great and that his rise to greatness—to immortality, even—was simply the application of his native "genius" to the problems around him? If we assume that, I think we do him an injustice. For Lincoln's genius was not a product of his genetic makeup. Certainly there was no evidence of any particular genius in either his ancestors or descendants. Lincoln's greatness was not a gift at birth but rather the product of a lifetime of effort: of careful and thoughtful reading, of considering and reconsidering, of arguing (mostly with himself) both out loud and on paper, of making mistakes and learning from them. He developed the rare strength of character necessary to suppress his own ego to higher causes. And this process of learning, arguing, and adjusting continued throughout his life. He was more of a political genius in 1865 than he was in 1861 when, it must be said, he made a number of rookie mistakes as president. But he seldom made them twice, and when he did, he acknowledged so publicly and changed course.

This is what allowed Abraham Lincoln to tackle issues that were completely foreign to him and, after some trial and error, to emerge as a genius in those fields, too. Certainly he devoted little time to questions of strategy and tactics in the decades before he became president. As a western country lawyer, he was hardly expert in matters of the sea. "I know little about ships," he confessed to Secretary of the Navy Gideon Welles in 1861. But he had learned a lot about people, and—even more important—he was willing to learn. The point is that Lincoln's genius was more a process than a character trait.[2]

This essay will consider the role Lincoln played in the western campaigns during the first four months of 1862—especially the war on the western rivers—and outline the circumstances that led him to step into a void of leadership and become an activist commander-in-chief, a task he never sought and, indeed, barely imagined prior to 1861. Yet, in the end, it was Lincoln's strategic vision that emerged triumphant, though his role in that triumph is seldom acknowledged.

Lincoln began to think about Union grand strategy almost from the first day of the war. On April 25, the day that the 7th New York regiment marched into Washington to ease fears of a rebel *coup de main*, he mused aloud to his assistant secretary John Hay about how the administration could regain control of the crisis. "I intend at present," he declared, "to fill Fortress Monroe with men and stores; blockade the ports effectually; provide for the entire safety of the

Capitol; keep them quietly employed in this way, and then go down to Charleston and pay her the little debt we are owing her." What is missing from this summary, of course, is a western river campaign, a curious omission since Lincoln was both a westerner and a river man. At the time, Lincoln was still thinking of the conflict as a kind of police action to pacify an out-of-control minority.[3]

By the end of the year, with the capital secure and the blockade established, Lincoln had developed a more sophisticated and detailed concept of grand strategy, one that did include a western campaign. He began with the simple fact that the Union States had "the *greater* numbers" while the rebellious states, operating with interior lines of communication, had "the *greater* facility of concentrating forces upon points of collision." It seemed evident to him that the way to take advantage of these circumstances was to "menace" the enemy at several different points "at the same time." This would force the rebels to do one of two things: Either they would have to concentrate their forces in one place by temporarily abandoning the others, or they would have to split their forces into a number of smaller units and try to defend everywhere. If the enemy chose concentration, Union forces should "forbear to attack" the strengthened position and occupy the abandoned sites. If instead the enemy divided his forces into smaller units, they could be defeated in detail one by one. It was a clearheaded and straightforward analysis, but its success depended entirely on effective cooperation by the generals in the field, and as Lincoln already knew, achieving such cooperation was problematic at best.[4]

Lincoln was not eager to manage that coordination himself. According to John Hay, Lincoln was sufficiently frustrated in the aftermath of the Gettysburg campaign to declare: "If I had gone up there I could have whipped them myself."[5] That, however, was more a measure of his disappointment than of any genuine intent and in any case was intended only for private ears. Unlike his Confederate counterpart, Lincoln never cherished the vision of donning a uniform, riding to the front, or even moving chess pieces about on a strategic map. His first hope had been that General Winfield Scott would assume that role, but it had become clear that despite Scott's brilliant success in earlier wars, the current task was beyond the elderly hero. It was precisely to achieve the kind of coordination that he believed to be essential that Lincoln turned to the younger George B. McClellan, endowing him with command of not only the Army of the Potomac but of all Union armies. By January 1862, McClellan had brought a sense of purpose and direction to the mobilization of the Army of the Potomac, but he had not as yet demonstrated any eagerness to test that army in battle, and his oversight of the nation's other armies was largely pro forma. Worse, McClellan had fallen seriously ill with typhoid fever, leaving a void at the top of the command pyramid.

With War Secretary Simon Cameron on his way out and McClellan in his sickbed, there was no sense of purpose or direction to the Union war effort. A delegation from eastern Tennessee filled Lincoln's ears with tales of Union patriots "being hanged and driven to despair," and a joint congressional committee met with Lincoln to complain about the absence of a "vigorous prosecution of the war." When Lincoln wrote Major General Henry W. Halleck, his chief western general, to ask how soon he might be able to move southward, Halleck replied with a lengthy lecture on the principles of war. At the bottom of this unhelpful dissertation, Lincoln wrote: "It is exceedingly discouraging. As everywhere else, nothing can be done." That same day, he dropped in on Montgomery Meigs, the army's quartermaster general, to whom he unburdened himself. "The people are impatient," the president groaned. "The General of the Army has typhoid fever. The bottom is out of the tub. What shall I do?"[6]

It was under these circumstances that Attorney General Edward Bates began to urge Lincoln to take the strategic reins into his own hands. Bates even wondered why McClellan had been granted the title of general-in-chief when the nation already had a commander-in-chief. Whether Bates touched a nerve or the circumstances simply compelled it, Lincoln saw that someone had to provide direction and leadership, and since no one else was apparently willing or able to do it, he took it upon himself. He scheduled a meeting of what amounted to a council of war for January 10, inviting Secretary of State William H. Seward, Secretary of the Treasury Salmon P. Chase, and Thomas A. Scott (who sat in for the lame duck Simon Cameron), plus two of the army's senior officers: Irvin McDowell, favorite of the congressional spokesmen, and William B. Franklin, the senior division commander in McClellan's army.[7]

Lincoln met three times with this ad hoc war council, and, inevitably, word of it leaked to McClellan. When the group reassembled on January 13, Little Mac himself was present. He was pale and haggard, but he was finally out of bed and in uniform. His presence silenced the rest; even Lincoln waited for the general-in-chief to assume control of the meeting. But McClellan was sullen and silent. When Lincoln asked him what should be done, he relied that "the case was so clear a blind man could see it." When Chase asked him to be more specific, he refused to divulge his plans on the grounds that no one in the room could keep a secret. When, at length, Lincoln asked him directly if he had a plan of action for the Army of the Potomac, McClellan said that he did. "Then, General," he announced, "I shall not order you to give it." And with that, he adjourned the meeting. As long as the commanding general was willing and able to do his job, Lincoln would not wrest it from him. Not yet.[8]

Of course, even if McClellan was successful in Virginia, it would not achieve what Lincoln still saw as the essential key to Union success: the coordination of all Union armies, east and west. If and when McClellan advanced, the two western armies would have to synchronize their activities as well to prevent the Confederates from concentrating on him. Moreover, both western armies would be heavily dependent on the river system for transportation and supply. In the West, railroads were useful, but railroads could be wrecked and railroad bridges could be burned, and in any case railroads did not have the capacity of river transport. Whatever happened in the western theater, therefore, would depend not only on the coordination of the two main field armies but on cooperation between those armies and river gunboats, and this led to a great deal of confusion and uncertainty about command authority on the rivers.

Tradition held that the authority of the U.S. Navy stopped at the high tide mark. The navy assumed jurisdiction over warships operating on the Potomac, the York, the James, and other tidal rivers on the east coast, but Secretary of the Navy Welles assumed that the western rivers were the army's problem. Alas, constructing and commanding gunboats required specialized knowledge that few army officers had, and even fewer were interested in volunteering for such a duty. Welles therefore agreed to send a naval officer to Cincinnati to help the army prepare a riverine force for the western campaign. But this created confusion, too, for while navy officers in the West were administratively under the Navy Department, they took their orders from the War Department, and there was no protocol to determine which department bore the responsibility for pay and supplies. According to the Constitution, there was only one person in the entire nation who had command authority over both the army and navy of the United States: the tall, overworked, and currently despondent man who occupied the White House. In his effort to effect a coordinated campaign in the West, Lincoln would find that he not only had to synchronize the movements of his generals; he also had to coordinate the army and the navy, a task that proved roughly equivalent to mixing oil and water.

The man Welles sent to Cincinnati was Commander John Rodgers. Like most naval officers of his era—or any era—Rodgers' professional goal was command at sea, and he looked upon his assignment to Cincinnati as a kind of banishment, especially since Welles made it clear that while his job was to establish a riverine force, he was to do so "under the direction and regulation of the Army." Nevertheless, Rodgers got to work at once, finding three suitable vessels, which he purchased and began to convert to military use by strengthening their decks to bear the weight of naval armament, replacing their thin bulwarks with five-inch oak planks, dropping the boilers from the deck into the lower hold, and rerouting the steam pipes to make them less vulnerable to enemy fire.[9]

Those first three river gunboats—*Tyler, Lexington,* and *Conestoga*—were destined to play crucial roles in the western campaigns, but when Welles learned what Rodgers had done, he was furious. He fired off a telegram informing Rodgers that he had overstepped his authority. "The movements on the Mississippi are under the direction and control of the Army," Welles declared. Therefore, "All purchases of boats . . . must be made by the War Department." Welles' concern was mainly financial. The gunboats "are not wanted for naval purposes," he asserted. "If they are required for the army," the army must "make requisitions on the War Department." Showing how distant he was from Lincoln's vision of a coordinated offensive, Welles informed Rodgers that "the two branches of service" must not "become complicated and embarrassed" by "any attempt at a combined movement on the rivers of the interior."[10]

Rodgers might have survived Welles' pique if he had managed to get along with the army commander in the West, John C. Fremont, but Fremont became annoyed with him, too. Naval constructor Samuel A. Pook was fabricating half a dozen armored gunboats under army contract, an effort that Frank Cooling has labeled "a Civil War prototype for latter military-industrial linkages in modern America." If so, those linkages were remarkably fragile in 1861. Rodgers' efforts to ensure navy participation in the planning and construction of these gunboats led Fremont to decide that the navy officer was meddling in army affairs, and he complained about it to Welles. Largely to gratify Fremont, Welles decided to supersede Rodgers with the newly promoted Navy Captain Andrew Hull Foote, whom Welles had known since boyhood when they had both attended the same prep school.[11]

As he had with Rodgers, Welles made it clear to Foote that he was "under the direction of the War Department" and that any requisitions for his flotilla must go to the army. By now, however, the weakness, not to say folly, of having navy officers draw on the

War Department for logistic support was becoming evident. Welles expected that the men of the gunboat flotilla would be paid by the army, but Fremont decided they should be paid by the navy, and the result was that the men didn't get paid at all. Nor did Foote have a secure source of supplies. He told Welles he was "embarrassed about powder and shot, having been positively refused these both by the Army and Navy." He wrote to Cameron, but the lame duck secretary had more pressing problems than meeting the needs of some navy officer out west and ignored him. The fact was that, important as it was, no one accepted responsibility for Foote's orphan command. As Edward Bates put it in his diary, "the boats are under the War Dept, and yet are commanded by *naval* officers. Of course they are neglected—no one knows anything about them."[12]

For the first nine months of the war, Lincoln did not involve himself with this jurisdictional confusion on the western rivers. In January 1862, however, at the same time that he established his council of war, the president learned that a large number of flat-bottomed mortar vessels that had been ordered months before and that were intended for the western campaign were still unready and that no one seemed to be exercising any oversight of the project. These boats, also called bomb vessels, were essentially flat-bottomed rafts, forty to fifty feet long, each of which boasted a single large and very heavy weapon that looked something like a witches' brewing pot in the exact center of its flat deck. The squat, ugly mortars fired enormous thirteen-inch shells (bombs) in a high arcing trajectory to rain down on enemy fortifications three or more miles away.

Lincoln may have first considered the capabilities of mortar boats as a result of a visit from Lieutenant David Dixon Porter. Welles had brought Porter to the White House in November 1861 to discuss an expedition to New Orleans. The notion of seizing New Orleans was not a new one, but Porter's idea of using mortar boats to accomplish it was. Once Porter had explained his plan, Lincoln leaned back in his chair and said: "This reminds me of a story." As Porter later remembered it, it went like this: There was an old woman in Illinois who missed some of her chickens, and couldn't imagine what had become of them. Someone suggested that they had been carried off by a skunk so she told her husband he must sit up that night and shoot the "critter." The next morning the husband came in holding two pet rabbits that he had shot during the night. "Them ain't skunks!" the old woman complained. "Well, then," the husband replied, "if them ain't skunks I don't know a skunk when I sees it." After a good laugh (Lincoln always laughed at his own jokes; it encouraged others to join in), the president observed that so far in the war the navy had been hunting pet rabbits. The easy victories at Fort Hatteras and Port Royal were all very well, but it was New Orleans—the South's biggest city and most important seaport—that was the real prey, and perhaps it was time to go hunting skunks.[13]

Indeed, the plan to seize New Orleans fit perfectly into Lincoln's overall strategic view of menacing the enemy in several places at the same time. If Foote's flotilla on the upper river system could advance southward at the same time that a force from the Gulf of Mexico pushed upriver, it would compel the rebels either to divide their forces or choose which threat to oppose. Lincoln not only approved the idea; he arranged to meet Welles and Porter at McClellan's head-quarters to convince his chief general to provide forces to occupy the Crescent City once it had been seized. McClellan was leery of the whole idea until he realized that Lincoln was not asking for an assault force of, say, fifty thousand men but only an occupation force of per-haps ten thousand. That he could manage, and at once he gave his blessing. Subsequently, Welles decided that Captain David Glasgow Farragut, Porter's older foster brother, would command the expedi-tion, and Porter himself would take charge of the mortar flotilla that would reduce the rebel forts and allow Farragut's warships to ascend the river.

As always, however, issuing the orders did not lead to immediate action. Porter, in New York, went to work acquiring some suitable vessels and converting them into mortar boats, but the foundry in Pittsburgh lagged in producing the weapons. Nor did Foote, in Cairo, seem to be making any significant progress with mortars. Lacking anything like the Industrial Mobilization Board that emerged in the next century to coordinate the various elements of the force buildup for both world wars, preparations in 1862 were ad hoc and inhibited by the traditional boundaries that separated the different services. Unwilling to be stymied by such traditions, Lincoln ordered Assistant Secretary of the Navy Gustavus Vasa Fox to find out what was going on. Fox wired Foote to tell him "The president desires immediately a full report . . . and full particulars relative to the mortar boats, number in commission, number of mortars mounted, number of mortars ready to mount, etc., the time of completion of all boats, etc." And as if to punctuate the urgency, he added: "Acknowledge this."[14]

Foote replied that only four mortars had been completed at Pittsburgh, and they were being sent to New York for Porter's squadron. No mortars or mortar rafts had been prepared for the western flotilla. Seeing that someone had to step into the void, Lincoln decided to take over management of the project himself. He told Navy Lieutenant Henry A. Wise of the Ordnance Bureau, "Now I am going to devote a part of every day to these mortars, and I won't leave off until it fairly rains Bombs." He directed Wise to tell Foote to get the mortars ready "at the earliest possible moment," asking him at the same time: "What can be done here to advance this? What is lacking?" Just as Lincoln had asked Scott to send him daily reports on the military situation in the early days of the war, so now did he order Foote to send him daily reports on the preparation of the mortar boats. "Telegraph us every day," he ordered, "showing the progress, or lack of progress in this matter."[15]

By stepping into the vacuum of authority in the western theater, Lincoln became not only the commander-in-chief but effectively the chief of staff with Lieutenant Wise acting as his aide. At Lincoln's direction, Wise, whose office was at the Washington Navy Yard, carried Foote's telegrams to the White House every day the moment they arrived. The president looked them over, made a decision, and handed the telegram back to Wise, who issued the necessary orders. Foote sensed the new urgency at once. "The President," he wired Pittsburgh, "is in a hurry for mortar boats." And if the president wanted mortar boats, he would have them. Over the next few weeks, a flurry of telegrams passed back and forth between Cairo and Washington as Lincoln managed the mobilization of the western mortar boats from the White House.[16]

Foote was concerned about the problem of on-board accommodation. After all, the mortar boats were simply flat-bottom barges with no hold or cabin; crewmen had to pitch a tent on the deck to keep the rain off. "The men must have a steamer for their accommodation," Foote wired. "Shall I purchase or hire a steamer for them?" Wise checked with Lincoln and reported back: "The president directs me to say that he approves . . . and desires you to go ahead." When Foote sought ammunition for the new craft, Lincoln directed the army's ordinance chief "to supply whatever ammunition may be required." Lincoln told Wise he wanted Foote to have enough shells "to rain the rebels out" with "a refreshing shower of sulphur and brimstone." When the army balked at paying the salaries of soldiers who transferred into the gunboat service, Lincoln ordered the War Department to pay up. Wise reported to Foote that "Uncle Abe, as you already know, has gone into that business with a will. . . . The wires have not ceased vibrating . . . nor will they until the thing is done."[17]

By involving himself directly in the construction, preparation, and fitting out of the mortar boat flotilla and by encouraging Foote to complete work on the gunboats, Lincoln demonstrated how to cut through the traditional institutional barriers between army and navy. As Wise put it, "He is an evidently practical man, understands precisely what he wants, and is not turned aside by anyone when he has his work before him." Though Bates and Fox continued to argue that it would be better simply to turn the river flotilla over to the Navy Department, Lincoln did not direct it. Instead he showed by example how to overcome the barriers between the services.[18]

One week after telling Wise that he wanted Foote to "rain the rebels out" of their forts along the western rivers, Gideon Welles arrived at the White House waving a telegram announcing that they had done just that. The mortars had played no role in the triumph—despite Lincoln's efforts, they were still not ready—but the gunboats had achieved a signal victory. Foote reported that after a short, sharp fight, Fort Henry, the principal rebel defense on the Tennessee River, had surrendered unconditionally to his gunboat flotilla. Spurred by Lincoln's order, later rescinded, to conduct a coordinated advance by February 22, Halleck had authorized Brigadier General Ulysses S. Grant at Cairo to cooperate with Foote's gunboats in the assault. After being dropped off a few miles below the fort by army transports, Grant's soldiers had approached Fort Henry overland while Foote's gunboats opened fire from the river. Perceiving the weakness of their position, however, the Confederate garrison evacuated the fort leaving behind only four score artillerists to battle the gunboats. Four armored gunboats took the fort under fire, and although the *Essex* received a shot through its boiler that scalded several men, well-directed fire from the rest of the flotilla overwhelmed the gunners on shore, who raised the white flag.[19]

Lincoln was "joyful" when he heard the news; the "navy boys" had not let him down. Welles wired Foote that his news gave the president "the highest gratification," though his gratification might have been even greater had the operation coincided with simultaneous advances by Halleck and Buell, not to mention McClellan. Still, a victory was a victory, and this one not only broke the Confederate defensive line in Tennessee, but it also boded well for future operations since it was clear that the new river ironclads could more than hold their own against rebel forts.

Having kicked down the door, Foote barely paused before sending three gunboats steaming upriver past Fort Henry to pursue the enemy's small flotilla of armed craft, all of which were captured, burned, or destroyed. One of them ascended the river all the way to Florence, Alabama, capturing a half-finished rebel warship and hundreds of tons of supplies. Another burned the Memphis & Bowling Green Railroad bridge over the Tennessee River, which cut Confederate communications between its two principal field armies in the West. Welles was delighted and praised Foote for surmounting "great and insuperable difficulties" to create the river force, ignoring the fact that Welles himself had been the author of some of those difficulties. Since January, however, Lincoln's active support for the river flotilla generally, and the mortar boats in particular, had caused Welles to adjust his outlook, and the victory at Fort Henry washed away the last of his reluctance to embrace the riverine flotilla as part of the navy.[20]

The success at Fort Henry also elevated the flotilla in the eyes of the army. Halleck wired Foote congratulations for his "brilliant success," and McClellan, too, took a new interest in the campaign. Prodded by Lincoln, Stanton had sent Assistant Secretary of War Thomas Scott out west, and Scott asked Foote solicitously to let him know what "additional force and equipment you need." From being an orphan, the riverine fleet now had two doting parents.[21]

Fort Donelson was next. The rebels had constructed two forts to guard the northward-flowing rivers in central Tennessee and Kentucky: Fort Henry on the Tennessee and a much larger and better-sited fortification named Donelson on the Cumberland River. Halleck was eager to keep the momentum going and ordered Grant to march his force across the narrow "land between the lakes" to Fort Donelson where, presumably, the Grant-Foote team would win another victory.

Lincoln followed developments by telegraph. The early news was encouraging, but then it often was. On February 12—his fifty-third birthday—he learned that "General Grant has invested Fort Donelson from the land side." Three days later Halleck wired that "Everything looks well." There was a note of panic, however, in a second telegram that afternoon in which Halleck insisted, "I must have more men. It is a military necessity." A similar wire arrived that night: "Give me the forces required and I will ensure complete success." This was precisely the kind of pledge that Lincoln was used to hearing from McClellan, and he may have been becoming inured to it.[22]

Halleck's nervous telegrams from St. Louis had been triggered by news that Foote made an attack on the fort with his gunboats on February 15 and had been repulsed. Foote reported that he had been on the verge of driving the enemy from his batteries when plunging fire disabled the steering on two of his ships, causing them to drift downriver and out of the fight. Foote himself had been wounded, painfully if not seriously, when a rebel shell exploded near where he was standing.[23] Was the early promise of victory about to be dashed, as it had at Bull Run?

To bolster his nervous western commander, Lincoln sent Halleck a reassuring telegram: "You have Fort Donelson safe," he wrote. The only real threat was that the enemy might somehow manage to concentrate against Grant, and to prevent that Lincoln suggested that Halleck might strike at the rail lines that the enemy could use to effect such a concentration, and, as always, he reiterated that the key to success was "full co-operation" between the Union generals. By the time Halleck received this advice, however, the issue had been decided. The very next day a wire arrived in Washington from Halleck's chief of staff with the news that "the Union flag floats over Fort Donelson." The entire garrison of 15,000 men had been taken prisoner; only a few of the defenders had escaped with Confederate General John B. Floyd, who had fled like a thief in the night.[24]

It was the best news in the war so far. But in contrast to his "joyful" reaction to the news of Fort Henry, Lincoln was unable to join in the celebration. For more than a week, Lincoln's two younger sons, Willie and Tad, had been bedridden with what the doctors called "bilious fever" but which was almost certainly typhoid, which was endemic in the city because of the pollution of the city's water. The president and his wife spent much of their days—and their nights— sitting by their semiconscious children. Two days after news of the victory at Donelson arrived in Washington, Lincoln staggered out of Willie's room devastated with grief, and in an emotion-strained voice told his young secretary, "Well, Nicolay, my boy is gone—he is actually gone." And then he burst into tears.[25]

Meanwhile, the victories at Fort Henry and Fort Donelson had not only smashed the rebel defensive line in the West; they had also proved the value of armored gunboats on the western rivers and the importance of cooperation between the services. The Mississippi was next, and Halleck was eager to employ the proven stratagem of combined operations against Columbus, Kentucky, the so-called Gibraltar of the West. Foote was willing enough, but he had to repair his ships, which meant pulling them back to Cairo. Halleck wanted to keep them on the river. Foote complained to Wise that "the generals" were "detaining two boats up the river . . . which I want to repair." Wise took the complaint to Lincoln, who resolved the dispute in Foote's favor, directing Halleck to send the boats "to Cairo for repairs." For all his initial reluctance to get involved, Lincoln was not only adjudicating conflicts between the services; he was also directing the movement of ships. Bates had urged Lincoln "to restore all the floating force of the command of the Navy Department with orders to cooperate with the army, just as the Navy on the sea coast does." That, in effect, is what happened, but it happened mainly because Lincoln had effectively taken charge.[26]

Despite the tragedy in his personal life, by the end of March Lincoln was beginning to hope that his vision of a simultaneous advance by Union forces might soon be realized. Even McClellan's Army of the Potomac was at last lurching into motion, transferred in the largest military sealift ever attempted from the Potomac to Fort Monroe at the tip of the Virginia Peninsula. A thousand miles to the west, Grant's smaller army also used army transports (escorted by the gunboats *Lexington* and *Tyler*) to ascend the Tennessee River to Pittsburg Landing just above the Mississippi state line near a little country church called Shiloh. Meanwhile on the Mississippi, Foote partnered with Major General John Pope for a push down the big muddy, and a fourth squadron gathered off the mouth of the Mississippi under Farragut and Porter to threaten New Orleans. McClellan's movement in Virginia was unlikely to affect the other three in any significant way, but if Grant, Foote, and Farragut all moved more or less simultaneously, it would fulfill Lincoln's strategic vision and challenge the ability of the Confederacy to defend itself from all three assaults. When Lincoln explained the idea to Bates on March 15, Bates saw it at once and recorded it in his diary: "The enemy is really in a strait. If he move his iron boats up stream to meet Foote, then he leaves the lower river open to Farragut and Porter—and [if] he send them down to meet the gulf force, the coast is clear for Foote."[27]

Once again, Lincoln kept track of the campaign via the telegraph. Much of the president's attention was focused on McClellan's vast army on the Virginia Peninsula, but he also kept up with Foote's operations on the Mississippi. The contrast could hardly have been greater. McClellan's messages complained of bad weather, poor transportation, and a need for more troops. The news from the West was more upbeat. Every day Wise brought him the latest information sent downriver from Island Number Ten to Cairo and forwarded it to Washington. Lincoln had told Wise to bring him the latest news regardless of the time of day, and taking him at his word, Wise showed up at two o'clock in the morning on March 17 to report that Foote's flotilla was "in line of battle" and "within 2 miles of the enemy." Lincoln may have been especially interested to learn that the mortar boats had fired their first shots in anger that day, lobbing "a few shells to try the range." The next day came news that the firing had begun in earnest, and soon Foote was reporting that the rebel fortifications were being battered "all to pieces," though he also noted that a gun had burst on board the *St. Louis*, killing four sailors. Perhaps for Lincoln's benefit he added: "The mortars are doing well." Indeed, the next day a mortar shell landed squarely on the Confederates' floating battery and "cleared the concern in short meter." But after raising expectations of another quick victory, within a few days Foote reported: "This place, Island No. 10, is harder to conquer than Columbus." Indeed, he did not think it could be taken at all without a land assault from the rear.[28]

For more than two weeks, Foote's mortar rafts rained down "sulphur and brimstone," to use Lincoln's phrase, on the rebel defenses. At the same time, however, Foote was looking for a way to bypass the rebel fortifications altogether. Halleck wanted him to get at least a few of his ironclads downriver to New Madrid, Missouri, on the west bank, where Major General John Pope was seeking transport for his army so that he could cross the river and attack the rebels from the rear. Foote even tried to carve a canal through an old slough in the hope of finding a way around the enemy strong point. As in Virginia, progress slowed to a stop.

Then all of a sudden there was an avalanche of news. On April 6, Foote reported that one of his ironclads, Henry Walke's *Carondelet*, had run past the batteries at Island Number Ten "without injury" and arrived safely at New Madrid. Another vessel made the run the next night, and together the two gunboats successfully escorted Pope's army across the river. The cabinet was in session on April 8 when news arrived that Island Number Ten had surrendered. At almost the same moment, another telegram brought news of "the most terrible battle of the war." The telegraph operator at Cincinnati reported that a rebel army had attacked Grant's force at Pittsburg Landing "in overwhelming force." Not until the next day did Lincoln learn that after a two-day fight, the attacking rebels had given way and that the battle at Shiloh Church was a Union victory.[29]

Suddenly all things seemed possible. The despondency of January gave way to near-euphoria in April. Though McClellan was still stalled on the Virginia Peninsula battling mud and his own fears, Union forces in the West had seized all three Confederate bastions on the major rivers, and their main field army had been soundly beaten. Surely Foote's gunboats would now speed southward to take Memphis and then on to New Orleans. With luck, they would meet Farragut's squadron coming upriver from the Crescent City.

It took longer than expected for Farragut to get his big oceangoing warships over the sand bars of the Mississippi delta. Not until April 15 did he manage to assemble his flotilla of seventeen wooden warships plus Porter's twenty mortar boats at the Head of Passes below the rebel forts. Throughout the rest of the month, while he kept track of McClellan's lack of progress on the peninsula, Lincoln also waited for news from Farragut. It came on April 29. Fox reported that Southern newspapers were carrying stories that New Orleans had fallen to the Yankees. There were no particulars yet, and there was still no news from official sources, but Lincoln could dare to hope.[30]

Confirmation came two days later. Under Porter's direction, Lincoln's mortars had pounded away at Fort Jackson and Fort St. Philip for four days, but despite inflicting a lot of physical damage, they were not able to neutralize the forts. Farragut, who had suspected from the beginning that it would come to this, took the bit in his teeth and steamed past the forts anyway, breaking the log-and-chain boom across the river at 2:00 am on April 24 and triggering a middle-of-the-night pyrotechnic eruption as the gunners in both forts fired at the dark shapes on the river and as the ships fired back at the muzzle flashes from the forts. Farragut did not plan to shoot it out with the forts, however. Like Walke at Island Number Ten, his goal was to get past them uninjured. The rebels sent fire rafts downstream, one of which briefly set Farragut's flagship, the *Hartford*, on fire. They also attacked with their small flotilla of gunboats. But the fire on the *Hartford* was suppressed, the Union warships forged past the forts easily dispatching the enemy's small craft, and by dawn most of Farragut's flotilla was safely upriver.[31]

Barely pausing to inspect the damage, Farragut left Porter behind to keep an eye on the rebel forts and steamed upriver to New Orleans. That afternoon he anchored off Jackson Square and demanded the surrender of the city. There was no resistance. Confederate authorities had all but stripped New Orleans of troops to concentrate against Grant at Pittsburg Landing, and the troops that were left evacuated the city when Farragut's dark ships anchored off the levee. Though the civil population shouted epithets and shook their fists at Farragut's vessels, it was all sound and fury. Captain Theodorus Bailey led a small group of marines through a crowd of angry and frustrated civilians to the custom house to raise the American flag.

The American flag soon flew over Memphis, too. As Lincoln had foreseen, simultaneous attacks at different places had forced the rebels to choose what to defend. Hoping that their forts would contain the threat from the river, they had concentrated their western armies for an all-out attack on Grant at Shiloh, and though they had come close, the gamble had failed. That decision had stripped both Memphis and New Orleans of troops and left them ripe for conquest.[32]

In the first four months of 1862, Lincoln was compelled by circumstance more than predilection to become an activist commander-in-chief. He had begun by proposing a strategic vision to his field commanders, but when they had responded with objections and explanations, he began to embrace a more active role. His involvement with the production and delivery of mortar boats for both Foote's squadron on the upper rivers and Porter's squadron in the Gulf of Mexico was a symptom of his new willingness to involve himself personally in the management of military affairs. In the end, the mortar boats he had sponsored had not proved decisive either at Island Number Ten or at Fort Jackson and Fort St. Philip, but the strategic vision he had articulated in January had been validated. The Confederates proved incapable of defending both the upper and lower reaches of the Mississippi River at the same time. Grant survived their furious attack at Shiloh while both Memphis and New Orleans fell to the Union. Tennessee and Louisiana had been reclaimed. At both the northern and southern ends of the river, Union forces had established a grip they would never relinquish. Indeed, the Confederacy never fully recovered from the reverses of these four months, and at least some of the credit belonged to the Union president who was beginning to act the role of commander-in-chief in fact as well as in name. He had become admiral-in-chief.

Jefferson Davis and Robert E. Lee
Reluctant "Traitors"
William C. Davis

THE EPITHET "TRAITOR," WHEN APPLIED TO ANYONE WHO sided with the Confederacy, can get a speaker or writer in big trouble, fast. As sensitive as it was to the men of the Confederacy themselves, it seems to be even more inflammatory among the self-appointed defenders of Confederate heritage and memory today. Article III, Section 3, of the Constitution is succinct and explicit in its definition: "Treason against the United States, shall consist only in levying War against them." Speaking critically of the government does not constitute treason. By this definition, even attempting to secede is not in itself a treasonous act. One must "levy war" to be a traitor. From the outset secessionists protested that all they wanted was to be left alone. They had no hostile intentions, and in seceding they sought only to defend themselves. Yet immediately upon seceding they turned around and seized forts and arsenals, armories and customs houses, warships and navy yards, federal post offices and mints, and revenue. And of course, they fired on the U.S. flag, first on January 9, 1861, when Charlestonians fired on the *Star of the West*, and then on April 12, with the attack on Fort Sumter.

Thereafter Confederate armies conducted multiple invasions of states that had rejected secession and remained loyal to the Union—Maryland, Kentucky, Missouri, the New Mexico Territory—all with the intent of conquest against the wishes of their citizens. They even had plans to seize California, or part of it, and of course they also invaded Pennsylvania, Indiana, and Ohio, even Vermont, while sending agents to practice arson in New York City. All of this is like "levying war," an aggressive war that went a long way beyond mere self-defense. Of course it all came down to a question simply stated but so complex and contentious that after decades of debate it remains unsettled. Was secession lawful? If it was, then the moment a state seceded, its citizens were henceforth incapable of committing treason against the United States even if they did levy war against it. It if was not, then they were committing treason with every seizure of federal property and every shot they fired. The question has never come before the Supreme Court, and the U.S. government has not recognized secession as a lawful act.

Jefferson Davis had a hard time making up his mind, though never when it came to the legality of secession. His father and his older brother decided for him where he would get his education. When he went to the Military Academy at West Point in 1824, he commented that "it was no desire of mine to go." By 1828, however, he believed the academy had made him a soldier for life. A year later in 1829 he wanted to resign if he could find something else to do.[1] Instead he stayed in the army, but three years later wanted to leave to try railroading. His brother told him not to. Another three years passed, and he finally did resign, but in a fashion that gave him six months to change his mind. Instead, again his brother Joseph made him a planter, with nine hundred acres of cotton land and slaves to work them. Then in 1837 he tried to get back into the army. When he finally entered the world of politics, friends persuaded him to go to a state Democratic convention and then nominated him for a seat in the legislature; Davis himself remained a passive participant. In 1845 his brother Joseph maneuvered him into meeting and courting

Varina Howell, whom he married. That same year, without his involvement, friends nominated him for a seat on the House of Representatives. Yet he had barely won and taken his seat in 1846 when he resigned to reenter the army, raising a regiment of Mississippi volunteers to fight in Mexico.

When he came home a wounded hero in 1847, he took an appointment to serve out an unexpired term in the Senate and won reelection, but he then resigned when friends persuaded him to run for the governorship when the current nominee resigned two months before the election. Defeated, he was offered a place in President-elect Franklin Pierce's cabinet, which he declined, then changed his mind and accepted. Leaving that post in 1857, he was elected to the Senate again, but resigned in January 1861 when Mississippi seceded and instructed him to leave Washington. A few weeks later, without his active involvement and against his wishes, delegates of the seceded states made him president of their new Confederacy. He seems never to have wanted what he had, but when he quit or resigned he also usually tried to leave a door open behind him. No wonder that on September 27, 1865, barely five months after the collapse of the Confederacy, its one-time secretary of the navy Stephen R. Mallory recorded in his diary some thoughts on his former chief, President Jefferson Davis, then a prisoner in Fort Monroe. "By all who have ever been associated with him in public affairs," said Mallory, "he is probably known to be singularly cautious, if not dilatory" in making up his mind.[2]

How then did Jefferson Davis decide to become a "traitor" in the eyes of many of his friends and former associates in the old Union by attempting to leave that Union and taking arms against it as president of the Confederate States?

From his earliest recorded statements on the nature of the Union, it is clear that he firmly believed secession to be an intrinsic right, that a state, having surrendered sovereignty to the federal government in return for assumed benefits, could reassume that sovereignty if its people chose to do so by means of an elected convention. Secession, in Davis's eyes, could not be treason. What set Davis apart from the Fire-Eater secessionists like William L. Yancey or Robert Barnwell Rhett was that he did not regard secession as a desirable end in itself but only as a last remedy after all other efforts to make a state's relationship with the Union work to the mutual benefit of both. In that last generation before the Civil War there were a great many men in the South and the border states who fell between the secessionists and the moderates, and Davis was one of them. He was all for the Union as long as it could be made to last, but he would accept secession as an alternative rather than remain in a Union that had become onerous.

Hence, from his earliest utterances on the question, Davis was neither a radical nor a moderate but an amalgam of both. As early as 1849, when he returned to Mississippi from his first session in the Senate, he railed against the attacks of the antislavery forces against the South, warning that if slavery could not spread into the new territories that would form future states, then the free states of the North would soon so outnumber the slave states that they would be able to alter the Constitution at will, which meant they could attack slavery where it already existed. Yet he denied any "spirit of disunion" in himself or his fellow Southerners and dismissed those who were calling for what he termed "hasty action." He condemned the idle talk of disunion and even armed conflict, warning that "we should make no ultimatum which we do not mean," adding that "when all other things failed then was left the stern appeal—*to arms*."[3]

A year later, during the heated debates over the several bills that came together as the Compromise of 1850, Davis repeatedly denied that he favored secession over remaining in the Union. "I have not spoken of disunion to the Senate," he declared, for that to him was "an alternative not to be anticipated—one to which I could only look forward as the last resort." He rejected the loose talk of civil war as just so much political fulmination. Yet there was always a "but" in his protestations of devotion. Hard as it is for us today to grasp, Davis and a host of his generation felt two concurrent yet inevitably conflicting loyalties.

"I, sir, am an American citizen," he said in the Senate. "I belong to no State and no section, when the great interests of the Union are concerned." But, "when the Union attempts to trample upon her rights," he went on, "I belong to the State which is my home."[4]

Davis actually took that a step farther by asserting that he and those sharing his views were the true Unionists, for they were loyal to the Union as it was intended and created by its founders and not as it was being perverted by the Yankee antislavery forces of the North. Even in being willing to accept the eventuality of secession, Davis argued that he was being true to the Union as it was. The Constitution had not denied the right of a state to leave the compact, and the Virginia and Kentucky Resolutions of 1798 and 1799 were the clear expressions of founders Jefferson and Madison themselves of the sovereignty of the states. If they did not actually assert the right of peaceful secession, they were still the bedrock of all pro-secession argument since. "Whilst we assert the right," he said in 1851, "we consider it the last remedy, the final alternative."[5]

Five years later, after the appearance of the Republican Party and the outbreak of sectional violence in Kansas over the issue of slavery in the territories, Davis still maintained his allegiance to the Union and still always attached a subordinate clause to the declaration. He supported Fire-Eater Preston Brooks's cowardly action on the floor of the Senate when Brooks attacked Charles Sumner from behind and beat him senseless with a cane in response to Sumner's earlier intemperate remarks about South Carolina. Yet Davis kept his distance from other Fire-Eaters like the hot-headed Rhett and numbered among his closest friends William Seward, a leading light of the new Republican Party. "My idea of our present condition is, that we should make all the preparations proper for sovereign States," he said in October 1856, but in words redolent of painful and deliberate decision, he went on to add that "we should make haste slowly, and be temperate in all things."[6] Secession was there for the South to use as recourse if it must, and they should prepare themselves for the *possibility* of its necessity—but prepare only, and that with careful and thoughtful deliberation.

In 1858 Davis made a tour of the Northeast largely for his health and was called on several times to speak before crowds. What he said surprised many in the South, especially the radicals. He called any who would try to divide the Union "trifling politicians" who could never succeed. "We became a nation by the constitution," he said; "whatever is national springs from the constitution; and national and constitutional are convertible terms."[7] He condemned those who promoted sectional agitation, and without actually saying so, it was implicit that he saw them as chiefly Northern antislavery forces. The South was not agitating; it was merely defending itself against hostile assaults on its institutions. Even then, he predicted that scheming sectionalists would be ground to dust by the inherent patriotism of good Americans, just as the waves pounded themselves futilely against the granite coast of New England.[8]

When Davis came home to Mississippi from that trip northeast, he found himself vilified by the states' rights radicals and even some of the more mainstream Southern press for his public remarks on the Union. Defending himself, he responded that he did not advocate and never had advocated breaking up the Union except when all else had failed, and that time had not yet come. But then he gave them a warning. In two years, in 1860, they would elect a new president. If the victory went to a Republican in sympathy with the avowed purposes of the abolitionists to contain slavery where it currently existed and ultimately attack it there, then they would have an enemy in the White House. It would be a "revolution": that would pervert the purposes of the government the Founding Fathers had formed, and, in that case, Mississippi and other states would have a duty to pursue their security and best interests outside the old Union, and to prepare they ought to turn their attention now to building railroads and armories. No one could miss the import of that.[9]

A year later Davis was still proclaiming his love for the Union, but his "buts" were becoming more frequent and strident. A Republican victory in 1860, then a year off, would lead to "the despotism of a majority," he said, and the people of Mississippi and the South would face a choice: become subjects of "a hostile government" or take action. If a Republican became chief executive, he said, he would "appeal to the God of battles at once" rather than live in such a Union. He repeated more urgently his call for the extension of rail lines and the raising of militia, yet still he argued that it was all in the hands of the Republicans. If they elected a candidate who would respect their rights, he would not be their enemy. He said, yet again, that Southerners should not give in to "the brainless intemperance of those who desired a dissolution of the Union, and who found in every rustling leaf fresh evidence of volcanic eruption."[10]

When the convention season came in 1860, and while men like William L. Yancey and Robert Rhett actively worked to divide and break up the Democratic Party over slavery extension, knowing that a divided party would lead to Republican victory and subsequent secession, Davis still strove to keep the Union whole. Yancey led a walkout that broke up the Democrats at their Charleston convention in April, and when they reconvened in May in Baltimore, Yancey did it again. This time the remnant nominated Stephen Douglas, who was unacceptable to the states' rights men of the South. Across town, those who left with Yancey nominated John C. Breckinridge, a moderate who felt little sympathy with them. Meanwhile a conglomeration of old Whigs, Unionist Democrats, and others called themselves the Constitutional Union Party and nominated John Bell on a platform calling for compromise without saying how it could be achieved. The fragmentation of the only national party in the country was guaranteed to achieve exactly what Yancey and the Fire-Eaters wanted. Seeing that, Davis took it on himself to try to effect the withdrawals of Douglas, Breckinridge, and Bell, all in favor of a compromise candidate like Horatio Seymour of New York, who might unite all factions of the old party and still make it possible to defeat the Republican candidate Abraham Lincoln and avert disaster. Breckinridge and Bell willingly agreed, but Douglas refused, virtually guaranteeing Lincoln's election.

During the ensuing campaign, Davis repeatedly declared that electing Breckinridge was the only hope for preserving the Union, at the same time stating forthrightly now that the election of Lincoln would justify Mississippi taking whatever action it felt necessary in cooperation with other states to protect itself. That could include, but was not limited to, secession. Hours before the election he took a further step, telling an audience that if Lincoln were elected and Mississippi decided to "resist the hands that would tarnish her star on the National Flag, then I will come at your bidding, whether by day or by night, and pluck that star from the galaxy, and place it upon a banner of its own. I will plant it upon the crest of battle, and gathering around me Mississippi's best and bravest, will welcome the invader to the harvest of death."[11] For years he had been making haste slowly in his gradual progress toward becoming an outright advocate of secession and of forceful resistance to any attempt by the Union to enforce its authority, and now he had very few options left, if any, before he crossed the line.

Lincoln was duly elected, and that started the secession juggernaut on its last sprint to the finish. "No human power can save the Union," Davis was heard to say.[12] Fatalistically, he declined at first to serve on the Senate Committee of Thirteen appointed to find a compromise to avert disaster. Then he changed his mind, stating that he would try anything to prevent what he saw coming. On the committee he advocated the Crittenden Compromise, which would have guaranteed that slavery could spread west below a resurrected Missouri Compromise line, but it came to nothing given the intransigence of the Republicans on the committee. At that point Davis finally abandoned all hope. On January 5, 1861, he met with senators from seven Deep South states and agreed that they should secede immediately and send delegates to meet in Montgomery, Alabama, within six weeks to form a new government.[13]

The strain of it all led to a collapse of his health, and he spent much of January in a sickbed. Mississippi became the second state to secede on January 9, and Davis learned of it that day or the next. Eleven days later he sadly said his farewell in the Senate. Privately he confided to a friend that "we have piped but they would not dance, and now the Devil may care."[14] Traitor or not, he had not wanted this. Jefferson Davis did not rush to leave the Union. Rather, events and the tenor of his own convictions pushed him to it. He had never been a radical or a secessionist, yet less than three weeks after he walked out of the Senate he was President of the Confederate States of America.

That other "traitor" was a far different man and came to his decision via a much different route. We actually know very little about Robert E. Lee's political views on the men and events of his time. He said virtually nothing publicly and very little even to friends or family that has survived. We have no certain knowledge of any political party identification, and we have no evidence whatever as to how he voted prior to the war or even if he voted at all. Officers in the professional army then, as now, were certainly not immune to politics. They acted under the same influences of family, friends, regional origin, popular fears, and enthusiasms. But they lived in a different environment from other citizens, detached from the real world. They worked together, lived together, formed their friendships almost exclusively among their peers, and even intermarried among military families to a greater extent than other professions. A culture developed in the broader profession and within its individual components, and with it a tendency to view outside events chiefly through the lens of those events' effects on that profession. Officers felt underappreciated, frustrated at slow career advancement, and operated under a degree of a siege mentality in the face of perceived underfunding and lack of public appreciation and respect.

Lee expressed these feelings privately, putting him in the mainstream of the officer corps, which in his time numbered fewer than a thousand men. Lee, like all the others, felt the precarious position of the professional military. Much of the public resented the cost of maintaining a standing army. Many politicians, especially from the South, objected to the Military Academy at West Point, which provided education at public expense. The War Department represented overwhelmingly the lion's share of the federal budget every year, even during peacetime, and to many, the army seemed a costly extravagance providing employment for officers, who were the sons of the privileged, and the dregs of saloons and immigrant ships, who made up the enlisted ranks. To speak out on any political matter risked losing the good will of this politician or that, and the result could hurt the profession and the officer personally.

Consequently, Lee observed almost complete silence on political matters prior to the war. What separates him from most of the others, however, is that he carried that reticence even into his personal correspondence, or at least what survives of it. Other than a few comments on secession and slavery, he is all but mute on major issues like expansionism, tariffs, internal improvements, and above all the extension of slavery into the territories, the driving irritant leading to secession. In the process, Lee was revealing that he had learned well from his reading of Clausewitz that soldiers were subordinate to the civil government and should remain quiet on political matters.

According to his cousin Cassius Lee, Robert E. Lee told him around 1850 that he favored the Whig Party and its principles.[15] That would be entirely consistent with his family background and his own personal experience and interest. His father Henry Lee was a Federalist in the years after independence. They stood for a strong central government, a national bank, protective tariffs, and the judicious expenditure of treasury funds on public projects to promote security and prosperity. They also, in large part, represented upper-class families like the Lees and bitterly opposed Thomas Jefferson's Republican Party. In fact, it was a Republican mob that attacked and beat Henry Lee in 1812, leading to his death several years later. That fact alone must have influenced his son to reject the people who virtually killed his father.

By the time Lee left West Point in 1829, the Federalists were dead, and Jefferson's party had split into a new alignment. The conservative elements formed the new Democratic Party, and their more liberal wing joined with most of the old Federalists to create the Whig Party. Lee was commencing his professional career just as the country entered public debate marked by the Whigs' advocacy of Henry Clay's "American System," promoting industrial and economic growth through a national bank, internal improvements through roads and canals, creation of public schools and colleges, and modernization in general, all of which best suited Northern interests. The Democrats, on the other hand, were committed to an agrarian society and culture and small government, which at the time best suited Southern interests.

Lee naturally considered himself a Southerner, yet it is not hard to see why he identified more with the Whigs. They were the party of his father and many of his family as well as of many of the First Families of Virginia. Lee always showed an awareness that his class, the old landed families, had an obligation to lead by example. He never disdained the common people, but he did not entirely trust their wisdom or morals. Jackson's Democrats, by enfranchising uneducated commoners, masses of them recent immigrants, risked handing government over to a rabble. In 1839, Lee told a friend that "the lower class are a swaggering, noisy set," and too many of the people recently thrust into prominence were what he called "new money." They were not like his Virginians.[16]

Professionally, Lee's best interests obviously lay with the Whigs. The internal improvements they wanted to fund would be constructed largely by the Army Corps of Engineers, his own branch of the service, which meant that while many Democrats resented the professional army, the Whigs were anxious to keep him employed. In short, the Whigs buttered his side of the bread. When the war with Mexico came, it was Democratic President James K. Polk's war, one bitterly opposed by the Whigs. Lee remained scrupulously silent as to his feelings on the war, once again showing that he well understood the military's subordination to the civil authority. He left only one known comment at the time, in May 1846, when he put himself squarely in the Whig camp by commenting that he was not entirely satisfied as to what he called "the justice of our cause." But then he added that a soldier's duty was to implement government policy, not to try to influence it, a lesson well learned that would make him the commander most respected by Jefferson Davis and the one who in return got the most cooperation from the Confederate president.[17]

"I think the military and civil Talents are distinct, if not different, and full duty in either sphere is about as much as one man can qualify himself to perform," he would declare.[18] Beside that, his opinion of the men who sought and held public office was never high. "Politicians are more or less so warped by party feeling, by selfishness, or prejudices, that their minds are not altogether balanced," he wrote privately. "They are the most difficult to cure of all insane people."[19]

And then came the final moments that were themselves a part of his training for command—resignation and duty—even to the point of self-sacrifice. When Southern states called conventions to consider secession after the election of Lincoln, Lee wrote a week before South Carolina's convention was to meet that "I am not pleased with the course of the Cotton States."[20] "Secession is nothing but revolution," he told his son Rooney Lee six weeks later, after Louisiana became the sixth state to secede. Arguing that in the early days of the republic secession had been considered treason, he asked his son, "What can it be now?"[21]

Even before then, on December 3, 1860, he had written that "I prize the Union very highly, & know of no personal sacrifice that I would not make to preserve it, *save that of honour*."[22] Through more than thirty years of military service to his country, through administrations he liked and some he deplored, one fixed point in his ever-changing universe was his unwavering loyalty to the Union. But now, and apparently for the first time, he expressed a condition to that loyalty: "*Save that of honour*." He did not say precisely what there was relating to his honor that might cause the exception, but that was soon coming.

On January 16, 1861, Lee wrote to a cousin that "If the Union is dissolved, I shall return to Virginia & share the fortune of my people." At that point, of course, the Union was already dissolved, given that four states had seceded, Georgia was on the verge, and conventions in Louisiana and Texas were virtually certain to follow suit. So it was something more than just the secession of several states that constituted in Lee's mind a dissolution of the Union, but he did not say what, nor did he say in what capacity he would return to Virginia, though the only inference is that he would no longer be a soldier. A week later, with Georgia seceded, he cleared the matter when he wrote to another cousin that "If a disruption takes place, I shall go back in sorrow to my people & share in the misery of my native state."

Just why Virginia should be miserable because other states had seceded he did not say. However, the only meaning that fits is that Virginia herself might secede. That was the "dissolution" Lee had in mind. For him, the Union was broken up when and if Virginia seceded, and with that would be severed his allegiance to the United States. He went on to remove any doubt as to what his course would be when he added that "save in her defense there will be one soldier less in the world than now."

That was clear enough. If Virginia seceded, Lee intended to resign his commission and be "one soldier less" unless he had to take arms to defend his state. If there were any remaining doubt as to what he intended to do, on January 29 he wrote to his son Rooney that "save in her [Virginia's] defense, I will draw my sword no more." Thus by the end of January 1861 Lee had decided that if Virginia seceded and the Union attempted by force of invasion to keep her in the Union, he would fight against the men who were now his comrades-in-arms and against the flag he had so nobly served all of his adult life.[23] Everything for him now hinged on Virginia's secession, and unless and until that happened, he would remain in the army, still rigidly adhering to his duty and responsibilities as a soldier and his well-founded resolve to steer clear of politics.

Two weeks after the new Confederate government formed in Montgomery, Alabama, Lee said "I must try & be patient & await the end for I can do nothing to hasten or retard it."[24] Lee was like hundreds of thousands of men in the middle, torn between their genuine love of and loyalty to the Union, their suspicion or even dislike of the extremists on both sides who they saw as promoting a crisis for their own ends, and their heartfelt allegiance to the places of their nativity, the friends, family, and extended cords of loyalty to the people of their home states.

On March 28, 1861, Robert E. Lee received and accepted his promotion to colonel of the 1st United States Cavalry, a commission signed by the new president, Abraham Lincoln. By that time he had already received an overture from Secretary of War Leroy Pope Walker in Montgomery, Alabama, offering him a commission as brigadier general in the army being raised by the new Confederate States of America. So far as we know, Lee never responded to Walker, which would have been proper for a serving U.S. army officer. And Lee owed no allegiance to Walker or the new Confederate government. Lee had only two loyalties—to the United States, and to Virginia—so it was easy to ignore approaches from Montgomery without any strains on his conscience.

But then those two loyalties collided. The firing on Fort Sumter on April 12 led to Lincoln's call the next day for volunteers to put down the rebellion. On April 17, even as the Virginia convention went into secret session one more time to debate seceding after several failed attempts, Lee received a summons from General Winfield Scott and a request for a meeting from Francis Preston Blair. The next day Lee met first with Blair, who informed him that Lincoln had authorized Blair to offer Lee command of the new 75,000-man army to be raised to put down the uprising, and with that command would go the two stars of a major general. After more than thirty years in the army, Lee had gained only four advances in rank thanks to the glacial pace of promotion. Now he faced the possibility of three promotions in just three weeks, a rise to the pinnacle of his profession.

Yet Lee politely but firmly declined, asserting his opposition to secession along with his even greater unwillingness to participate in an invasion of the South and, in particular, of Virginia. Then he went to his interview with Scott and informed him of what he had told Blair. Lee had hoped to be able to stay in the army so long as Vir-

ginia did not secede, but now Scott told him that an officer unwilling
to be actively employed in any assignment ought to resign his commission, and under the circumstances Lee should do so immediately.

Lee met with his brother Sydney Smith Lee and others that day
and evening as he tried to see his way through the sudden chaos.
Interestingly, the course of Lee's brother Sidney Smith Lee closely
paralleled his own. After a long and distinguished career in the navy,
he, too, faced a choice as Virginia confronted secession and war. As
his wife wrote her cousin Daniel Murray Lee on May 27, Sidney Lee

> pondered it over & over in his mind. It was a severe struggle
> with him & if you could have seen him during that week you
> would have pitied him, for he w[a]s giving up a profession he
> was devoted to & proud of, & sure independence for a dim
> uncertainty. He thought when it came to taking sides, North
> or South, to fight against his own people or for them, there
> was but one thing to do—& you my dear Murray ask yourself
> the question candidly what could he do? What would you
> have done, under similar circumstances—fight against your
> State, where your kindred & children were, or with them.

Smith Lee's wife declared that

> there is no one on earth who deplores this state of things
> more than I do, or who fought harder to stay in the Union, &
> be one people united under our beautiful Flag than I did,
> but when it narrowed down to a war between the North &
> South, then my Southern blood showed itself. We have given
> up every thing, our home, our position, our income, certainly
> for nothing we expect [to be] better on the other side.[25]

The next morning, April 19, Robert E. Lee went into Alexandria
and had the decision forced upon him when he learned that Virginia's
convention had voted to secede. It was the talk on everyone's lips that

day, and when Lee stopped in a pharmacy to pay a bill and heard yet more fulminating on leaving the Union, he sadly told the apothecary that "I am one of those dull creatures that cannot see the good of secession."[26] That night, sometime after midnight, he wrote a single sentence to the government resigning his commission, in a stroke ending the professional career that had occupied all his adult life. He enclosed it with a heartfelt letter to Scott, saying he would have resigned immediately during their last meeting "but for the struggle it has cost me to separate myself from a service to which I have devoted all the best years of my life." He hoped now never to don uniform or take arms again "save in defense of my native state."[27]

A few days later, but before Lee's act was publicly known, the editor of the Alexandria *Gazette* declared that in this crisis, Lee's "reputation, his acknowledged ability, his chivalric character, his probity, honor, and—may we add, to his eternal praise—his Christian life and conduct—make his very name a 'tower of strength.'"[28]

Whether it was right or wrong, Lee had shown that strength in his final act as a soldier of the Union, an act grounded in long and careful thought, after careful weighing of pros and cons, born in an immutable sense of duty, and above all driven by a character molded from birth through more than half a century of experience. It was also an act of supreme self-sacrifice: he ended the career that had been the joy of his life rather than adopt a course that ran counter to his sense of his self, his blood, and his ancestral loyalties. Most of all, it was an act that was bold and decisive.

A few days later on April 21, when Virginia offered him the command of state forces, he accepted. He was ready to lead. The very next day, another reluctant "traitor," now a president in Montgomery, wrote to Governor John Letcher and asked the whereabouts and intentions of Colonel Robert E. Lee.[29] Jefferson Davis, the Confederacy, and history were waiting for him.

"The Battle Hymn of the Republic"
Origins, Influence, Legacies

John Stauffer

"THE BATTLE HYMN OF THE REPUBLIC" IS AMERICA'S UN-
official anthem. You all know the song, but what you might not know
is that the "Battle Hymn" is far more popular today than it was during
the Civil War, beloved by Northerners and Southerners, conservatives and radicals, whites and blacks. About the only thing that Glenn
Beck and Rush Limbaugh have in common with Al Sharpton and
Jeremiah Wright is that the "Battle Hymn of the Republic" is one of
their very favorite songs.[1]

Origins

The origins of the "Battle Hymn" have long been shrouded in obscu-
rity. The tune is often attributed to William Steffe, a native of South
Carolina who settled in Philadelphia. Steffe was an unflagging
self-promoter, and he claimed, decades after the fact and without
any evidence, that he had composed the tune in the mid-1850s for a
Baltimore fire company then visiting Philadelphia. Steffe said he
called the tune, "Say, Bummers, Will You Meet Us."[2] Even today, you

see some sheet music and arrangements that attribute Steffe as the tune's creator.

But these attributions are simply wrong. The "Battle Hymn" tune dates back to early nineteenth-century Southern camp meetings and slave culture. Camp meetings were the chief form of worship in the early nineteenth-century South. Most Southerners lived in small, backwoods communities and lacked the resources to construct churches. Camp meetings were open-air services, attended by whites and blacks, slaves and free. The liturgy consisted mainly of hymns.[3]

The "Battle Hymn" tune was adapted from "Say, Brothers, Will You Meet Us/On Canaan's Happy Shore," a Southern camp-meeting spiritual. The "Say Brothers" hymn was first published in an 1807 Virginia hymnbook by the Methodist "circuit-rider" Stith Mead. In the introduction of his hymnbook, Mead said that popular hymns were the most effective way to bring sinners to Christ. They could "melt and move the most obdurate heart" or "cheer and comfort the most dejected mind." Hymn 50, "Grace Reviving in the Soul," soon became known as the "Say Brothers" or "O Brothers" hymn. It is a folk hymn, meaning that it adapted sacred words to a secular tune. It has a simple AAAB structure, and like other folk hymns, it was easily memorized, and it circulated orally. (As a result, there are frequent, usually modest, changes in the published lyrics.) Mead probably heard the hymn sung in camp, liked it, and included it in his hymnbook.[4]

What's especially fascinating about this first known publication of "Say Brothers" is that it includes call-and-response directions:

> *Question:* O brothers will you meet me [repeat 2x], On Canaan's happy shore?

> *Ans:* By the grace of God I'll meet you [repeat 2x], On Canaan's happy shore.

Call-and-response directions between minister and congregants typified the basic form and structure of African American spirituals. The

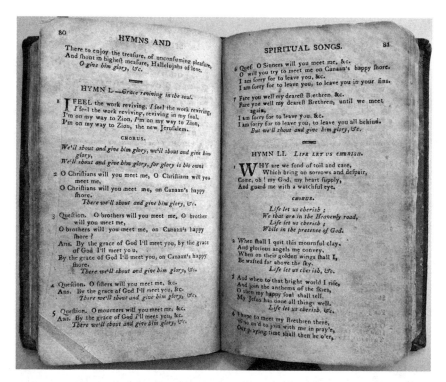

Hymn 50, "Grace Reviving in the Soul," later known as the "Say Brothers" or "O Brothers" hymn. From Stith Mead, *A General Selection of the Newest and Most Admired Hymns & Spiritual Songs* (1807). (Collection of Richard H. Hulan)

black roots of the "Say Brothers" hymn are further suggested by numerous eyewitnesses who described slaves singing "Say Brothers" in a ring shout, an African religious ritual in which people gathered in a circle, sang (or shouted), danced in a counterclockwise direction, and used a call-and-response structure. Additionally, the "glory, glory Hallelujah" chorus, which soon replaced "We'll shout and give him glory," was especially popular in black spirituals. And we know that Mead preached to slaves. The hymn's call-and-response structure, the interracial makeup of camp meetings, Mead's documented preaching to blacks, and eyewitness observers' describing slaves singing the hymn in a ring shout all suggest that the origins of "Say Brothers" were probably as much African as white American.[5]

But whites and blacks interpreted "Say Brothers" quite differently in the antebellum South. For white Southerners, Canaan, a heavenly place, was "a metaphor of the South," according to the religious historian Christine Heyrman. "Canaan's happy shore" offered deliverance from sin without touching slavery. It was a heavenly vision of whites' own moral universe. But for slaves, "Canaan's happy shore" meant deliverance from bondage. Canaan was both a heavenly place and a place in the world. For example, when Frederick Douglass first schemed to run away from slavery, he and his conspirators repeatedly sang "O Canaan, sweet Canaan,/I am bound for the land of Canaan." Canaan meant "something more than a hope of reaching heaven," Douglass noted; "we meant to reach the *north*—and the north was our Canaan."[6]

The "Say Brothers" hymn began circulating in the North via hymnbooks in the 1840s. By the late 1850s, it was popular especially in Boston, then the cultural and publishing center of the nation. Northerners were introduced to it through hymnbooks, without the call-and-response structure. They understood it as a white spiritual and associated it with Methodists, owing to the sect's explosive growth.[7]

In 1861, one Northerner in particular would become closely associated with the "Say Brothers" hymn: the militant abolitionist John Brown. Brown had become famous (or infamous) for his raid on the federal arsenal at Harpers Ferry, Virginia, with a small army of blacks and whites in October 1859. He had hoped to distribute arms to slaves and spark a major insurrection that would result in freedom. But federal troops led by Robert E. Lee killed or captured Brown and his men, tried the survivors for treason and murder (except for five who escaped), and executed them in December 1859 and March 1860. Brown's memory would spread the tune that had begun as a Southern spiritual in the form of "John Brown's Body."

Martin M. Lawrence, *John Brown*, 1858. Salt Print. This is the last known photograph of John Brown and the basis of the engraving that appeared on the cover of *Frank Leslie's Illustrated Newspaper* after his capture at Harpers Ferry. (Author's collection)

How did "Say Brothers" become "John Brown's Body"? Following the South's bombing of Fort Sumter in April 1861, the 2nd Battalion, known as the "Tigers," garrisoned in Fort Warren in Boston Harbor. The soldiers talked of John Brown, as did almost every other Bostonian, for Brown's raid was widely considered a major catalyst leading to secession and war. Most Bostonians considered Brown a martyr rather than a murderer. John Andrew, a rising Republican in the 1850s, had known Brown and defended his raid: "John Brown himself is right. I sympathize with the man . . . because I sympathize and believe in the eternal right." Andrew's defense of Brown catapulted him to the forefront of Massachusetts politics. He was elected governor of Massachusetts by a large majority.[8]

One of the Tigers at Fort Warren, a Scottish immigrant, was also named John Brown. He and some fellow soldiers formed a choral group, and Brown's comrades frequently needled him for his name. "This cannot be John Brown," they quipped. "John Brown is dead." Another soldier would add: "His body lies mouldering in the grave." Soon six stanzas were created, set to "Say Brothers," one of their favorite hymns. In May 1861 the Tigers Battalion merged with the Massachusetts 12th Regiment, and "John Brown's Body" (also known as "the John Brown song") became its signature anthem. In June, the Boston abolitionist C. S. Hall published the "John Brown Song" as a penny ballad, with the six verses and the "Glory, glory Hallelujah" chorus. Hall's sheet quickly sold out. On July 18, the 12th Regiment sang "John Brown's Body" on Boston Common while under review. One week later they sang it while marching down Broadway in New York City. Onlookers seemed "crazy with enthusiasm and delight." A reporter for the *New York Tribune* published the lyrics, and by August 1861 "John Brown's Body" was the most popular song in the Union army.[9]

The song's popularity coincided with the First Confiscation Act, which authorized the Union army to confiscate all slaves of rebel masters who had reached Union lines, effectively freeing them, as Jim Oakes has emphasized.[10] Perhaps it is not coincidental that

Sergeant John Brown of Boston, Scottish immigrant and soldier in the
Second Battalion ("Tigers"), garrisoned at Fort Warren in Boston Harbor,
undated photograph. (West Virginia State Archives)

"John Brown's Body" became a mascot of the Union army at the
very moment the war became an emancipation war, for the lyrics
are unambiguous in its abolitionist message. The song evokes John
Brown as martyr: his body "lies a mouldering in the grave," but his

"John Brown's Body" sheet music, 1861, arranged by C. B. Marsh. This is the first publication of the song with music. (Courtesy Boston Public Library)

soul is "marching on." The second stanza is even more explicit in its articulation of Brown as a martyr:

> He's gone to be a soldier in the army of the Lord,
> He's gone, & c.
> He's gone, & c.
> His soul's marching on

The fifth stanza seeks vengeance against slaveholders: "We will hang Jeff Davis to a sour apple tree." And the last stanza calls for "three rousing cheers for the Union."

Despite its immense popularity, "John Brown's Body" was never thought of as a national anthem. It was too coarse and needed to be elevated. This happened in November 1861, when Julia Ward Howe went to Washington, D.C., with her husband, Samuel Gridley Howe, who had joined the U.S. Sanitary Commission, along with her Unitarian minister James Freeman Clarke and Governor John Andrew. Julia had grown up in New York City, the daughter of one of the nation's wealthiest financiers. Beautiful and impeccably educated, she had moved to Boston when she married Samuel. The travelers had all known John Brown. Clarke had introduced him to Massachusetts Senator Charles Sumner. Samuel had been one of the "secret six" leading fundraisers of Brown's raid. And Julia had hosted Brown in their home. She was one of America's most highly respected poets, having already published two books of poetry. Even Nathaniel Hawthorne, who is not often remembered as a friend of women writers, called her the "poetess of America."[11]

While in Washington, Julia witnessed a review of troops across the Potomac. A Confederate raiding party broke up the review, creating the equivalent of a nineteenth-century traffic jam. To pass the time as her carriage inched its way toward the city, Julia joined soldiers in singing "John Brown's Body." The soldiers were much impressed with her beautiful, operatic voice, shouting "Good for you!"—or in effect, "Go girl!" Reverend Clarke, who was with her, suggested that she "write

Julia Ward Howe, facsimile of a photogravure by
Josiah Hawes, ca. 1861. From Julia Ward Howe,
Reminiscences, 1819–1899 (Boston: Houghton, Mifflin
and Company, 1899). (Author's collection)

some good words for that stirring tune." Julia replied that she had
often thought of doing so but had not yet received the inspiration.[12]

Inspiration came that night at the Willard Hotel, where she was
staying. As she later recalled, "I awoke in the gray of the morning
twilight; and as I lay waiting for the dawn, the long lines of the
desired poem began to twine themselves in my mind." She jumped
out of bed, found the old stump of a pen, and scrawled the verses on

the back of a piece of Sanitary Commission stationary, "almost without looking at the paper." In Howe's telling, the suddenness of the inspiration suggested a supernatural visitation. Her creation myth echoed that of Harriet Beecher Stowe, who said, "I didn't write" *Uncle Tom's Cabin*; "God wrote it."[13]

Howe's lyrics are deeply indebted to Revelation. The first stanza comes directly from Revelation 14, in which an angel "gathered the vine of the earth, and cast it into the great winepress of the wrath of

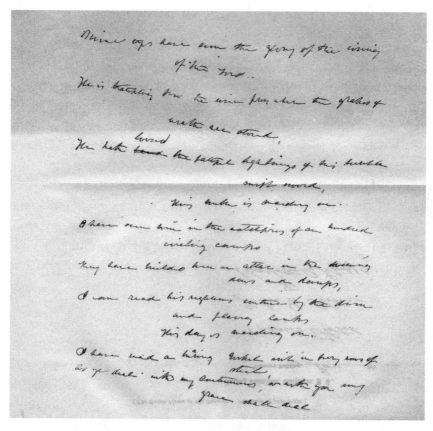

Facsimile of the first draft of the "Battle Hymn of the Republic," as written by Julia Ward Howe at Willard's Hotel, Washington, D.C. From Julia Ward Howe, *Reminiscences, 1819–1899* (Boston: Houghton, Mifflin and Company, 1899). (Author's collection)

God." Throughout Revelation, God or his angels cast lightning bolts and thunder into the earth, inducing an earthquake. Howe places the narrator of her poem *within* Revelation, personalizing its phantasmagoric imagery and turning it into a narrative lyric:

> Mine eyes have seen the glory of the coming of the Lord:
> He is trampling out the vintage where the grapes of wrath
>   are stored;
> He hath loosed the fateful lightning of His terrible swift sword:
> His truth is marching on.

It may seem strange that a Unitarian would know the Book of Revelation almost by heart. But Howe's intimate familiarity with it was representative, reflecting the degree to which most Americans interpreted the Civil War in apocalyptic terms. Revelation explained the ravages of war in religious terms and offered hope for the future. If the war was the apocalypse, then a new age of peace and harmony was not far away.[14]

The "Battle Hymn" was published in February 1862 on the front page of the *Atlantic Monthly*, one of the nation's most influential magazines. The published version was largely unchanged from Howe's inspired scrawl in the middle of the night, with one notable exception: Howe deleted the sixth (and last) stanza, and in doing so the song ends with the climactic power of the fifth stanza.

Influence

Despite its publishing prominence, the "Battle Hymn" was never as popular during the war as "John Brown's Body." This was largely because of the "Battle Hymn's" sophistication. Having been written for the college bred, soldiers on the march found it difficult to memorize. (Even today, few people know it by heart.) Moreover, Howe squeezed a lot of words into each bar of music, requiring singers to enunciate them quickly. The words are almost too big for the music.

THE

ATLANTIC MONTHLY.

A MAGAZINE OF LITERATURE, ART, AND POLITICS.

VOL. IX.—FEBRUARY, 1862.—NO. LII.

BATTLE HYMN OF THE REPUBLIC.

MINE eyes have seen the glory of the coming of the Lord :
He is trampling out the vintage where the grapes of wrath are stored ;
He hath loosed the fateful lightning of His terrible swift sword :
    His truth is marching on.

I have seen Him in the watch-fires of a hundred circling camps ;
They have builded Him an altar in the evening dews and damps ;
I can read His righteous sentence by the dim and flaring lamps :
    His day is marching on.

I have read a fiery gospel writ in burnished rows of steel :
" As ye deal with my contemners, so with you my grace shall deal ;
Let the Hero, born of woman, crush the serpent with his heel,
    Since God is marching on."

He has sounded forth the trumpet that shall never call retreat ;
He is sifting out the hearts of men before His judgment-seat :
Oh, be swift, my soul, to answer Him ! be jubilant, my feet !
    Our God is marching on.

In the beauty of the lilies Christ was born across the sea,
With a glory in his bosom that transfigures you and me :
As he died to make men holy, let us die to make men free,
    While God is marching on.

"Battle Hymn of the Republic," as published on the cover of *The Atlantic Monthly*, February 1862. (Widener Library, Harvard University)

The wartime popularity of "John Brown's Body" stemmed partly from the fact that it is a simple ballad, easy to memorize with its AAAB structure, and soothing to march to. Moreover, it emphasizes the image of bodily decay coinciding with spiritual rebirth, which was immensely popular during the Civil War. Then, too, by 1860 sheet music was the most profitable printed medium. Publishers knew that "John Brown's Body" made money, and the ballad rolled off the presses in countless variations.

The "John Brown" song was also open-ended enough to be interpreted in a variety of ways. It was a heroic song, an inspirational song, a revenge song, and a comradeship song. It inspired soldiers to fight, and possibly die, for the abstract causes of freedom and Union. But it also helped build esprit de corps among troops, encouraging them to seek revenge for a friend who had been killed. One Union officer said that the ballad "made heroes of all his men." Another officer required his troops to sing it every day, in order to imbue them with "Cromwellian earnestness." And a New Hampshire lieutenant said simply: "The effect of 'John Brown's Body' when heard in camp or on the march was simply indescribable."[15]

There is one final explanation for the popularity of a song that enshrined an abolitionist hanged for murder and treason. "John Brown's Body" became a Union mascot at the very time that a war waged to preserve the Union had also become a war to abolish slavery. The two discrete aims had converged into one: preserving the Union *required* abolishing slavery and vice versa. In essence, the war *mainstreamed* John Brown, reflecting the social revolution that it brought about. The Boston physician and writer Oliver Wendell Holmes Sr. described this apotheosis of John Brown. Brown's raid should not be seen as a failure but heralded as posthumous campaign. "His soul marched at the head of half a million men, shaking the continent and the world with the chorus of Glory Hallelujah."[16]

Understandably, "John Brown's Body" was especially popular among African Americans. The soldiers of the 1st Arkansas (Colored) Regiment were so inspired by it that they created a new adaptation, which Sojourner Truth sang to inspire recruits. In February 1865, when the Massachusetts 55th Colored Regiment marched triumphantly into Charleston, South Carolina, they sang "John Brown's Body" as thousands of freedmen and women cheered them on. For most Northerners, this was the symbolic end of the war.[17]

The "Battle Hymn" also had its champions. It was widely promoted by Charles McCabe, a Methodist minister who became chaplain of the 122nd Ohio Volunteer Infantry. He read Howe's poem in the *Atlantic* and was so taken with it that he committed it to memory. It was not until he heard the "Battle Hymn" sung at a war rally that he realized the poem had been written to accompany the tune of "John Brown's Body." In June 1863 he was captured by Confederate troops and sent to Libby Prison in Richmond. A month later, the prisoners heard of a great battle at Gettysburg and were initially told that it had been a decisive Confederate victory. But then an old slave

"'Marching On!': The Fifty-Fifth Massachusetts Colored Regiment Singing John Brown's March in the Streets of Charleston," February 1865. Engraving from *Harper's Weekly*, March 18, 1865. (Author's collection)

who sold newspapers brought the latest editions and announced, "Great news in de papers!" McCabe jumped onto a box and led the men in the "Battle Hymn": "the very walls of Libby quivered in the melody as five hundred" prisoners sang the "Glory, Hallelujah" chorus. He likened the scene to a mass resurrection.[18]

News in Libby Prison, engraving of the scene, made popular by Chaplain McCabe, when inmates in the Confederate prison learn that Gettysburg was a Union victory and sing the "Battle Hymn" to celebrate. Published in Edward P. Smith, *Incidents of the United States Christian Commission* (Philadelphia: J. B. Lippincott & Co., 1869). (Widener Library, Harvard University)

In 1864 McCabe turned Lincoln into an ardent fan of Howe's song. Having been released from Libby after suffering a bout of typhoid fever, he sang the "Battle Hymn" at a Christian Commission meeting at the U.S. Capitol, with Lincoln in attendance. McCabe had a rich, baritone voice, and Lincoln was especially moved by the fifth stanza, which equated Christ's sacrifice on the cross with the Union troops' sacrifice on the battlefield. Tears welled in his eyes after the final chorus, and he yelled, "Sing it again!" He told McCabe: "Take it all in all, the song and the singing, that was the best I ever heard."[19]

Legacies

Before the "Battle Hymn" could become a *national* anthem, it had to be embraced by both Southerners and Northerners. This transformation began in the 1880s. It coincided with the quest for reconciliation and reunion between white Northerners and Southerners and the uncoupling of the "Battle Hymn" from "John Brown's Body," with which it had been closely associated. "John Brown's Body" remained popular through the end of Reconstruction. But as Southerners began to control the story of the Civil War, John Brown and his song began to get sidelined. Increasingly, "John Brown's Body" was sung only by blacks and radicals.

The sidelining of "John Brown's Body" opened the way for the "Battle Hymn" to be reinterpreted. Whereas the former song invokes a militant abolitionist and calls for hanging Jeff Davis, the lyrics of "Battle Hymn" are wonderfully vague and thus adaptable. God is the main actor, advocating freedom. Southerners, too, believed that they had fought for God and freedom. As a result, the University of Georgia adopted the "Battle Hymn" as its anthem in the 1890s, and it remains the university's anthem today. In 1911, an early silent film, "The Battle Hymn of the Republic," was especially popular in the South. The film focused on the hymn's millennialist themes, and its artistic innovations helped revitalize the "Battle Hymn" for a modern age.[20]

There were many other legacies of the "Battle Hymn." At the turn of the century, it became a Progressive Party anthem. Theodore Roosevelt, the head of the party, treated the "Battle Hymn" as his personal anthem. To him, it encapsulated his advocacy of a sacred, strenuous life. Roosevelt was so in love with the "Battle Hymn" that he led a campaign among congressmen to adopt it as the official national anthem, but he could not convince enough Southern politicians.[21]

America's entry into World War I further helped nationalize, and indeed internationalize, the hymn. It became the anthem of countless Northern and Southern soldiers, as well as British soldiers, as they fought to defend freedom. Winston Churchill served on the western front, and partly owing to this experience, the "Battle Hymn" became his favorite song.[22]

The "Battle Hymn" became the workers' anthem in 1915, when Ralph Chaplin, a leading Wobbly (the common name for the Industrial Workers of the World or IWW) wrote "Solidarity Forever" to the tune of "John Brown's Body" and "Battle Hymn." Wobblies explicitly defined themselves as "the modern abolitionists, fighting against wage slavery." Like the abolitionists, they were racial egalitarians and millennialists. Chaplin retained the note of millennialism in his version of "Solidarity Forever," reflected in the song's last lines before the refrain: "We can bring to birth the new world from the ashes of the old,/For the Union makes us strong." The song enabled workers disenchanted with the "Battle Hymn," which obscures material conditions, to couple their millennial aspirations with social and economic transformation. Indeed Chaplin, like his socialist friends Eugene Debs and Upton Sinclair, imagined the Wobbly or socialist revolution as the material manifestation of Christ's second coming on earth. As Sinclair phrased it: "It was the new religion of humanity—or you might say it was the fulfillment of the old religion, since it implied but the *literal* application of all the teachings of Christ."[23]

Throughout the twentieth century, the "Battle Hymn" has also been an evangelical anthem. It was the theme song of both Billy Sunday and Billy Graham, the two greatest revivalists in American history. In fact Sunday, Graham, and the "Battle Hymn" ensured that evangelical Christianity would remain a vital force in the twentieth century.[24]

During Sunday's 1917 revival in New York, a city often considered "modern Babylon" and the graveyard of evangelists, he preached to one-quarter of the population. Over one hundred thousand New Yorkers "hit the sawdust trail," walking down aisles covered with wood shavings, to signify their acceptance of Jesus as their personal savior. The "Battle Hymn" was performed at every service. It was the perfect anthem for Sunday's revivals, for it fit his militant, triumphant, and patriotic style of "muscular Christianity." A former professional baseball player, Sunday owned the record for most bases stolen in one season until Ty Cobb broke it. He brought his athleticism to his sermons; he shadowboxed Satan, slid home to Jesus, and climbed onto the pulpit and waved an American flag as his orchestra performed "Battle Hymn."[25]

Billy Graham, the spiritual advisor to eleven presidents, from Harry Truman to George W. Bush, preached to more people around the world than perhaps anyone else in history. During a career that spanned from World War II through the end of the Cold War, he led some 450 crusades in 185 countries, disseminating the "Battle Hymn" and evangelical Christianity throughout the world. For several decades, millions of listeners heard "Battle Hymn" on Graham's weekly radio program, *Hour of Decision*. The "Battle Hymn" "exemplified the heart of Billy's crusades," noted Cliff Barrows, Graham's director of music: "His truth is marching on," "His day is marching on," "Since God is marching on," "Our God is marching on," "While God is marching on." The music "framed the theme" of Graham's message.[26]

Graham's love of the "Battle Hymn" also reflected his background as a Southerner haunted by the Civil War. Both grandfathers had been wounded as Confederate soldiers; his maternal grandfather lost a leg and an eye at Seminary Ridge at Gettysburg, and his paternal grandfather died with a Yankee bullet in his leg. It was his mother who recommended the "Battle Hymn" as his theme song. Just as the hymn had transcended its Northern, abolitionist origins, it also helped Graham transcend his roots and become a national and then international revivalist rather than another Southern preacher.[27]

The "Battle Hymn" was also a civil rights anthem and one of Martin Luther King Jr.'s favorite songs. In March 1965 King led a group of 25,000 blacks and whites from Selma to Montgomery, Alabama, and then delivered a speech on the grounds of the Alabama capital that ended with a millennialist vision of racial justice: "How long?" he asked. Not long, because:

> Mine eyes have seen the glory of the coming of the Lord
> He is trampling out the vintage where the grapes of wrath are
>   stored;
> He has loosed the fateful lightning with his terrible swift sword;
> His Truth is marching on.

He quoted the second stanza as well and then concluded with the "Glory, glory, hallelujah!" chorus. The hymn, like his speech, offered a vision of a unified nation. And the final line of King's last public address, on the night before he was assassinated, captures the degree to which the song embodied his millennialist vision: "Mine eyes have seen the glory of the coming of the Lord."[28]

Progressives, Wobblies, evangelicals, and civil rights activists were never united in their vision of America. Many evangelicals (though not Graham) opposed Wobblies and civil rights radicals, and progressives hated the Wobblies. "I would stand every one of the ornery, wild-eyed I.W.W.'s, Anarchists, crazy Socialists, and other types of Reds up before a firing squad," Billy Sunday declared. In fact, he said that Julia Ward Howe, the author of his anthem, was burning in hell, because as a Unitarian she did not properly acknowledge Christ's divinity.[29]

Despite their lack of unity, progressives, Wobblies, evangelicals, and civil rights activists especially are the legacies of the abolition movement—and these legacies have been previously ignored or downplayed. Members of these groups, like the abolitionists, saw themselves as holy warriors, uniting their religious faith with their visions of social reform. And much like the abolitionists, they spoke truth to power and were willing to sacrifice themselves for the cause of freedom. Wobblies and civil rights activists also advocated, like the abolitionists, equality under the law for all people.

These legacies also highlight the degree to which the "Battle Hymn" is America's unofficial anthem. Perhaps it is a blessing that it is not the national anthem, for it has been freed from countless obligatory performances at sporting events. Its influence is felt at more solemn occasions. For decades it has been sung as the finale of the national Democratic and Republican conventions. And it has been performed at the funerals of presidents Kennedy, Johnson, Nixon, and Reagan, along with those of Robert Kennedy, Teddy Kennedy, and Winston Churchill. Most recently, the Brooklyn Tabernacle Choir performed "Battle Hymn" at President Obama's second inaugural. It remains a popular closing hymn at funeral services for many ordinary Americans.[30]

The hymn also served as the finale of the 9/11 memorial service at Washington National Cathedral, where the heads of state heard Billy Graham deliver one of his last public sermons. And appropriately, it has a *physical* presence in America's unofficial church. In the Lincoln Bay of the National Cathedral, seven ornamental keystones depict the "Battle Hymn's" most vivid images, including grapes of wrath being trampled and lightning loosed, trumpets sounding forth, lilies growing where Christ was born, and soldiers singing the Hallelujah chorus.[31]

Why has the "Battle Hymn" been a national anthem for so long? There are several reasons. First, it is a song that both unites and divides, distinguishing "us" from "them" and thus clarifying a sense of

Four of the seven ornamental keystones depicting images from "The Battle Hymn of the Republic" at Washington National Cathedral. (Washington National Cathedral Collection)

national identity. It is an ideal song for a nation at war, which is when it is most popular, and the United States has been at war for most of the last century. Like the Gettysburg Address, it encourages individuals to sacrifice themselves for a greater, collective good. The fifth stanza brilliantly emphasizes the theme of sacrificing oneself for freedom:

> In the beauty of the lilies Christ was born across the sea,
> With a glory in his bosom that transfigures you and me:

As he died to make men holy, let us die to make men free,
His truth is marching on.[32]

Second, the "Battle Hymn" has long functioned as a template of America's "civil religion," in which Americans act out what they believe is God's will for their country. As the fifth stanza implies, Christ is both an exemplar and an object of faith. His will can be known. And since he (rather than humans) is the catalyst of social change, he lightens reformers' burdens.[33]

Third, the "Battle Hymn" has been immensely adaptable. Throughout its history, as its legacies reveal, it has served violent and nonviolent, postmillennial and premillennial, Northern and Southern, conservative and radical ends.

Fourth, the song exploits the millennialist strain in American culture, revealing the degree to which the United States is exceptional among developed nations; it stands apart from Europe and Canada in its religiosity. Throughout the twentieth century, between one-quarter and one-third of Americans believe that Christ's second coming will occur in their lifetime, according to Gallup polls. For Europeans and Canadians, such a belief borders on lunacy, but Americans accept it as a distinctive aspect of their culture.[34]

Fifth, it is an aspirational hymn, much like the Declaration of Independence. "The Battle Hymn" envisions a future good society, a reign of peace and harmony. It is thus sublime, which some critics have called an American aesthetic. The song evokes a terrible delight; it unites afflictions of the present with future joy.

Perhaps most importantly, the "Battle Hymn" is a musical masterpiece, especially when performed in *largo*—a slow, dignified tempo—as it was by the Mormon Tabernacle Choir, which won a Grammy in 1959, and the U.S. Army chorus. In these arrangements, the melody notes have been expanded in order to allow the words the chance to express themselves. Even listeners who disagree with the song's apocalyptic message cannot help but be transported by its aesthetic power.

The Emancipation of Abraham Lincoln

Eric Foner

ABRAHAM LINCOLN IS THE MOST ICONIC FIGURE IN AMERICAN history. He exerts a unique hold on our historical imagination as an embodiment of core American ideals and myths—the self-made man, the frontier hero, the liberator of the slaves. Thousands of works have been written about Lincoln, and almost any Lincoln you want can be found somewhere in the literature. Lincoln has been portrayed as a shrewd political operator driven by ambition, a moralist for whom emancipation was the logical conclusion of a lifetime hatred of slavery, and a racist who actually defended and tried to protect slavery. Politicians from conservatives to communists, civil rights activists to segregationists, have claimed him as their own.

Lincoln is important to us not because of his melancholia or how he chose his cabinet but because of his role in the vast human drama of emancipation and what his life tells us about slavery's enduring legacy. With the 150th anniversary of the Emancipation Proclamation it is important to focus on that document. The title suggests double emancipation—how Lincoln's decision to make slavery a target of the Union war effort represented both a fundamental change in the nature of the war and an emancipation from unsuccessful ideas and policies for Lincoln himself. With the proclamation, Lincoln launched himself on a journey, tragically cut short, in which he began to rethink his assumptions about how to rid the nation of slavery and the role of blacks in American life.

Like all great historical transformation, emancipation during the Civil War was a process, not a single event. It played out over time, arose from many causes, and was the work of many individuals. It began at the war's outset when slaves, ignoring Lincoln's insistence that the struggle was about national unity, began to seek refuge behind Union lines. It did not end until December 1865, with the ratification of the Thirteenth Amendment, irrevocably abolishing slavery throughout the reunited nation. But the Emancipation Proclamation was certainly the crucial step in this process.

In approaching the subject of Lincoln's views and policies regarding slavery and race, the first thing to bear in mind, as emphasized in *The Fiery Trial*, is that it is fruitless to identify a single quotation, speech, or letter as the real or quintessential Lincoln. At the time of his death, Lincoln occupied a very different place with regard to these issues of slavery and race than he did earlier in his life. That Lincoln changed, of course, is hardly a new idea. But the story is forward, not backward—not as a trajectory toward a predetermined goal but as an unpredictable progress, with twists and turns along the way, and the future always unknown.[1]

Lincoln's relationship with abolitionists and with Radical Republicans, who in effect represented the abolitionist point of view in party politics, is essential in understanding his "emancipation." They often criticized him, and he made some unflattering remarks about them. Lincoln was not an abolitionist and never claimed to be one. Yet he saw himself as part of a broad antislavery movement that included both abolitionists and more moderate politicians like himself. He was well aware of the abolitionists' significance in creating public sentiment hostile to slavery. And on issue after issue—abolition in the nation's capital, wartime emancipation, enlisting black soldiers, amending the Constitution to abolish slavery, allowing some African-

Americans to vote—Lincoln came to occupy positions the abolitionists had first staked out. The destruction of slavery during the Civil
War offers an example, as relevant today as in Lincoln's time, of how
the combination of an engaged social movement and an enlightened
political leader can produce far-reaching social change.

Unlike the abolitionists, most of whom sought to influence the
political system from the outside, for nearly his entire adult life Lincoln was a politician. In the 1830s and 1840s, he was a prominent
Illinois Whig, a member of the legislature and, for one term, of Congress. During this part of his political career, Lincoln said little about
slavery. Most of his speeches dealt with the economic issues of the
day—banking, the protective tariff, and government aid to internal
improvements, a program to which Lincoln was so passionately
devoted that he helped push through the Illinois legislature a
far-reaching plan of building roads, canals, and railroads that bank-
rupted the state.

Lincoln did not elaborate his views on slavery until the 1850s,
when he emerged as a major spokesman for the newly created Republican party, committed to halting the westward expansion of slavery.
In speeches of eloquence and power, Lincoln condemned slavery as
a fundamental violation of the founding principles of the United
States, as enunciated in the Declaration of Independence—the affir-
mation of human equality and of the natural right to life, liberty, and
the pursuit of happiness. To Lincoln, equality meant the equal right
to the fruits of one's labor, in a society that offered opportunity for
advancement to what he and others called the "free laborer."

There are many grounds for condemning the institution of
slavery—moral, religious, political, economic. Lincoln referred to all
of them at one time or another. But ultimately, he saw slavery as a
form of theft—stealing the labor of one person and appropriating it
for another. Lincoln was frequently charged by Democrats with sup-
porting "Negro equality." He firmly denied the charge, as we will
see. But he explained the kind of equality in which he did believe,
using a black woman as an illustration: "In some respects she cer-

tainly is not my equal; but in her natural right to eat the bread she earns with her own hand without asking the leave of anyone else, she is my equal, and the equal of all others."[2] The natural right to the fruits of one's labor was the grounding of equality, not bounded by either race or gender.

Lincoln could declare, "I have always hated slavery, I think as much as any Abolitionist."[3] He used language similar to that of abolitionism—he spoke of slavery as a "monstrous injustice," a cancer that threatened the lifeblood of the nation.[4] Why then was he not an abolitionist? The shadow of Lincoln should not obscure the contribution to the end of slavery of men and women like Wendell Phillips, Frederick Douglass, and Abby Kelley, who fought against overwhelming odds to bring the moral issue of slavery to the forefront of national life. But before the Civil War, abolitionists were a small, despised group. Outside a few districts, no one with political ambitions could be an abolitionist. If you were from central Illinois, abolitionism was hardly a viable political position.

But Lincoln was not a secret abolitionist restrained by political pragmatism. Abolitionists believed that the moral issue of slavery was the paramount issue confronting the nation, overriding everything else. This was not Lincoln's view. In a famous letter to his Kentucky friend Joshua Speed, in 1855, Lincoln recalled their visit in 1841 to St. Louis, where they encountered slavery: "That sight was a continual torment to me; and I see something like it every time I touch the Ohio [River, the boundary between free and slave states]. . . . You ought . . . to appreciate how much the great body of the northern people do crucify their feelings, in order to maintain their loyalty to the constitution and the Union." Just before this sentence, Lincoln commented on fugitive slaves: "I confess I hate to see the poor creatures hunted down, and caught, and carried back to their stripes, and unrewarded toils; but I bite my lip and keep quiet."[5] Why did he keep silent? Because the right to recover fugitives is in the Constitution.

William Lloyd Garrison burned the Constitution because of its clauses protecting slavery. Lincoln revered the Constitution. He believed the United States had a mission to exemplify the institutions of democracy and self-government for the entire world. This, of course, was the theme of the Gettysburg Address. He was not, to be sure, a believer in "manifest destiny"—the idea that Americans had a God-given right to acquire new territory in the name of liberty, regardless of the desires of the actual inhabitants. Lincoln saw American democracy as an example to the world, not something to be imposed on others by unilateral force.

The combination of hatred of slavery and reverence for the Constitution created a serious dilemma for Lincoln and for many others. In his great Peoria speech of 1854, Lincoln explained that slavery "deprives our republican example of its just influence in the world—enables the enemies of free institutions, with plausibility, to taunt us as hypocrites—causes the real friends of freedom to doubt our sincerity." Slavery, in other words, was an obstacle to the fulfillment of the historic mission of the United States. Yet, the nation's unity must be maintained, even if it meant compromising with slavery. Certainly, the compromises of the Constitution, including very distasteful ones like the fugitive slave clause, could not be violated lest the entire edifice fall to pieces.[6]

Another key difference between Lincoln and abolitionists lay in their views regarding race. Abolitionists insisted that once freed, slaves should be recognized as equal members of the American republic. They viewed the struggles against slavery and racism as intimately connected. Lincoln saw slavery and racism as distinct questions. Unlike his Democratic opponents in the North and pro-slavery advocates in the South, Lincoln claimed for blacks the natural rights to which all persons were entitled. "I think the negro," he wrote in 1858, "is included in the word 'men' used in the Declaration of Independence" and that slavery was therefore wrong.[7] But inalienable natural rights—life, liberty, the pursuit of happiness—he insisted, did not necessarily carry with them civil, political, or social equality. Persistently charged with belief in "Negro equality" during his campaign for the Senate against Stephen A. Douglas, Lincoln responded that he was not "nor ever have been, in favor of making voters or jurors of Negroes, nor of qualifying them to hold office, nor to intermarry with white people."[8] Lincoln refused to condemn the notorious Black Laws of Illinois, which made it a crime for black persons to enter the state.

Throughout the 1850s and for the first half of the Civil War, Lincoln believed that "colonization"—that is encouraging black people to emigrate to a new homeland in Africa, the Caribbean, or Central America—ought to accompany the end of slavery. We sometimes forget how widespread the belief in colonization was in the pre–Civil War era. Henry Clay and Thomas Jefferson, the statesmen most revered by Lincoln, outlined plans to accomplish it. Rather than a fringe movement, it was part of a widely shared mainstream solution to the issues of slavery and race.[9]

Colonization allowed its proponents to think about the end of slavery without confronting the question of the place of blacks in a postemancipation society. Why should freed slaves leave the country? Clay had a reason: he spoke of free blacks as a "debased and degraded set" and insisted that multiplying their numbers would pose a danger to American society.[10] Lincoln never said anything like this—he did not verbally abuse black people as so many Northern politicians, including some Republicans, did. Jefferson had a different reason. As he explained in his famous letter to Edward Coles about the prospects for ending slavery, while the institution must come to an end, if the two races lived together as free people, "amalgamation" would follow.[11] Jefferson practiced amalgamation but feared its consequences. Lincoln never said anything about this either. Instead, Lincoln emphasized the strength of white racism. Because of it, he said several times, blacks could never achieve equality in the United States. They should remove themselves to a homeland where they could fully enjoy freedom and self-government.[12]

Many scholars have been puzzled by Lincoln's public advocacy of colonization or have simply ignored it, insisting that Lincoln could not have been serious when he advanced the idea, which does not fit easily with the image of the Great Emancipator. It is important to remember that for Clay, Lincoln, and many others, colonization was part of a broader program for ending slavery in a political system that erected seemingly insuperable legal and constitutional barriers to abolition.

To oversimplify, slavery can be abolished in one of three ways. One is individual manumission, some of which occurred in the United States but not nearly enough to threaten the system's viability. Second is emancipation by legal means. This can proceed where owners lack the political power to prevent it, as happened in the Northern states after the American Revolution, and in the British empire. Where the owners are more powerful, legal abolition requires their consent. Lincoln, like Clay, long believed that this could be obtained only through a program of gradual emancipation, coupled with monetary compensation to the owners for their loss of property in slaves, and a plan to encourage (or, in the case of Clay and Jefferson, require) blacks to leave the country, as it seemed impossible that slaveholders would ever consent to the creation of a vast new population of free African-Americans.

The third mode of emancipation is military emancipation. War destabilizes slavery; it strips away its constitutional protections. Contending sides make slavery a military target to weaken their opponents. They enlist slave soldiers. This happened many times in wars in the Western Hemisphere, including during the American Revolution. It would happen during the Civil War. But in the 1850s, no one knew war was on the horizon. No one could conceive of a way of ending slavery without the cooperation of slaveholders. The Constitution barred interference with slavery in the states where it already existed. For Lincoln, as for most Republicans, antislavery action meant not attacking slavery where it was but working to prevent slavery's westward expansion. (I suppose there is a fourth mode of emancipation—slave revolution, as in Haiti. But this was highly unusual and certainly no one in the United States thought it was a likely occurrence except perhaps John Brown.)

Lincoln, however, did talk about a future without slavery. The aim of the Republican party, he insisted, was to put the institution on the road to "ultimate extinction," a phrase he borrowed from Henry Clay. Ultimate extinction could take a long time: Lincoln once said that slavery might survive for another hundred years.[13] But to the South, Lincoln seemed as dangerous as an abolitionist because he was committed to the eventual end of slavery. This was why it was the election not of Garrison or Phillips but of Lincoln—a mainstream Republican politician—that led inexorably to secession and civil war. The Southern secession conventions made it clear that they feared Lincoln's administration would be a threat to the future of slavery.

During the Civil War, of course, Lincoln had to do more than talk about slavery. He had to act. How did he become, if indeed he did become, the Great Emancipator?

The Civil War, of course, did not begin as a crusade to abolish slavery. Almost from the beginning, however, abolitionists and Radical Republicans pressed for action against slavery as a war measure. Faced with this pressure, Lincoln began to put forward his own ideas. I do not wish to rehearse in detail the complicated chronology of events in 1861 and 1862. In summary, Lincoln first proposed gradual, voluntary emancipation coupled with colonization—a plan that would make slaveowners partners in abolition. Lincoln has been criticized for delay in moving toward emancipation. This is not correct. In August 1861, he willingly signed the First Confiscation Act, which emancipated slaves employed for military labor by the Confederacy. In November 1861, only a few months into the war, when no significant battle had yet been fought, he met with political leaders from Delaware to present his plan. Delaware was one of the four border slave states (along with Maryland, Kentucky, and Missouri) that remained in the Union. In 1860, it had only 1,800 slaves. Delaware, Lincoln said, could have the glory of leading the way to the end of slavery. It would be gradual and compensated, and the government would encourage the freed slaves to emigrate. Delaware was not interested. Slaveowners do not wish to relinquish their slaves, even for compensation. (Ironically, Delaware, with Kentucky, were the last states to see slavery end—only the ratification of the Thirteenth Amendment abolished the institution there.) Undeterred, throughout the spring and summer of 1862, Lincoln promoted his plan with the border states, and any Confederates willing to listen, to no avail.[14]

Lincoln's plan also fell apart at the other end—among blacks. In August 1862, he held a famous meeting with black leaders from Washington, D.C. Lincoln was only the second president to meet with blacks in a capacity other than slaves or servants. The first time came half a century earlier, when James Madison met with the black sea captain Paul Cuffe, who wanted to promote emigration to Africa. Lincoln's purpose was the same. At the meeting he issued a powerful indictment of slavery—blacks, he said, were suffering "the greatest wrong ever inflicted on any people." But he refused to issue a similar condemnation of racism; nor did he associate himself with it: "whether it is right or wrong I need not discuss." Racism was intractable. "Even when you cease to be slaves, you are yet far removed from being placed on an equality with the white race. . . . It is better for us both, therefore, to be separated."[15] But the large majority of black Americans refused to contemplate emigration from the land of their birth. They insisted on their right to remain here and fight for equal rights.

In mid-1862 Congress moved ahead of Lincoln on emancipation, although he signed all their measures: the abolition of slavery in the territories; abolition in the District of Columbia (with around $300 compensation for each slaveowner); the Second Confiscation Act of July 1862, which freed all slaves of pro-Confederate owners in areas henceforth occupied by the Union army and slaves of such owners who escaped to Union lines. Meanwhile, Lincoln was moving toward his own plan of emancipation. A powerful combination of events propelled him:

The failure of efforts to fight the Civil War as a conventional war without targeting the bedrock of Southern society. Military stalemate generated support in North, first among abolitionists, then more broadly, for making slavery a military target. A war of army against army must become a war of society against society.

Many Northerners feared that Britain might recognize the Confederacy or even intervene on its behalf. Adding emancipation to preserving the Union as a war aim would prevent this.

Slavery itself was beginning to disintegrate. From the beginning, the slaves saw the Civil War as heralding the long-awaited dawn of freedom. Hundreds, then thousands, ran away to Union lines. Slaves realized that the war had changed the balance of power in the South. Their actions forced the administration to begin to devise policies with regard to slavery.

Enthusiasm for enlistment was waning rapidly in the North. By 1863, a draft would be authorized. At the beginning of war, the army had refused to accept black volunteers. But the reservoir of black manpower could no longer be ignored.

All these pressures moved Lincoln in the direction of general emancipation. He first proposed this to his Cabinet on July 22, 1862. Lincoln presented a draft order consisting of three sentences. The second reaffirmed Lincoln's support for compensated, gradual emancipation. The third, invoking his authority as commander-in-chief, declared that on January 1, 1863, "all persons held as slaves within any state or states" still under Confederate control "shall then, thenceforward, and forever, be free."[16] Presented without fanfare and appearing almost as an afterthought, this final sentence constituted the initial version of the Emancipation Proclamation. The Cabinet seemed stunned. Not all approved of Lincoln's decision, although all recognized its momentous significance. Secretary of State Seward warned that issuing the proclamation might seem an act of desperation—he advised Lincoln to wait until the Union achieved a military victory. Lincoln agreed to shelve the order for the time being.

Two months later, in September 1862, after General George McClellan's army forced Confederates under Robert E. Lee to retreat from Maryland at the battle of Antietam, Lincoln issued the Preliminary Emancipation Proclamation—essentially a warning to the South to lay down its arms or face emancipation in one hundred days. In the interim, Lincoln continued to pursue his colonization idea (which was specifically mentioned in the Preliminary Proclamation), issued his famous public letter to Horace Greeley insisting that whatever action he took regarding slavery was motivated by a desire to save the Union, and saw his party suffer reverses in congressional elections. When Congress reconvened on December 1, 1862, Lincoln's annual message said nothing about the impending proclamation but devoted a long passage to reiterating his commitment to gradual, compensated emancipation and colonization. He asked for constitutional amendments authorizing Congress to appropriate funds for any state that provided for emancipation by the year 1900. It was a final offer to the border and Confederate states of a different mode of abolition than immediate emancipation.

Lincoln closed the message with a stirring peroration: "The dogmas of the quiet past, are inadequate to the stormy present. . . . As our case is new, so we must think anew, and act anew. We must disenthrall our selves, and then we shall save our country." These eloquent words, wrote one magazine, should be "committed to memory and constantly recalled by every man."[17] But they referred not to the impending Emancipation Proclamation but to Lincoln's thirty-seven-year plan of compensated emancipation. The message revealed Lincoln's thinking at a crucial moment of transition. He clung to a proposal he had been promoting for a year with no success. But on January 1, 1863, Lincoln abandoned the dogmas of the past and moved to free the nation from the institution of slavery.

The Emancipation Proclamation is perhaps the most misunderstood important document in American history. Certainly, it is untrue that Lincoln freed four million slaves with a stroke of his pen. The proclamation had no bearing on the slaves in the four border states. Since they remained in the Union, the constitutional protections of slavery remained in place for them. The proclamation exempted certain areas of the Confederacy that had fallen under Union military control, including parts of Virginia and Louisiana and the entire state of Tennessee (this was at the request of Military Governor Andrew Johnson—it was a significant exaggeration to say all of Tennessee was in Union hands). All told, perhaps eight hundred thousand of the nearly four million slaves were not covered by the proclamation. But 3.1 million were. This was the largest emancipation in world history. Never before had so many slaves been declared free on a single day. The proclamation did not end slavery everywhere when it was issued, but it sounded the death knell of slavery in the United States— assuming the Union won the war (were the Confederacy to emerge victorious, slavery would undoubtedly last a long time). Everybody recognized that if slavery perished in South Carolina, Alabama, and Mississippi, it could hardly survive in Tennessee, Kentucky, and a few parishes of Louisiana.

A military measure whose constitutional legitimacy rested on the "war power" of the president, the Emancipation Proclamation often proves disappointing to those who read it. Unlike the Declaration of Independence, it contains no soaring language, no immortal preamble enunciating the rights of man. Couched in dull, legalistic language, much of it consists of a long quotation from the preliminary proclamation of September. Only at the last moment, at the urging of Secretary of the Treasury Salmon P. Chase, an abolitionist, did Lincoln add a conclusion declaring the proclamation not only an exercise of "military necessity" but "an act of justice."[18]

Nonetheless, the proclamation was the turning point of the Civil War and in Lincoln's understanding of his own role in history. Lincoln was not the Great Emancipator if by that we mean someone who was waiting all his life to abolish slavery. He was not the Great Emancipator if this means that he freed four million slaves in an instant. One might better say that Lincoln *became* the Great Emancipator—that he assumed the role thrust on him by history and henceforth tried to live up to it. Lincoln knew he would be remembered for this act. The Preliminary Proclamation had included a long excerpt from the Second Confiscation Act, leaving the impression that Lincoln was acting on congressional authority. The Emancipation Proclamation made no mention of any congressional legislation. Lincoln claimed full authority as commander-in-chief to decree emancipation and accepted full responsibility.

Lincoln had said, "We must disenthrall ourselves, and then we shall save our country." He included himself in that "we." The Emancipation Proclamation was markedly different from Lincoln's previous statements and policies regarding slavery. It abandoned the idea of seeking the cooperation of slaveholders in emancipation and of distinguishing between loyal and disloyal owners. It was immediate, not gradual; contained no mention of compensation for slaveowners; and made no reference to colonization. For the first time, it authorized the enrollment of black soldiers into the Union army. The proclamation set in motion the process by which two hundred thousand black men in the last two years of the war served in the Union army and navy, playing a critical role in achieving Union victory.

Lincoln would, on occasion, refer to elements of his previous thinking, such as gradualism and compensation, during the next two years. But from January 1, 1863, onward, he never again mentioned colonization in public. And while his administration continued to offer assistance to blacks who voluntarily decided to emigrate, colonization was no longer part of a larger program of abolition. Since emancipation no longer required the consent of slaveholders, colonization had become irrelevant. Moreover, putting black men into the army implied a very different vision of their future place in American society. You do not ask men to fight and die for the Union and then send them and their families out of the country.

One of the pleasures of working on Lincoln is simply reading, slowly and carefully, his writings. He was an extremely careful writer with a remarkable command of the English language. Even the familiar Emancipation Proclamation itself produces surprises when read with care. The Preliminary Proclamation had aroused criticism for seeming to encourage violence by the slaves. Even Chase had feared, when Lincoln presented his emancipation order to the Cabinet in July, that it would lead to "depredation and massacre." In the final version, Lincoln enjoined the former slaves to refrain from violence, but he added, "except in necessary self-defense." Lincoln was not cowed by widespread charges that emancipation would be followed by a racial bloodbath. Lincoln did not have to say that blacks had a right to defend their freedom by violence if need be, but he did so. And, repudiating his earlier commitment to colonization without quite saying so, he urged freed slaves to go to work for "reasonable wages"—in the United States. Not just wages but reasonable wages. Lincoln wanted to make clear that the former slaves had a right to compete in the marketplace as free laborers, to judge for themselves the wages offered them. In other words, in the proclamation, Lincoln addressed African-Americans directly, not as the property of the nation's enemies but as men and women with volition and whose loyalty the Union must earn.[19]

Overall, the proclamation fundamentally changed the character of the Civil War. It made the destruction of slavery a purpose of the Union army. It liquidated without compensation the largest concentration of property in the United States. It crystallized a new identification between the ideal of liberty and a nation-state whose powers increased enormously as the war progressed. As Karl Marx, then in London writing newspaper columns about the war, observed, "Up to now we have witnessed only the first act of the Civil War—the constitutional waging of war. The second act—the revolutionary waging of war, is at hand."[20]

Lincoln came to emancipation more slowly than the abolitionists desired. But having made the decision, he did not look back. In 1864, with casualties mounting, there was talk of a compromise peace. Some urged Lincoln to rescind the proclamation, in which case, they believed, the South could be persuaded to return to the Union. At the least, some Republican leaders insisted, such a step could defuse opposition to his reelection, which was very much in jeopardy that summer. Lincoln would not consider this. Were he to do so, he told one visitor, "I should be damned in time and eternity."[21] (Had McClellan defeated Lincoln in 1864, it is quite possible to imagine the Union being restored with slavery still existing in some places.)

Lincoln knew full well that the proclamation depended for its effectiveness on Union victory, that it did not apply to all slaves, and that its constitutionality was certain to be challenged in the future. In the last two years of the war he worked to secure complete abolition, pressing the border states to take action against slavery on their own (which Maryland and Missouri did), requiring that Southerners who wished to have their other property restored pledge to support emancipation, and working to secure congressional passage of the Thirteenth Amendment. None of these measures, when adopted, included gradualism, compensation, or colonization.

Moreover, by decoupling emancipation from colonization, Lincoln in effect launched the historical process known as Reconstruction—the remaking of Southern society, politics, and race relations. Lincoln did not live to see Reconstruction implemented and eventually abandoned. But in the last two years of the war, he came to recognize that if emancipation settled one question, the fate of slavery, it opened another—what was to be the role of emancipated slaves in postwar American life?

In 1863 and 1864, Lincoln for the first time began to think seriously about the role blacks would play in postslavery America. Two of Lincoln's final pronouncements show how his thinking was evolving. One was his "last speech," delivered at the White House in April 1865 a few days before his assassination. Of course, Lincoln did not know this was his last speech—it should not be viewed as a final summation of policy. In it he addressed Reconstruction, already underway in Louisiana. A new constitution had been ratified, which abolished slavery yet limited voting rights to whites. The state's free black community complained bitterly about their exclusion from the ballot, with support from Radical Republicans in the North. Most Northern states at this point, however, did not allow blacks to vote, and most Republicans felt that it would be politically suicidal to endorse black suffrage. In this speech, Lincoln announced that he would "prefer" that limited black suffrage be implemented. He singled out not only the "very intelligent"—the free blacks—but also "those who serve our cause as soldiers" as most worthy. Moreover, he noted that blacks desired the right to vote—an indication that their opinions were now part of the political equation. Hardly an unambiguous embrace of equality, this was the first time that an American president had publicly endorsed any kind of political rights for blacks. Lincoln was telling the country that the service of black soldiers, inaugurated by the Emancipation Proclamation, entitled them to a political voice in the reunited nation.[22]

Then there is one of the greatest speeches in American history, Lincoln's second inaugural address, of March 4, 1865. Today, it is remembered for its closing words: "with malice toward none, with charity for all . . . let us strive to bind up the nation's wounds." But before that noble ending, Lincoln tried to instruct his fellow countrymen on the historical significance of the war and the unfinished task that still remained.

It must have been very tempting, with Union victory imminent, for Lincoln to view the outcome as the will of God and to blame the war on the sins of the Confederacy. Yet Lincoln said he would not even discuss events on the battlefield; rather he dwelled on the deep meaning of the war. Everybody knew, he noted, that slavery was "somehow" the cause of the Civil War. Not the black presence, as he had said in his meeting with the blacks from Washington, D.C., in 1862, but slavery as an institution. Yet Lincoln called it "American slavery," not Southern slavery, underscoring the entire nation's complicity. No man, he continued, truly knows God's will. Men wanted the war to end, but God might wish it to continue as a punishment to the nation for the sin of slavery, "until all the wealth piled by the bond-man's 250 years of unrequited toil shall be sunk, and until every drop of blood drawn with the lash, shall be paid by another drawn by the sword."[23] Here was a final reaffirmation of his definition of slavery as a theft of labor and also one of the very few times that Lincoln spoke publicly of the physical brutality inherent in slavery. (Lincoln generally discussed slavery as an abstraction, a matter of principle, rather than dwelling on its day-to-day brutality.) Lincoln was reminding his audience that the "terrible" violence of the Civil War had been preceded by 250 years of the terrible violence of slavery. Violence did not begin with the firing on Fort Sumter in April 1861.

In essence, Lincoln was asking the entire nation to confront unblinkingly the legacy of the long history of bondage. What are the requirements of justice in the face of this reality? What is the nation's obligation for those 250 years of unpaid labor? What is necessary to enable the former slaves, their children, and their descendants to enjoy the "pursuit of happiness" he had always insisted was their natural right but that had so long denied to them? Within a few weeks, Lincoln was dead. He did not provide an answer. And 150 years after the Emancipation Proclamation, these questions continue to bedevil American society.

Lincoln and the Struggle to End Slavery

Richard Striner

FOR A VERY LONG TIME, AMERICANS HAVE THOUGHT ABOUT Abraham Lincoln as a patriot above all else. Many see him as a quintessential "moderate"—a man who rescued our polity and saved our most precious institutions.

And there is surely much truth in this portrait. But there is quite a lot of truth left out of it. For Lincoln was more than just a patriotic Unionist, as most of his pre-presidential speeches and pronounce- ments (including his speeches in the Lincoln-Douglas debates and his "House Divided" speech) make abundantly clear. And his appar- ent moderation in the Civil War years was in some respects a dis- guise. Lincoln's Unionism—transcendental though it sometimes appears—was contingent on America's progress in phasing out slav- ery. And when it came to his long-term antislavery program, this American leader was brilliant to the point of audacity.[1]

There was a fiery and charismatic side to this man that is long overdue for analysis. In Lincoln the United States produced an extraordinary moral strategist—both fervent and Machiavellian— who saved the Union by *changing* it.

Lincoln constantly insisted in the 1850s that America should stop the geographical expansion of slavery. This program was a very real threat to the Southern way of life, so called. For with a quarantine placed around the slavery system, the free-state majority in Congress would grow toward a supermajority. That being the case, the final triumph of the antislavery movement would be very hard for Southerners to stop: a congressional supermajority (together with a supermajority of free states) could sweep aside Southern opposition and amend the Constitution to destroy the institution of slavery altogether. Consequently, it was Lincoln's election itself—with his "free soil" pledge to prevent any further extension of slavery to western lands—that pushed the slave states into secession.

Lincoln's earliest strategy for ridding the nation of slavery was incremental. "Phase One" was the containment of the evil. "Phase Two" would be a long-term phaseout program, a concept in many ways derived from the British antislavery method of the 1830s. Lincoln also (at least until 1864) supported the principle of voluntary colonization for blacks as a way to defuse the incendiary racial issue among the electorate. What he wanted, he explained more than once, was to phase out the evil of slavery and then let the races go their separate ways in peace.

Some observers, such as Lerone Bennett Jr., have argued that Lincoln was an overt racist. They cite his emphasis on colonization and they quote certain statements that he made in the 1850s—statements that in many ways *sound* like the talk of a man who harbored racial aversions.

But if Lincoln were a racist, we are left with a bit of a conundrum. For he denounced the oppression of blacks. In his famous Peoria speech of October 16, 1854, he pleaded with the whites in Illinois to acknowledge the truth that the "negro has some natural right to himself" and that "those who deny it, and make mere merchandise of him, deserve kickings, contempt, and death."[2] He said the same sort of thing many times.

Why on earth would a bigot even trouble his mind about the subject? Why would any racist candidate for office tell his racist constituents that slavery was evil and that blacks deserved liberation?

One obvious reason was the deep humanitarianism of Lincoln. He wrote privately in 1855 that the status of the slaves was "a continual torment to me." He added that he and other antislavery Northerners "crucify their feelings" on the issue.[3]

But there was more to this than tenderhearted feeling. Lincoln also called for the cessation of race-conscious thinking in America. In 1858, he urged supporters to "discard all this quibbling about this man and the other man—this race and that race and the other race being inferior, and therefore they must be placed in an inferior position. Let us discard all these things, and unite as one people."[4]

Lincoln actually strove to *attack* racist doctrines on occasions when he could get away with it. In the autumn months of 1859, for instance, he made a number of speeches that attacked his political rival Stephen Douglas for propounding the notion that blacks were equivalent to beasts. These speeches were direct attacks upon the heart of white supremacist doctrine.

In a speech in Columbus, Ohio, Lincoln lashed out at those who said that blacks were "sub-human." In some notes that he made before drafting this speech, he reviewed a statement Douglas had made within the previous year: "At Memphis," Lincoln wrote,

> Douglas told his audience that he was for the negro against the crocodile, but for the white man against the negro. This was not a sudden thought spontaneously thrown off at Memphis. He said the same thing many times in Illinois last summer and autumn, though I am not sure it was reported then. It is a carefully framed illustration of the estimate he places on the negro and the manner in which he would have him dealt with. It is a sort of proposition in proportion. "As the negro is to the crocodile, *so* the white man is to the negro."

> As the negro ought to treat the crocodile as a beast, so the
> white man ought to treat the negro as a beast.[5]

These were preparatory *notes* for his speech; now consider the passion that Lincoln displayed when he spoke in Columbus, Ohio, on September 16, 1859: "Did you ever five years ago, hear of anybody in the world saying that the negro had no share in the Declaration of National Independence, that it did not mean negroes at all; and when 'all men' were spoken of negroes were not included? . . . . I have been unable at any time to find a man in an audience who would declare that he had ever known any body saying so five years ago. But last year there was not a Douglas [supporter] in Illinois who did not say it."

How far had this fundamental change of opinion proceeded in Ohio, Lincoln asked his audience. How many now believed that the Negro was excluded from the Declaration of Independence? "If you think that now," Lincoln said,

> and did not think it then, the next thing that strikes me is to
> remark that there has been a *change* wrought in you [laugh
> ter and applause], and a very significant change it was, being
> no less than changing the negro, in your estimation, from
> the rank of a man to that of a brute. They are taking him
> down, and placing him, when spoken of, among reptiles and
> crocodiles, as Judge Douglas himself expresses it. . . . I ask
> you to note that fact, and the like of which is to follow, to be
> plastered on, layer after layer, until very soon you are pre
> pared to deal with the negro everywhere as with the brute.
> If public sentiment has not been debauched already to this
> point, a new turn of the screw in that direction is all that is
> wanting.[6]

Once again, the pointed question must be asked: why would a racist be inclined to say these sorts of things at all? It was surely not for reasons of expediency: white supremacist feeling was a powerful presence in the North and especially so in Lincoln's own political base, Illinois. If anything, political expediency would have pushed men like Lincoln in the *opposite* direction: to say the sorts of things that would protect them from a white supremacist backlash. And there is reason to believe this was exactly the case in regard to the *particular* statements by Lincoln that latter-day critics like Bennett have produced to substantiate their charge that Lincoln was a racist.

Lincoln's paramount goal in the 1850s was to counteract the program of Senator Stephen A. Douglas of Illinois. Douglas and other politicians had rolled back the barriers to slavery expansion with the Kansas-Nebraska Act of 1854. This law permitted slavery to spread into parts of the Louisiana Purchase in which it had been banned for many years.

Lincoln was afraid that the adaptability of slavery could bring the institution into all the Northern states over time. This worst-case scenario should not be dismissed from our own rather comfortable vantage point. The case can be made that Lincoln *stopped* such a worst-case future.

As early as 1847, the institution of slavery had proven its worth in the industrial workplace. When a group of white workers tried to go on strike at a factory in Richmond, Virginia, the owner fired them all and then ran his factory with slaves.

It was against this background that Lincoln charged Douglas and other leaders of the Democratic Party—including presidents Franklin Pierce and James Buchanan—of working with the slaveholding South to spread slavery to national dimensions. Lincoln made these charges in his famous "House Divided" speech in 1858.

Douglas fought back by asserting that Lincoln was a "negro-lover" who intended to undermine the status of whites. Listen to Douglas in action; consider this excerpt from the Lincoln and Douglas debates that shows the white supremacist tactics of Stephen A. Douglas in all of their nakedness. (The audience reactions were recorded on the spot by reporters from several newspapers using shorthand). "I ask you," he queried the Illinois electorate in 1858,

are you in favor of conferring upon the negro the rights and
privileges of citizenship? ("No. no.") Do you desire to strike
out of our State Constitution that clause which keeps slaves
and free negroes out of the State, and allow the free negroes
to flow in, ("never") and cover your prairies with black settlements? Do you desire to turn this beautiful State into a free
negro colony, ("no, no") in order that when Missouri abol-
ishes slavery she can send one hundred thousand emancipated slaves into Illinois, to become citizens and voters, on
an equality with yourselves? ("Never," "no.") If you desire
negro citizenship . . . then support Mr. Lincoln and the Black
Republican Party . . . For one, I am opposed to negro citizenship in any and every form. [Cheers.] I believe this government was made on the white basis. ("Good.") I believe it
was made by white men, for the benefit of white men and
their posterity forever.[7]

So much for Stephen Douglas and his open, unambiguous, and
popular expressions of bigotry. The state of Illinois was a white
supremacist bastion in the 1850s. Free blacks had been barred under
law from setting foot in the state since 1853, when this policy was
written into the new state constitution and intermarriage had been
made illegal. It was in this context—in response to the open racial
demagoguery of Douglas—that Lincoln made certain statements that
appeared to be the sort of thing his audience insisted on hearing with
regard to the subject of race, but often with slippery qualifications.

Consider one of the most frequently used examples of Lincoln's
putative "racism." It consists of a statement that he made (under
pressure from Douglas) in the course of the 1858 Lincoln-Douglas
debates. Here is the statement in full: "I have no purpose to introduce political and social equality between the white and black races.
There is a physical difference between the two, which in my judgment will probably forever forbid their living together upon the footing of perfect equality, and inasmuch as it becomes a necessity that

there must be a difference, I, as well as Judge Douglas, am in favor of the race to which I belong, having the superior position."[8]

A clever ploy, if he meant to be deceptive. For all he said on this particular occasion was this: he had *no plans* ("no purpose") to endorse (or, as he put it, to "introduce") civil rights legislation since the *likelihood* of placing the races on the "footing" of perfect equality was poor given the widespread hatred arising from their "physical difference." Meanwhile, Lincoln continued, if there *had* to be difference in the power positions of the black and white races—if there "*must* be a difference," as he put it—neither Lincoln nor any other man would *choose subjection.*

In all, it *sounded* like a racist manifesto, at least at first blush. But it was probably just a clever trick by a crafty attorney—a tissue of words that could not withstand critical analysis. Lincoln, when he wished, could be temporizer *par excellence.* He was a master of language that contained *alternate meanings,* and his enemies knew it. For good reason his rival Stephen Douglas complained that Mr. Lincoln had "a fertile genius in devising language to conceal his thoughts."[9]

Here's another example from the 1858 campaign. "Certainly," Lincoln explained in a speech to some skeptics, "the negro is not our equal in color—perhaps not in other respects; still, in the right to put into his mouth the bread that his own hands have earned, he is the equal of every other man, white or black. . . . All I ask for the negro is that if you do not like him, leave him alone."[10]

On the surface Lincoln's words could seem racist. But his language was slippery indeed. Consider sentence one, for example: "Certainly the negro is not our equal in color" and "perhaps not in other respects." What did he mean? Let us start with the very first word of this particular sentence—"certainly," a very clear term. But what was "certain," in Lincoln's opinion? That the negro is "not our equal in color." But Lincoln never bothered to define what he meant by the vexed term "equal," which was crucial to the meaning of his statement. Was he saying, in effect, that the darker pigmentation of blacks was less *worthy* than the skin tone of whites? Or was he saying that the skin tone blacks was merely *different* (not *equal* in the sense of *not the same*)? If so, then this particular difference was trivial. If we happen not to *like* the appearance of others, we can *certainly* leave them alone, as Lincoln pointed out clearly.

But we are still not finished with the passage. Recall Lincoln's further observation that "perhaps" other racial differences existed. A very interesting qualifier term—"perhaps"—which was no doubt easily missed if Lincoln's speech were enunciated quickly. But perhaps what he intended was to place between the lines of this speech a very pointed admission of *doubt*. Perhaps he meant to imply that *he did not really know* whether blacks were really different, with the obvious exception of their skin tone. So remember that Lincoln said *"perhaps."* And make *certain* to remember what Douglas had said: he had *no doubts at all* about the matter.

Under circumstances such as these—Illinois was perhaps the most racist state above the Mason-Dixon line—Lincoln's stance was almost innocuous. The mere fact, for example, that he disavowed plans to support civil rights *at the moment* left him free to endorse civil rights later on—as he did, when conditions had improved. His preliminary goal was to deliver the most fundamental of rights: the right to be free. Other rights could be addressed in due sequence.

Now listen to the fervor of Lincoln as he spoke at a torchlight rally in Chicago on July 10, 1858:

> Those arguments that are made, that the inferior race are to be treated with as much allowance as they are capable of enjoying; that as much is to be done for them as their condition will allow. What are these arguments? They are the arguments that kings have made for enslaving the people in all ages of the world. . . . They always bestrode the necks of the people, not that they wanted to do it, but because the people were better off for being ridden. . . . This argument . . . is the same old serpent that says you work and I eat, you toil and I

will enjoy the fruits of it. Turn in whatever way you will—
whether it come from the mouth of a King, an excuse for
enslaving the people of his country, or from the mouth of men
of one race as a reason for enslaving the men of another race,
it is all the same old serpent. . . . I should like to know if taking this old Declaration of Independence, which declares
that all men are equal upon principle, and making exceptions
to it, where will it stop? If one man says it does not mean a
negro, why not another say it does not mean some other man?
If that declaration is not the truth, let us get the Statute book,
in which we find it and tear it out! Who is so bold to do it!
[Voices—"me" and "no one," &c.] If it is not true let us tear it
out! [cries of "no, no,"].[11]

As his fame grew to national dimensions, Lincoln entered the
ranks of the contenders for the 1860 Republican presidential nomination. His capture of the White House unleashed the secessionist
movement in the South.

Lincoln quickly assembled a war coalition for the purpose of
defeating the Confederates while keeping his firm and non-negotiable
commitment to stop the spread of slavery. Lincoln's famous commitment to "preserving the Union" was *half*—and *only* half—of his policy when war began. The other half was slavery containment.

In the first two years of the war, Lincoln launched the second
phase of his antislavery program: the voluntary phaseout. His hope
was to start within the border states.

He met secretly with abolitionists at the White House. He told
them he intended to escalate his antislavery measures as political
contingencies permitted. He would pose as a leader who had pledged
to save the Union by any means necessary—repeat, any means necessary—and thus pave the way for liberating actions.

In his memoirs, the abolitionist Moncure Daniel Conway recalled
a meeting with Lincoln in January 1862. He asked Lincoln whether
"the masses of the American people would hail you as their deliverer

if, at the end of the war, the Union would be surviving and slavery still in it?" Yes, said Lincoln, "if they were to see that slavery was on the downhill." Conway pressed a little harder, and Lincoln responded with a stunning political confession. "I think the country grows in this direction daily, and I am not without hope that something of the desire of you and your friends may be accomplished. Perhaps it may be in the way suggested by a thirsty soul in Maine who found he could only get liquor from a druggist. As his robust appearance forbade the plea of sickness, he called for a soda, and whispered, 'Couldn't you put a drop o' the creeter into it unbeknownst to yourself?'"[12] Lincoln's cunning left hand would spike the soda with emancipation—"unbeknownst to himself"—as his right hand strove to save the Union.

Lincoln acted within a few months: he got Congress to authorize funds for the purpose of paying off the owners of slaves (not only in the rebel states but also in the loyal border slave states) who would set their human property free. No president had ever attempted to do such a thing before.

But Lincoln got no takers—none whatsoever, in spite of his pleading over several months.

When his plans for the phaseout of slavery were thwarted, he revised his strategy quickly: he took the radical step of using wartime measures to liberate the slaves in the rebel states *without compensation* by means of the Emancipation Proclamation. He pretended to the public that defense of the Union was his *sole* motivation for the policy. But this was nonsense: there were many other ways in which the Union could have been saved without attacking the slavery system. Lincoln's Democratic enemies, for instance, would have tried to end the war by just patching things up with the South.

Lincoln was tricky for political reasons: he feared that the white supremacist consensus in the North might sweep him out of office if he seemed to be a "Negro-lover." So he worked behind the scenes for black interests. In public, of course, he kept posing as a leader whose *only* motivation was the patriotic cause of the Union.

As the emancipation program went into effect, Lincoln struggled to lock in the progress he had made before he had to face the risks of reelection. His worst-case approach to the contingencies that faced him in the election year of 1864—military stalemate resulting in political defeat—was to change the constitutions of the occupied slave states and turn them into newly minted free states. This strategy was aimed at protecting his emancipation policy from later court challenges. And it was largely done in a manner that produced what political strategists today would call "deniability." "Give us a free-state reorganization . . . in the shortest possible time," Lincoln secretly told his occupation commander in Louisiana.[13] Meanwhile, he offered a lenient Reconstruction plan (his famous 10 percent plan) if the rebels would lay down their arms.

It bears noting, however, that this plan was in reality another blow against slavery. For Lincoln's plan required an oath of allegiance—not only to the Union *but also to the Emancipation Proclamation and all antislavery acts by Congress.* In other words, *the only people whom Lincoln would allow to cast votes* in the occupied Confederate states would be Southerners opposed to slavery. A mere 10 percent of the voting population would suffice for this purpose—which meant that a tiny minority of antislavery whites could topple a 90 percent pro-slavery majority in ex-Confederate states for the purpose of turning those states into free states. And this plan was supposedly *lenient!* Here was Lincoln the Machiavellian strategist at his most brilliant. The supposedly lenient 10 percent plan was in many ways precisely the reverse of what it seemed. It was a tough and audacious ploy by Lincoln to *force* emancipation on a state-by-state basis—and to force it *fast.*

Lincoln also argued openly and angrily with racists as he praised black valor on the battlefield in 1863. Peace, he told his racist detractors

> does not appear so distant as it did. I hope it will come soon, and come to stay; and so come as to be worth the keeping in

all future time. . . . And then, there will be some black men who can remember that, with silent tongue, and clenched teeth, and steady eye, and well-poised bayonet, they have helped mankind on to this great consummation; while, I fear, there will be some white ones, unable to forget that, with malignant heart, and deceitful speech, they have strove to hinder it.[14]

Few Americans today are aware of the ordeal that Lincoln faced in the summer of 1864 when it looked as if the Northern electorate would throw him out of office. The other side of this scenario, election of a Democratic president—in all probability a *racist pro-slavery* Democrat—could wipe away everything that Lincoln had achieved. The nineteenth-century Democratic Party was a haven for white supremacy. A Democratic president would probably attempt to save the Union on terms that would satisfy the South at the expense of the freedmen. The Emancipation Proclamation would of course be abrogated: perhaps the freedmen would be shipped back to bondage. Lincoln met secretly with the black abolitionist Frederick Douglass in the summer of 1864. Lincoln urged Douglass to incite a great exodus of runaway slaves who would cross Union lines in the hope that many millions of blacks could be freed in the dying months of Lincoln's term.[15]

As this worst-case strategy developed, however, Lincoln kept his hopes alive with some best-case political planning. In secret, he encouraged the occupation governor of Louisiana to consider the idea of phasing in voting rights for blacks.[16] And he silently backed away from black colonization even as a voluntary measure.

The battlefield victories of General William T. Sherman and Philip H. Sheridan in the autumn months of 1864—victories that resulted in a massive Republican triumph—led Lincoln to accelerate his antislavery strategy. He began to work openly with Radical Republicans and played the determining role in persuading the outgoing Congress to pass the new Thirteenth Amendment to the Constitution, which eliminated slavery forever and throughout the nation. He even toyed with the notion of *paying* all the slave states to ratify—to the tune of several hundred million dollars.[17] He let stand an extraordinary order by General William Tecumseh Sherman giving thousands of acres of seized plantation lands to former slaves. He signed the Radical Republicans' bill to create a new social welfare agency, the Freedmen's Bureau, to provide direct assistance to blacks in the occupied South.

In the final speech of his life, Lincoln advocated voting rights for blacks who had fought to save the Union. And he warned that his lenient Reconstruction plan might have to be retracted. He went so far as to say that "as bad promises are better broken than kept, I shall treat this as a bad promise, and break it, whenever I shall be convinced that keeping it is adverse to the public interest." He then continued: "In the present 'situation' as the phrase goes, it may be my duty to make some new announcement to the people of the South. I am considering, and shall not fail to act, when satisfied that action will be proper."[18] John Wilkes Booth was in the audience when Lincoln made that speech.

If the Booth plot had failed—if Lincoln had survived to complete his second term—the civil rights revolution might have happened a hundred years sooner. "The colored man," Lincoln intoned from the White House balcony on April 11, 1865, should be "inspired with vigilance, and energy, and daring."[19] This was the Lincoln whom Frederick Douglass would praise just a few months later as "emphatically the black mans [sic] President: the first to show any respect for their rights as men."[20]

If this portrait of Lincoln is surprising, the reason is simple: Lincoln masked his revolutionary impulse as much as he could in his presidential years. He was a Machiavellian idealist—a reformer with exceptional "street smarts."

His admirers called him "Father Abraham." His young secretary called him "the Tycoon." It is time to appreciate this leader for his brilliance and discard all the myths of "moderation." Lincoln was a brilliant moral strategist—perhaps the greatest one of all in modern times. In outmaneuvering his foes, he delivered the results that saved America.

Lincoln's Emancipation Proclamation
A Propaganda Tool for the Enemy?

Amanda Foreman

IT IS WELL KNOWN HOW MUCH CONTROVERSY SURROUNDED President Lincoln's Preliminary Emancipation Proclamation after the battle of Antietam. Who can forget the words of John Hughes, archbishop of New York, who warned: "We Catholics . . . have not the slightest idea of carrying on a war that costs so much blood and treasure just to gratify a clique of Abolitionists in the North."

But less well known or understood is the controversy that the proclamation attracted abroad. Both Union and Confederate supporters in Britain tried to use it as a propaganda tool, and in the beginning at least, it was the Confederates who benefited the most.

The reasons for this were laid down at the beginning of the war, when England was still pondering its response to the conflict. A poem in *Punch*, on March 30, 1861, neatly expressed Britain's cotton dilemma:

> Though with the North we sympathize, It must not be forgotten,
> That with the South we've stronger ties, Which are composed of
> cotton.

The revelation by the London *Times* journalist, William Howard Russell, that the South hoped to exploit these ties, along with his poignant descriptions of slave life, provoked outrage in England when his reports started to appear in April. But the North gained less support than Southerners feared once Britons learned that President Lincoln had promised not to interfere with slavery in his inaugural address.

The British attitude in general dismayed the U.S. ambassador Charles Francis Adams. "People do not quite understand Americans or their politics," he wrote to his son Charles Francis Jr. "They think this a hasty quarrel. They do not comprehend the connection which slavery has with it, because we do not at once preach emancipation. Hence they go to the other extreme and argue that it is not an element of the struggle."[1]

But Adams was himself guilty of mischaracterization. The English reaction was far more complicated than he allowed. Even the North's two biggest supporters in Parliament, the radical member of parliament (hereafter MP) Richard Cobden and his colleague John Bright, believed that Lincoln had made a mistake by not abolishing slavery at the outset. A leading abolitionist, Richard Webb, complained: "Neither Lincoln nor Seward has yet spoken an antislavery syllable since they took office."[2]

This was true: Seward had specifically instructed all U.S. ambassadors and consuls to avoid mentioning the word in connection with the Union. The deliberate omission was a grievous miscalculation. Seward had sacrificed the North's trump card in Britain, hoping it would appease the South. Instead, he had provided ammunition to his critics who accused the North of hypocrisy. *The Economist* declared: "The great majority of the people in the Northern States detest the coloured population even more than do the Southern whites."[3]

Yet for all the finger-pointing and public criticism of the North, the Southern envoys in Britain, William Lowndes Yancey and Ambrose

Dudley Mann, failed to make the slightest change to Britain's policy. "We are satisfied that the Government is sincere in its desire to be strictly neutral in the contest," Yancey told the Confederate government, "and will not countenance any violation of its neutrality."[4] Writing to a close friend in the South, Yancey admitted that the mission was not turning out the way he had envisioned: "In the first place, important as cotton is, it is not King in Europe." Furthermore, he added, "The anti-Slavery sentiment is universal. *Uncle Tom's Cabin* has been read and believed."[5]

However, not long afterward the British learned that Lincoln had rejected General John Fremont's emancipation proclamation in Missouri. Regardless of the problems at home, abroad, Lincoln's rebuke played into the Confederates' hands; without the slavery issue the North was simply a large country fighting a rebellion in its nether regions. "Look at the Southerners here," Henry Adams, the younger son of Charles Francis Adams, wrote indignantly on October 25, 1861. "Every man is inspired by the idea of independence and liberty while we are in a false position."[6]

A speech by the Liberal chancellor of the exchequer, William Gladstone, to an audience in Manchester, England, in April 1862 revealed the extent to which ambiguity over the slavery question benefited the South and damaged the North. There was, "no doubt," he declared, "if we could say that this was a contest of slavery and freedom, there is not a man within the length and breadth of this room, there is, perhaps, hardly a man in all England, who would for a moment hesitate upon the side he should take."[7] Gladstone felt vindicated after he received a letter from a Liberian diplomat named Edward Wilmot Blyden, who declared that he was "very glad of the position which England maintains with reference to the war. . . . Both sections of the US are negro-hating and negro-crushing."[8]

The South's chief propagandist in England, a journalist from Mobile, Alabama, named Henry Hotze, used every opportunity to blast the message that the war was about states' rights, not about slavery. Hotze was able to convince Britons that the new Anglo-American

Slave Trade treaty, which allowed the British Navy to search suspected American slave ships, and a bill abolishing slavery in Washington itself, were just window dressing. As proof he pointed to the fact that Lincoln had failed to win support from the border states for a gradual emancipation bill.

Then came the reports of the terrific slaughter at Antietam, which horrified the British. But just as shocking to them was Lincoln's Preliminary Emancipation Proclamation. As Seward had feared from the outset, the proclamation was widely denounced as a cynical and desperate ploy. Charles Francis Adams understood its symbolic importance, but even pro-Northern supporters could not understand why Lincoln had allowed the border states to keep their slaves unless the emancipation order was directed against the South rather than slavery itself. "Our people are very imperfectly acquainted with the powers of your Federal Government," explained the antislavery crusader George Thompson to his American counterpart, William Lloyd Garrison. "They know little or nothing of your constitution—its compromises, guarantees, limitations, obligations, etc. They are consequently unable to appreciate the difficulties of your president."[9]

The pro-Northern *Spectator* magazine declared itself to be disappointed with the proclamation: "The principle is not that a human being cannot justly own another," it insisted, "but that he cannot own him unless he is loyal to the United States." For the radical MP Richard Cobden, the moral contradiction proved that "the leaders in the Federal government are not equal to the occasion."[10]

Henry Hotze successfully planted propaganda stories and articles in the press that portrayed the proclamation as a ploy to encourage race riots, or at the very least force Southern soldiers to return to their homes to protect their families. *Punch* depicted Lincoln as a desperate gambler who was using the proclamation as his last card. The *Times* even accused Lincoln of inciting the slaves in the South to kill their owners, imagining in graphic terms how the president "will appeal to the black blood of the African; he will whisper of the pleasures of spoil and of the gratification of yet fiercer instincts; and when blood begins to flow and shrieks come piercing through the darkness, Mr. Lincoln will wait till the rising flames tell that all is consummated, and he will rub his hands and think that revenge is sweet."[11]

The effect of the proclamation on the British Cabinet—which was already debating whether it had a moral duty to stop the bloodshed—was almost catastrophic. Two of its leading members, Foreign Secretary Lord Russell and William Gladstone, became convinced that a humanitarian crisis was at hand. For Gladstone, the combination of his worries about the suffering of the Lancashire cotton workers and his disgust with the apparent hypocrisy of the Preliminary Emancipation Proclamation pushed him over the edge. On October 7, the day after the proclamation appeared in the *Times*, he made a speech in Newcastle in which he proclaimed: "We may have our own opinions about slavery; we may be for or against the South, but there is no doubt that Jefferson Davis and other leaders of the South have made an army; they are making, it appears, a navy; and they have made what is more difficult than either; they have made a nation." The speech was telegraphed all over Europe almost before Gladstone had sat down. The Confederate envoy Dudley Mann in Brussels wrote to Richmond that same night: "This clearly foreshadows our early recognition."[12]

Two years after the conclusion of the war, in 1867, Gladstone admitted his mistake: "I had imbibed, conscientiously if erroneously, an opinion that 20 or 24 millions of the North would be happier, and would be stronger . . . without the South than with it, and also that the negroes would be much nearer to emancipation under a Southern Government than under the old system of the Union," he wrote.[13]

At the time, however, Gladstone had not been alone in his confusion about the slavery question or in assuming that Southern nationhood was around the corner. A few weeks after his speech in Newcastle, the Confederate commissioner in England, James Murray Mason, attended a banquet given by the lord mayor of the City of London. "When my name was announced by the Mayor, it was received with a storm of applause," Mason wrote in his diary. He was invited to address the hall and elicited loud cheers each time he referred to the commercial ties between the City and the South, confirming his belief that he had acquitted himself rather well. A Southern supporter had been among the guests and was convinced that he had witnessed a momentous event.

"I was at the Mansion House last night," he wrote afterward, "and heard the Lord Mayor virtually recognize the South in the quietest and most inoffensive way that could be imagined. . . . As I came out I rubbed shoulders with Captain Tinker, Grinnell's partner and I said, jocularly, 'Well, you see the Lord Mayor has been and gone and done it.' He laughingly replied, 'Oh yes, it's all over now. Depend on it, this expression of opinion from the heart of England's middle classes must tell. It will reverberate thro' the land and find an echo.'"[14]

Well, Captain Tinker, and Gladstone, were wrong. There was no echo either in the Cabinet or "thro'" the land. Antietam and the Preliminary Emancipation Proclamation notwithstanding, the Cabinet agreed that England should remain neutral, and once the proclamation had become law without spawning any massacres of Southern whites, British public opinion began to alter in its favor.

An increase in the number of potential army volunteers calling at the American embassy reflected the changing perception of the war. "Applications for service in our army strangely fluctuate," wrote the assistant secretary, Benjamin Moran, on January 14, 1863. "For some time past they have been but few. Since the announcement of the President's determination to adhere to his emancipation policy they have again become numerous and today we have had a French and British officer seeking employment."[15] Another surprise was waiting for Moran when he went to church. The vicar had never mentioned the war before, but on this Sunday he announced during prayers, "our hearts in this great contest are with the North," which was answered with a deep "Amen" from the congregation.[16]

The U.S. consul in London, Freeman Morse, also noticed the change since Lincoln's proclamation. "Emancipation Meetings continue to be held in London every week, sometimes four or five a week at some of which two and three thousand people have been present and in a majority of cases unanimously with the North. Other portions of the country are following the example of this city and holding meetings with about the same result,"[17] he reported to Seward. The largest emancipation meeting of all took place at Exeter Hall on January 29, 1863. Henry Adams managed to secure a seat at the meeting and was thoroughly uplifted by the experience. The politicians, Henry told his brother afterward, were going to have to listen to their constituents or risk being "thrown over."

Pro-Southern supporters such as the Liverpool businessman James Spence now began to find it much harder to convince audiences that the South would also abolish slavery as soon as it won independence. Lincoln scored a further propaganda coup by sending a personal letter to the "Workingmen of Manchester" thanking the cotton workers for their patience and sacrifice. "Whatever misfortune may befall your country or my own," he declared, "the peace and friendship which now exist between the two nations will be . . . perpetual."[18] Jefferson Davis's silence on the matter of slavery spoke volumes.

Even though some veteran abolition campaigners like Bishop Samuel Wilberforce and Lord Brougham remained unconvinced (much to Henry Hotze's glee), the proclamation had finally succeeded in linking the cause of emancipation with that of a united America. The hitherto pacifist British and Foreign Anti-Slavery Society changed its stance and became actively involved in the counterpropaganda war, secretly supplying the U.S. embassy with information about Confederate activities in the financial markets. There was also a rise in pamphlets and books putting forward the case for the North. The economist John Elliot Cairnes published his attack on the South, *The Slave Power*, right after the Emancipation Proclamation. Cairnes was followed by the actress Fanny Kemble, who published her diary, *Journal of a Residence on a Georgian Plantation in 1838–1839*, written during her exile on her former husband's slave plantation in Georgia, and William Howard Russell, whose account of his stay in America, *My Diary*

North and South, verified many of her observations. The *Spectator* journalist Edward Dicey followed with a travelogue—*Six Months in the Federal States*—which tried to correct many of the distortions and caricatures about Northern culture that pro-Southern journalists had propagated.

The growing sense that the North was committed to abolition had just as big an effect on Southern supporters in England as it did on Northern supporters. The Confederates were horrified by the efforts of James Spence to propose an Emancipation Proclamation to Jefferson Davis. "I almost dread the direction his friendship and devotion seem about to take," Henry Hotze confessed to Confederate Secretary of State Judah P. Benjamin.[19] Spence had been so inspired by the Preliminary Emancipation Proclamation that he was convinced the South should issue one of her own. Hotze was outraged by the idea but unsure how to divert him without exposing the truth. In the end, Benjamin was forced to fire Spence as the South's official financial agent in England.

Determined to regain the moral high ground on the slavery question, Hotze managed to pull off the extraordinary feat of persuading a religious publishing house to include in every publication, religious and nonreligious, a Southern pamphlet entitled *Address to the Christians Throughout the World*. Signed by the ninety-six clergymen of Richmond, the *Address* urged fellow Christians to protest against Lincoln's Preliminary Emancipation Proclamation. Hotze estimated that it would be read by two million people.

Yet even that signal success failed to stem the tide created by the proclamation. Hotze's troubles with James Spence and others mirrored those of Confederate Commissioner James Mason with his Tory allies. They too tried to extract a pledge from him that the South would renounce slavery once independence was achieved. Camouflaging the South's total dependence on slavery was the only way that Mason was able to persuade the veteran abolition campaigner Lord Shaftesbury to give them his support. Even then, the relationship almost foundered when Shaftesbury asked, in all innocence, "if the

[Confederate] President could not in some way present the prospect of gradual emancipation. Such a declaration coming from him unsolicited would have the happiest effect in Europe." The Confederate commissioner insisted that abolition was an issue for the individual states to decide, not Richmond, which provided an answer but not the answer to Lincoln's proclamation.

However, fortunately for Henry Hotze, the Confederate finessing of the slavery question was enough to convince James Spence—so much so that he continued to propagandize on their behalf despite being relieved of his official position for being antislavery. But the bulk of the population proved to be less gullible, and increasingly the Confederates had to turn to violence to stop the emancipation message.

During the summer of 1863, when Parliament debated the question of Southern recognition for the final time, the Confederate lobby went all out in its propaganda efforts. Londoners found Waterloo Station placarded with posters depicting the British Union Jack crossed with the Confederate flag. Hackney cab drivers were encouraged to display the same emblems in miniature. Henry Hotze was working at a feverish pace, distributing posters, placards, and circulars up and down the country. The *Morning Herald* and the *Standard* agreed to print editorials demanding recognition every other day until the actual debate at the end of June.

But James Spence had a much harder time connecting with the general public. For this final push in Parliament, he set up two separate organizations. One was a respectable club, called the Manchester Southern Club, whose purpose was to distribute Confederate material in the north of England. The other was his own private army of agitators. The group successfully broke up an abolitionist meeting at the Manchester Free Trade Hall. "These parties are not the rich spinners but young men of energy with a taste for agitation but little money," Spence wrote to Mason. "It appears to my judgment that it would be wise not to stint money in aiding this effort to expose cant and diffuse the truth. Manchester is naturally the centre of such a move and you will see there are here the germs of important work—but they need to be tended and fostered. I have supplied a good deal of money individually but I see room for the use of 30 or 40 pounds a month or more."[20]

As Spence soon discovered, breaking up a few abolition meetings was not going to affect the debates in Parliament or change the growing perception that the South was not prepared to tackle the slavery question.

There were of course, diehards who insisted on the reverse: the novelist Mrs. Gaskell, for example, told Charles Elliot Norton in July 1864:

> I fully believe, because I know you; but what *facts* am I to give in answer to such speech as this: "It is a war forced by the Government on the people, hence the conscription orders for enlistment are not readily or willingly responded to. 2ndly, It is a war for territory. The pretext of slavery is only a pretext with a large majority. And then they refer to the Emancipation proclamation only setting the slaves of *rebels* free . . . I have one person in particular in my mind, who holds these opinions and uses these arguments—such a good noble conscientious man, though he is so wrong-headed,—he joined the Southern Association as soon as the Emancipation proclamation was published—for the reason I have given above—it's only including the slaves of rebels."

But even these holdouts were not necessarily advocating a change in the government's policy of neutrality. The celebrated Southern oceanographer Commodore Matthew Fontaine Maury was the first among the Confederates in England to realize that the Preliminary Emancipation Proclamation had struck at the heart of the Southern support. "Many of our friends here have mistaken British admiration of Southern 'pluck,' and newspaper spite at Yankee insolence as Southern sympathy. No such thing," he wrote to a friend. "There is no love for the South here. In its American policy the British Government fairly represents the people . . . there is no hope for recognition here, therefore I say withdraw Mason."[21]

The truth of Maury's statement was finally made plain to James Mason when he met with Lord Palmerston on March 14, 1865, in a last-ditch effort to secure British recognition of the South. Mason was shocked when he learned that Jefferson Davis was prepared to abolish slavery in return for recognition, and he did not want to carry out the order to relay the message to Palmerston. By Mason's own account, he prevaricated for almost twenty minutes before finally asking whether "there was some latent, undisclosed obstacle on the part of Great Britain to recognition."[22] Palmerston had already divined the real purpose of the conversation and replied without hesitating that slavery had never been the obstacle. Mason was elated until he recounted the conversation to a friend, Lord Donoughmore, who told him that Palmerston had said this precisely to forestall a last-minute appeal from the South: slavery had always been the chief impediment to recognition. The South had squandered her only chance of achieving it by not emancipating the slaves in 1863, when Lincoln had issued his final Emancipation Proclamation on January 1 and General Robert E. Lee was the undisputed victor on the battlefield. For a brief moment, Mason feared that he had been responsible for ruining the South's last hope of survival, and he wanted to see Palmerston again so he could be much clearer this time, but Donoughmore assured him that the opportunity had gone.

The history of Lincoln's Emancipation Proclamation in England is therefore a complex tale of bad first impressions followed by a gradual movement away from Southern support as the public realized the asymmetry between the two sides. The South almost succeeded in turning the North's moral victory into defeat but ultimately was unable to come up with an answer that satisfied English abolition sentiment. Although the Confederate propagandists in Britain continued to portray the South as a plucky underdog fighting for independence, without a comparable emancipation proclamation the slavery weapon was effectively out of their reach.

The Gettysburg Campaign and the New York City Draft Riots
Conspiracy or Coincidence?

Barnet Schecter

THE VOLCANIC FORCE AND FURY OF THE RIOTS THAT ERUPTED in New York City on July 13–17, 1863, can be explained only in part by the first federal conscription law in U.S. history, signed by President Abraham Lincoln on March 5—a law that exempted any man who could pay $300 or present a substitute. Equally threatening in the minds of white workingmen was the Emancipation Proclamation of January 1, which Lincoln's opponents warned would send a flood of freed slaves to compete for low-wage jobs in Northern cities. While poor men died in battle and their families starved, the rich would stay home, getting richer on war contracts. This linkage of class discrimination and labor competition by the Democratic press helped spark what still ranks as the deadliest riot—the largest civil insurrection—in American history. Aside from the Civil War itself, the riots in New York in the summer of 1863 are the largest rebellion in our national history.[1]

By the time the riots ended, the official death toll stood at 105 people, but the actual total was almost certainly larger, probably closer to five hundred, based on the evidence of contemporary accounts. And the impact of the riots fell most heavily on the city's free African Americans, a vulnerable but vibrant community of 12,500 people in a city of eight hundred thousand. About 40 percent of that 12,500—some five thousand African American men, women, and children—were burned out of their homes, pursued through the streets, and driven out of the city. Homeless refugees, they fled on foot or by ferry to New Jersey, Long Island, and New England. Those who did not escape were murdered, some by hanging. According to one African American newspaper, 175 blacks were killed.[2]

The draft riots of 1863 are a painful, shameful episode in the city's and the nation's history, but they are worth revisiting, in particular because these five days of arson, looting, and lynching that gripped the city present a sort of microcosm of the larger Civil War, a playing out some of the great issues that had polarized the country—the defining questions of the Civil War and the Reconstruction era—about the scope of federal power over states and individuals and about freedom and ultimate equality under the law for African Americans.

In proposing the Confederate incursion through Maryland into Pennsylvania that unfolded in late June 1863, General Robert E. Lee had displayed his attentiveness to politics as well as his military aggressiveness. He told President Jefferson Davis that an invasion of the North would strengthen the "rising peace party" in the North, those antiwar Democrats who wanted a negotiated settlement of the conflict. The advancing Army of Northern Virginia and the political pressure of the so-called Copperheads would create a double wedge, fracturing Northern public opinion even further, he hoped, and force Lincoln and the Republican Congress to sue for peace. Republican cartoonists depicted the Peace Democrats as snakes in the grass, traitors within the borders of the Union's loyal states. And many Northerners suspected that these Copperheads, acting in concert with Confederate leaders in Richmond, would be willing to go a step further, not merely to influence public opinion and take advantage of it but to foment riots in the streets of the Union's major port cities, creating a "fire in the rear" on the Union homefront as part of a military offensive.[3]

The timing of the riots in New York, which erupted just ten days after the Battle of Gettysburg on July 1–3, fueled the conspiracy theory—the suspicion that the riots were part of a concerted military strategy. The rioters cut telegraph lines and pried up train tracks leading in and out of the city, further suggesting that this was not simply a spontaneous popular rebellion but an attempt to isolate New York from outside help and destroy the financial, commercial, and industrial hub of the Union.[4]

Another factor worried Northerners as well. In the Midwest, the Confederate cavalry commander John Hunt Morgan led 2,500 troopers in a raid out of Kentucky and across the Ohio River to free Confederate prisoners in Indiana and Ohio. Morgan also hoped to capitalize on discontent and stir up rebellion in the lower Midwest among farmers and businessmen whose livelihoods had been destroyed by the Union blockade of the Mississippi River. If the timing was right, Morgan even hoped to move eastward through Ohio into Pennsylvania to join forces with Lee.[5]

In the eyes of Northern newspaper editors at the time, the confluence of events—Morgan's raid, the Gettysburg campaign, and the riots in New York City—seemed too powerful to be coincidence. Horace Greeley, the editor of the *New York Daily Tribune*, certainly saw a connection. He reported that the draft riots were originally supposed to occur at the same time as the Battle of Gettysburg, and that on the night of July 3, 1863, leaflets denouncing the Lincoln administration were found all over the streets of New York as a signal for the insurrection that was to take place on July 4, emphasizing the South's righteous struggle for independence from an overgrown, tyrannical federal government. The Union victory at Gettysburg had derailed the planned riots, Greeley explained, though the riots took place, after a delay of about ten days, apparently in the vengeful hope that they would offset the Confederates' military loss.[6]

If this had been the original plan, some influential Northerners shuddered to think of Picket's charge breaking through the Union line at Gettysburg, exposing Harrisburg and Philadelphia to attack; of Lee's army marching on to New York, where Confederate iron-clads, entering the Upper Bay would have joined in the battle, while the streets erupted in flames ignited by rioters. Indeed, the idea that the "New York mob" or the "Northern mobs" would constitute a strategic asset for the South in the event of secession was nothing new. Henry Raymond, Greeley's protégé who had left the *Tribune* to found the *New York Times*, pointed out that this vision had been in the air, and in Southern newspaper editorials, since the threat of war loomed in the late 1850s. During the actual riots, Raymond's *Times* asserted that there were "agents direct from Richmond" in the streets of New York orchestrating the violence but they concealed themselves "with devilish subtlety."[7]

South Carolina's Edmund Ruffin had even written a novel, *Anticipations of the Future*, published in 1860, in which the loss of trade with the South drove New York's angry, unemployed workers to loot the stores and bars and in a drunken rage put the entire city to the torch. Ruffin seemed clairvoyant by the middle of July 1863. After news of the New York riots reached him on July 18, Ruffin wrote triumphantly in his diary that they were more important than any military event, and he hoped that riots of the same magnitude would spread to other Northern cities, leading to the South's ultimate victory.[8]

The New York riots did indeed create a chain reaction of violence, not immediately as Ruffin envisioned but rather in the long term, in the decades after the war. At the time, the riots marked not a beginning but rather the culmination of a process, of forces and tensions that had been building both in the six months since the Emancipation Proclamation and in the decades leading up to the Civil War. The conspiracy theory, for which there is virtually no documentary evidence, is not necessary to explain the explosive power of the New York riots; the battle lines of race, class, religion, and politics had grown steadily since the late 1820s. Lincoln's wartime measures merely lit the fuse on a social powder keg.

Peace Democrats denounced the Emancipation Proclamation from the moment it was issued on January 1 and linked it to the conscription law in the minds of white workers throughout the Union: in the marble quarries of Vermont, in the coal fields in Pennsylvania, and in the cities and towns of the Midwest. During the enrollment for the draft in the spring of 1863, when the newly created Provost Marshal General's Bureau sent its agents from house to house taking the names of eligible men, the agents encountered violent resistance across the North. Draft officials had been killed in Indiana and then in Pennsylvania. In the coalfields, religious tensions were already acute since most of the workers were Irish Catholics while the owners and foremen were Irish Protestants; when the management turned over their names to the assistant provost marshal, the miners retaliated. New York City was unique in the density of its immigrant population, a tinderbox of resentment, with half a million people crowded into Lower Manhattan's dismal slums. The fear of labor competition, combined with the evident unfairness of the draft law, poisoned the mood in the city in the months leading to the draft lottery, which began on July 11.[9]

The government blundered in New York by starting the lottery on a Saturday. The drawing of names from rotating wooden drums by blindfolded clerks proceeded peacefully, and onlookers even joked "Ah, poor Jones," as men were called up to join the Union ranks. But on Sunday workingmen had their one day off and could review the lists of some 1,200 names that had been drawn. Their anger came into sharp focus, and many spent the day stockpiling weapons: bricks, cobblestones, and guns, which would be used the following day and for almost a solid week of mayhem and mob rule.[10]

In the predawn hours of Monday, July 13, thousands of protesters streamed out of the poorest neighborhoods in Lower Manhattan and swept up the west side to gather on a vacant lot near the southeastern corner of Central Park, which was still under construction. Some carried signs saying "No Draft." The crowd soon numbered in the tens of thousands as it headed down to the Ninth District draft office at Forty-Sixth Street and Third Avenue. Here, what had begun as a labor strike and street protest quickly degenerated into arson, as the draft office was stormed by the crowd and burned to the ground, along with the entire block. The mob then moved southward, killing soldiers and overwhelming platoons of policemen in its path, while targeting armories on Second Avenue to capture more weapons.[11]

As terrifying as the morning had been, the full horror of the riots began to unfold in the afternoon as the violence against government targets shifted to the city's African American community and became a racial pogrom.[12] The mob targeted individual abolitionists, including Henry Highland Garnet, a prominent clergyman, and James McCune Smith, the first accredited black physician in America. McCune Smith was the attending physician at the Colored Orphan Asylum, on Fifth Avenue between Forty-Third and Forty-Fourth Streets, which was burned to the ground. The leaders of the black community defied the racist stereotype of blacks as inferior and the prediction that emancipated slaves would inevitably become an impoverished, dependent population. Highly educated, politically active black men and women including Garnet and McCune Smith, who attended the African Free Schools founded by the New York Manumission Society in the late eighteenth century, had been waging a struggle for civil rights since the 1830s and 1840s and had high hopes on January 1, 1863, for a jubilee year—a year that was supposed to bring freedom. Instead, the riots dealt them a severe setback.[13]

Fortunately, the 233 children in the orphanage all escaped from the building with the help of their teachers and were brought to safety in the local police station. They were also helped by a group of young Irish streetcar drivers led by Paddy McCaffrey, as the *Times* reported the following day. Though some critics blamed the draft riots largely on the Irish instead of on the Democratic orators and newspapers, the young streetcar drivers and other Irish New Yorkers who aided and sheltered blacks reveal a more complex picture.[14]

The racial pogrom also included the lynching of at least eighteen black men; others were chased through the streets and off the docks into the rivers. The bodies, hanging from lampposts and trees, were shot, burned, and otherwise mutilated, as the rioters vented their fury. Today, such scenes are more commonly associated with the attacks by the Ku Klux Klan in the South after the Civil War, but they unfolded on the streets of New York City in July 1863.[15]

There were no black ghettoes in Lower Manhattan, which ironically might have helped African Americans band together and resist the mobs. Instead there were individual buildings or streets where blacks lived, and they fell prey to the marauding rioters. The Lyons family, for example, had achieved a kind of middle-class affluence, running a rooming house for black seamen, which was also a station on the Underground Railroad. They were an active part of the black community that was starting, in its own tentative ways, to thrive in this period before the riots. When the riots began, Albro and Mary Lyons armed themselves and attempted to defend their home, but it was ultimately attacked and heavily damaged. The black ghettoes would form later, partly as a result of the dispersion of blacks during the riots, this active attempt to drive them to the fringes of white society.[16]

During the week of rioting, a battle also raged in the press. Greeley, who had hectored Lincoln to hasten emancipation, locked horns with Manton Marble of the New York *World*, who, even as the city was burning, apologized for the rioters, saying that the violence was the inevitable result of the administration's attempts to elevate blacks to an unnatural position in white society. Marble poured fuel on the flames and practically invited the rioters to attack the *Tribune* offices.[17]

Nonetheless, Marble touched a nerve with his assertion of white fears of emancipation. The effort to free blacks and bring them into full citizenship predated the Lincoln administration; it had stirred up racial hatred for decades, ever since the abolition movement took root and spread out from New England with the Second Great Awakening of the 1830s. Much of that hatred had been expressed over the years through the Democratic press, McCune Smith noted, and this steady drumbeat of fear-mongering helped feed the New York riots. Garnet, too, blamed Democratic demagogues, saying that the Irish were not naturally racist; they were fellow sufferers of oppression who had been pulled into a racial caste system in America, which rewarded them for their whiteness by giving them the vote. They had been transformed by American politicians.[18]

The Democratic party at the time was essentially a white supremacist organization that still regarded the values of Andrew Jackson, a slaveholder, as its first principles. Fernando Wood, a three-term Democratic mayor of New York in the 1850s had also been a congressman and a disciple of South Carolina's Senator John Calhoun. Throughout his career Wood had been a leading voice in the clamor against emancipation, using the New York *Daily News*, which he owned with his brother Ben, to advance their racist message. Wood had gotten his start running a grocery-groggery on the waterfront, and his constituents were the Irish-, German-, and American-born workers on the docks and in the factories. He told them that in order to preserve their jobs, New York must do everything possible to preserve its economic ties to the Cotton Kingdom. For decades, New York had supplied the machinery for Southern agriculture, loaned hundreds of millions of dollars to planters, and insured their cotton while transshipping it to textile mills in Europe. As late as 1860, the most valuable commodity passing through the port of New York, and in the largest volume, was cotton.[19]

As New York came into its own as one of the world's busiest ports, starting in the late 1820s, it also developed some of the worst slums on earth. In the infamous Five Points, families lived in basement rooms below sea level, the walls covered with moss and mold. Mothers holding babies paid their last pennies to sleep on the floors of lodging cellars amid strangers. Nonetheless, these conditions were generally an improvement over Ireland, where the Great Famine of 1845–1852 had left more than a million dead and spurred more than a million to emigrate, many on so-called coffin ships where they died of disease or starvation. The United States had provided a haven from economic disaster and from political and religious persecution, so the Irish were grateful to the young republic. They volunteered readily when the war broke out, in units like the famous 69th Regiment of New York Volunteers, in Corcoran's Legion, and in Meagher's Irish Brigade. An estimated three hundred thousand Irish Americans served in the Union ranks. Men like Colonel Robert Nugent of the 69th were ardent Unionists who supported Lincoln and his policies unwaveringly throughout the war.[20]

However, the first two years of the war were filled with heavy casualties and horrific Union defeats. The fervor of the war's opening weeks quickly faded, and authorities resorted to cash bounties to fill the ranks. By the summer of 1862, the Confederacy had turned to conscription and the Lincoln administration instituted a militia draft (a prelude to the more sweeping federal draft of the following year), extending the time that state troops could be held in federal service from ninety days to nine months. In September Lincoln issued the Preliminary Emancipation Proclamation, to take effect January 1, 1863, in any states that remained in rebellion. Lincoln justified the proclamation on the grounds of military necessity: He was within the scope of his constitutional authority as president to take this action, which would clearly help win the war. It would liberate half of the South's workforce, creating a fire in the rear and draining their manpower.[21]

Lincoln's opponents in the North and many of his conservative supporters saw the Emancipation Proclamation as an outrageous extension of his power and a betrayal of the war's original purpose. Indeed, it was a revolutionary act that put the war on an entirely new footing. The struggle was no longer a conservative effort to preserve the Union but a radical crusade to destroy slavery, a fight to the bitter end against the Confederate armies that would require the destruction of much of the South. Many conservatives viewed this as a usurpation of his legitimate authority and a betrayal of the original agenda. Archbishop John Hughes, for example, the spiritual leader of New York's Irish Catholics, had been a strong supporter of Lincoln, serving as his envoy to France and to the Vatican earlier in the war. Reflecting the views of many of his flock, however, Hughes declared that while the Irish would fight to the death for the Union, they would not do so for abolition. The Democratic governor of New York, Horatio Seymour, denounced the Emancipation Proclamation as one more instance of Lincoln's abuse of power. The president had already suspended habeas corpus, censored the press, and locked up federal prisoners without due process in New York's Fort Lafayette off the Brooklyn shore. Lincoln should not be surprised, Seymour warned darkly, if the people took matters into their own hands and rebelled against his measures. Between emancipation and the draft, Marble declared, the United States was succumbing to military "despotism."[22]

Seymour encountered a storm of Republican criticism for arriving in Manhattan belatedly, on Tuesday July 14, to contend with the riots, and for reportedly addressing the crowd in front of City Hall as "My friends." Whether he used those words or not, he certainly took a conciliatory approach in dealing with the rioters, promising to pursue fairness in the draft law through the courts while urging them to disperse.[23]

In the end, however, the week of rioting was brought to a close by brute force, as Henry Raymond had urged: "Give them grape, and plenty of it." Entire platoons of federal troops fired into the crowds and also used artillery loaded with grapeshot and larger antipersonnel canister shot to clear the streets. The police, wielding locust-wood clubs, cracked the heads of rioters as they tried to storm the *Tribune* building and other targets. It had been an exhausting week for the police and the 550 federal troops deployed from the harbor forts. The emergency at Gettysburg had drawn some 16,000 New York militiamen to Pennsylvania (bolstering the theory that the battle and the riots were linked by a Confederate conspiracy), and the one thousand state troops in the city, poorly led, played only a small role in containing the riots. Not until Lee had retreated back across the Potomac River on July 14 did Secretary of War Edwin Stanton release five regiments from the battlefront to New York to flush out the last of the rioters, who still held parts of the city, and these troops did not arrive until the early morning of July 16.[24]

With order restored, Lincoln faced the question of how to resume the draft and assert federal authority. Staunch Unionists like George Templeton Strong and Frederick Law Olmsted telegraphed the White House, urging Lincoln to impose martial law in the city, launch a federal investigation, and break the power of Tammany Hall, the Democratic organization, if necessary by executing the ringleaders of the riots. Instead, County Supervisor William "Boss" Tweed forged a compromise that would assuage the angry public while providing Lincoln with troops: The city would issue $2 million of bonds and use the money to create a committee that would pay the $300 exemption fee for any man who could demonstrate hardship; the money would also be used to hire substitutes and fill the Union ranks. This solution was copied by other cities and towns, and the draft resumed peacefully throughout the North. Ultimately, the overall effect of the draft was to encourage enlistment. Of all Union troops raised after the passage of the conscription law—about 1.2 million men—only some 46,000 (fewer than 4 percent) were draftees.[25]

Nonetheless, the draft, the riots, and the compromise in their aftermath had some sinister effects that reached well into the twentieth century. Ultimately the riots did engender a chain reaction of violence. Perhaps the best illustration of this point is a cartoon by Thomas Nast entitled "This Is a White Man's Government." Dating from 1868, Nast's condemnation of the Democratic Party platform shows a Five Points Irishman, Nathan Bedford Forrest, and August Belmont joining forces to trample on a black Union veteran. In the background, on the left, rioters burn the Colored Orphan Asylum, while on the right the Klan burns a Freedmen's school in the South. Nast's anti-immigrant bigotry is on display, but he makes a cogent point: The draft riots were the beginning of a long campaign of violence aimed at depriving blacks of equality even though they had been freed. The cartoon suggests that Reconstruction—the radical Republican program of freedom and equality for African Americans—began with the Emancipation Proclamation and that the riots were the first battle of the Reconstruction era. The riots were a cry of rage against the tidal wave of social change that Lincoln had unleashed.

Lincoln accepted Tweed's compromise and turned his attention away from the Democratic threat in New York to prosecute the wider war, but he had opened the floodgates for the struggle of the next hundred years: to realize and enforce the full promise of emancipation: not only freedom but equality under the law.[26]

Lincoln and New York
A Fraught Relationship
Harold Holzer

THROUGHOUT HIS PRESIDENCY, ABRAHAM LINCOLN HAD A complex and curiously conflicted relationship with the nation's largest city and its largest state. Lincoln, of course, was an essentially western man—from Illinois by way of Kentucky and Indiana—but that accounts for only part of the complexity of his relationship with New York State. That relationship began well enough with the triumph of his famous Cooper Union address in February 1860, which, along with the Mathew Brady photograph taken of him at the same time, did much to make him president.[1]

Lincoln knew that New York was crucial to his election, and he could only hope that the majority he was likely to win in upstate New York would overcome the drubbing he would almost certainly receive in the city. Like the nation itself, prewar New York State was divided along a fairly rigid north-south border. Its own Mason-Dixon line stretched along what is now Route 287—the Cross Westchester Expressway—on the latitude of Tarrytown. Below that line the population was overwhelmingly Democratic, north of it, predominately Republican. In the end, the "Little Giant" Stephen Douglas beat Lincoln by 24,000 votes in Manhattan, five thousand in Brooklyn, and 2,500 in Westchester, but overwhelming upstate support allowed Lincoln to win a statewide fifty-thousand-vote majority.

Lincoln next visited New York during his lengthy and circuitous train ride from Springfield to Washington to assume his duties as president. On that trip, his train stopped in Westfield, New York, where Lincoln told the crowd how he had decided to grow a beard partly in response to a letter he had received from a little girl in that town. She had seen a photograph of him at a local fair and thought the absence of whiskers made him look too thin. So she wrote to Lincoln to say: "If you . . . let your whiskers grow . . . You would look a great deal better. All the ladies like whiskers and they would tease their husband's [*sic*] to vote for you and then you would be President."[2]

Lincoln initially wrote Grace Bedell a letter that seemed to reject the idea. "As to the whiskers," he asked her, "never having worn any, do you not think people would call it a piece of silly affect[at]ion if I were to begin it now?" But within a month, once elected to the White House, the "silly piece of affectation" was not only sprouting from his face but effectively changing his image from that of the frontier rail-splitter who scraped his way up the ladder in pursuit of the American dream to that of a wise, bearded statesman who at least *looked* equal to the secession crisis looming on the horizon.[3]

When the train carrying him to Washington for his inauguration stopped in Grace Bedell's home town on February 16, 1861, the president-elect devoted his very first speech in New York State to acknowledging her. Speaking from the back of his railroad car, he said:

> Some three months ago, I received a letter from a young lady here; it was a very pretty letter, and she advised me to let my whiskers grow, as it would improve my appearance; acting upon her suggestion, I have done so; and now, if she is here, I would like to see her. . . .[4]

Excited onlookers located Grace, shouted "Here she is!" and passed her forward above their heads to the tracks. Lincoln stepped from his train, and "gave her several hearty kisses . . . amid . . . yells of delight from the . . . crowd."[5] It was an auspicious upstate debut. As his secretary John Hay wrote, Lincoln was greeted here by crowds so large it seemed as if "the seas had been let loose and its billows transformed into patriots." Lincoln might have harnessed the sympathy it generated by turning to more substantive reassurances about the national future as his train steamed through upstate New York.

The crowds energized a politician long out of public circulation—ever since February 1860. But in nearby Dunkirk, he did little more than feebly protest: "Were I to stop and make a speech at every station, I would not reach Washington until after the inauguration." In Buffalo, he said he would remain silent to avoid disappointing "the reasonable expectations of those who have confided to me their votes."[6]

Moving east to Batavia, the exhausted and hoarse president-elect merely joked that he did not want to develop a reputation as "a talker." At Rochester he protested, "I have not the strength" for speeches. It was much the same in Clyde, Syracuse, Utica, Little Falls, and Fonda. The *Schenectady Evening Star* was being generous when it reported that "we were only able to obtain a few disjointed sentences" from the president-elect.[7]

Nonetheless, in nearby Albany, excitement around the train station built to a fever pitch on February 18, 1861. "All was confusion, hurry, disorder, mud, riot, and discomfort," wrote one reporter on the scene. Worse, when Lincoln emerged onto the platform, almost no one applauded. It was not because this was Seward territory. Rather, as one eyewitness explained: "Standing *uncovered* . . . [Lincoln] was barely recognized by the crowd, and anxiety to see him and to be certain that they saw the right man overcame any disposition to cheer." Those widely circulated portraits of a clean-shaven Lincoln may have been a bit *too* effective.

"Tired, sunburned, adorned with huge whiskers," a reporter on the scene complained, "[Lincoln] looked so unlike the hale, smooth shaven, red-cheeked individual who is represented upon the popular prints and is dubbed the 'rail splitter'; that it is no wonder that the people did not recognize him." Riding up State Street in an open carriage on a blustery winter day, one eyewitness said he "swayed like a tall cedar in a storm." Several commented that "his pictures do not do him justice." Lurking in the throng was a young actor who had just come to town to star in a play called *The Apostate*, and he told everyone there that Abraham Lincoln was pretty much an apostate himself. The actor's name was Booth—John Wilkes Booth.[8]

Lincoln took the curiously restrained welcome in stride. As he acknowledged at the depot: "The great Empire State at this time contains a greater population than did the United States of America at the time she achieved her national independence."[9] He spoke only briefly, addressing remarks to both Mayor George Thacher and Governor Edwin Morgan. His brevity was understandable; he had just learned that at another state capital, Montgomery, Alabama, Jefferson Davis had taken the oath as president of the Confederate States of America.

Secession was more a reality than ever. Lincoln begged to be excused from making a longer address. He had maintained strict silence since his election—the period known as the Great Secession Winter—while telling older and more experienced politicians in private letters that he would not compromise extending slavery, even if it meant war. He would not trade freedom for peace.

Having won only 39 percent of the national vote, he knew that he needed to keep Northern Democrats on his side, especially if he had to face down secession, so in Democratic Albany he expressed gratitude that his reception there had been proffered "without distinction to party" but out of a common desire "to perpetuate our institutions, and to hand them down to succeeding generations"—a reassuring reminder that he intended to be president of all Americans, the opposition of some notwithstanding.[10]

He may not have known that prior to his arrival, the legislature had deadlocked on how to welcome him. To avoid any partisan ugliness, the governor decided to entertain the president-elect privately at his home, so that no one else, a newspaper teased, got to see "his long legs under the executive mahogany." Lincoln was pawed at at an overcrowded public reception, and then a cannon misfired in an attempt to offer him a goodbye salute. A fellow traveler wrote that Lincoln and his wife left town "with feelings of gratitude for their safe deliverance." Upstate New York had elicited from him what he called "diffidence" and "awe" just thinking of "the history of this great state, the renown of those great men who have stood here and spoke here, and been heard here." It was his first speech in the capital in one of the original thirteen colonies and the beginning of a rhetorical comeback the visit inspired.[11]

Lincoln resumed his official silence as he headed south through Troy (where he was overwhelmed by what he called the "most immense gathering . . . I have ever seen before"), riding in the most ornate train yet put at his disposal: his parlor warmed by modern heaters and filled with easy chairs, walls paneled with curly maple and zebra-pattern inlay, and window panels adorned with thirty-four stars, one for each state. In this plush carriage he pushed on north to find a crossing over the icy river, then down through Cohoes, and through Hudson, Poughkeepsie, Fishkill, and Peekskill to New York City.

There, his triumphant 1860 Cooper Union experience notwithstanding, Lincoln was greeted coolly by a small crowd. Eyewitness Walt Whitman was mortified at the absence of what he called "the glad exulting thunder-shouts of countless unloos'd throats of men." On the other hand, he was relieved that no "outbreak or insult" had occurred, for as he put it, Lincoln "possessed no personal popularity in New York and not much political." Besides, as Whitman wrote, "many an assassin's knife and pistol lurked in hip or breast pocket" that New York day. Behind the chilly welcome was even colder frost. At a City Hall reception, Lincoln told Mayor Fernando Wood: "There is nothing that can ever bring me willingly to consent to the destruction of the Union, under which not only the commercial city of New York, but the whole country has acquired its greatness." At the time, the mayor was hatching a plan to have the metropolis secede and become an international port so it could maintain its profitable commerce with the slaveholding South. Lincoln merely drawled: "I reckon that it will be some time before the front door sets up housekeeping on its own terms."[12] As Lincoln predicted, the city remained part of the state, and during the ensuing war, New York State contributed more men and materiel to the Union cause than any other.

Two months after Lincoln's inauguration, Fort Sumter was bombarded. In response to Lincoln's call for troops, New York quickly massed its volunteers and sent them south. Parading down Broadway, the 7th Regiment marched past the hero of Sumter himself, Major Robert Anderson, and beneath the tattered flag of Fort Sumter, hauled down in surrender, carried to New York, and now floating over the city's broadest street to inspire its soldiers as they headed for war. Flags flew everywhere in Manhattan that day. And a few days later, the Fort Sumter flag was draped over the statue of George Washington in Union Square as thousands of patriots cheered—not unlike the night the World Trade Center flag was raised at Yankee Stadium to restart the delayed World Series and assure the 55,000 people there and millions watching from home that America had survived.

As the war dragged on inconclusively for more than a year, Lincoln came face to face with the old and the new rules of war. No battles ever raged in New York, but in June 1862, the commander-in-chief came quietly north from Washington to visit West Point. There he talked strategy with his former general-in-chief, the aged Mexican War hero Winfield Scott.

Later on that same trip, Lincoln visited Robert Parrott's furnace-like, high-tech munitions foundry in Cold Spring and observed Parrott's new, rifled cannon hurling shells across the Hudson River, exploding with accuracy onto targets painted on the cliffs on the opposite shore. Lincoln surely left West Point convinced that sophisticated, accurate, relentless modern weaponry would be the key to Union victory.

When the draft riots convulsed New York City in July 1863, Lincoln made no attempt to visit the city to help restore calm or to console loyal New Yorkers personally, even though he believed his own son was visiting the city at the time and surely worried that he might be in danger. Three months earlier, Lincoln's Confederate counterpart, Jefferson Davis, had made a heroic personal appearance at the site of the Richmond bread riots to plead for order. True, the Confederate disturbance occurred virtually in Davis's own backyard, and the rioters were female, far less dangerous than the marauding New Yorkers. But Davis *did* rush to the scene, where he made a personal appeal to protesters to disperse. Yet the New York City draft riots, the worst civil disorder in the entire history of the nation, save for the Civil War itself, did not seem urgent enough for the president of the United States to impose what he had once described in Albany as "the representative of the majesty of this great nation"—that is, the president himself.[13]

Five months later, he was invited to come to New York to attend a "friendly meeting of citizens." This might have been his opportunity to talk directly to New Yorkers about the war and to address the city's draft riots. This time, circumstances made a visit impossible. Soon after delivering his most famous speech at the dedication of the National Cemetery in Gettysburg, Lincoln had come down with a mild case of smallpox. It was not life threatening but was too severe to allow him to travel. He did, however, employ a device he had used before to communicate to the people. He sent a letter to be read aloud. In it, he offered "honor to him who braves, for the common good, the storms of heaven and the storms of battle."[14]

New York remained a major political objective for Lincoln as well as a target for enemies of the Union—including terrorists. Late in the war, Confederate agents hatched a kind of bioterrorism plot to spread yellow fever to New York. Believing that the disease could be spread through the things its victims touched, they planned to ship contaminated clothing—clothing worn by dead Southern fever victims—to New York, where, presumably, it would infect thousands. Medically, the plot could never have worked. And though we know that the plan was considered, we are not quite sure whether it was ever carried out.

Lincoln never ventured to New York again. But he could not avoid a major political controversy that erupted there in 1863 over the issue of civil liberties. In May 1863, a group of outraged New York Democrats staged a "mass indignation rally" in Albany to protest the military arrest of antiwar Democratic Congressman Clement Laird Vallandigham of Ohio, who had visited New York City to long and protracted cheers just two months earlier. The meeting had condemned Lincoln, warning that his policies would overthrow "our liberties." Lincoln countered with one of his most famous wartime letters, addressed to upstate Democrat Erastus Corning, the leader of the convention, but also released to the friendly Republican press and published nationwide. "He who dissuades one man from volunteering, or induces one soldier to desert," Lincoln wrote, "weakens the Union cause as much as he who kills a Union soldier in battle. Must I shoot a simple-minded soldier boy who deserts, while I must not touch a hair of a wiley [*sic*] agitator who induces him to desert? I think that in such a case, to silence the agitator, and save the boy, is not only constitutional, but a great mercy."[15]

Unconvinced, the Albany Democrats quickly replied that Lincoln was showing "pretensions to more than regal authority," and some scholars since have criticized Lincoln for his disrespect for judicial process. Similar arguments about the appropriate balance between security and civil liberties emerged in the wake of the 9/11 attack on New York's World Trade Center. Even now Lincoln's letter to Corning captures a complex issue in understandable terms and artfully seeks national consensus on the constitutionality of presidential powers. As Lincoln argued, Vallandigham had been arrested "not for damaging the political prospects of the administration, but because he was damaging the army, the existence and the vigor of which the life of the nation depends."[16]

In 1864, Lincoln received a request for the only handwritten copy of the Emancipation Proclamation still in his control. The request came from a charity fair, but it took considerable political wire-pulling to get the author to part with his work. The project was managed by the Albany, New York, Army Relief Association. Open from February 22 through March 30, 1864, in the teeth of one of Albany's dread winters, the event drew thousands of spectators to its barracks-like temporary structures at Academy Park. The magical setting, its special newspaper declared, had "risen like the palace of Aladdin." All the "palace" lacked was a crown jewel. Though organizers planned to raffle off a cuckoo clock and a Shaker doll, something more substantial was needed. The chairman of the fair's organizing committee, William Barnes, was well placed to aspire to a far loftier treasure: the original manuscript of the Preliminary Emancipation Proclamation. Though he never achieved a political station of his own higher than state superintendent of insurance, Barnes had married the daughter of Thurlow Weed, the Albany editor and Republican political boss who for years had served as chief sponsor of the onetime New York governor and senator, and now secretary of state, William Seward. Sidestepping the president, Mrs. Barnes appealed directly to her father's old friend. On January 4, Seward's son and secretary, Frederick W. Seward—who had also witnessed the New Year's Day signing of the proclamation at the White House—obliged by sending Mrs. Barnes "the original draft of the September proclamation," the "body" of the work "in his [Lincoln's] own handwriting."[17]

The document's arrival sparked huge interest in the Albany Fair, and organizers took maximum advantage of the publicity by delaying a raffle drawing for the treasure until closing night. Ill-advisedly, however, they announced that for added drama the winning ticket would be drawn from a lottery wheel used in the city only recently for conscripting soldiers.

Albany resistance was perhaps attributable not only to the anti-Lincoln, pro-Corning element in town but to the impolitic choice of lottery wheel. This reminder of the unpopular military draft perhaps contributed to poor sales. Five thousand raffle tickets were offered at one dollar each, but for a time, despite the document's value, sales languished. The fair's official newsletter did not help when it published a stunningly disobliging piece of doggerel that wickedly made this point.

In the little publication created to promote the fair, not criticize its most generous donor, an anonymous rhymester joked: "The President sent in a Draft—;/What else could be expected,/From one who's dealt in nothing else/Ever since he was elected?"[18]

The philanthropically minded abolitionist Gerrit Smith knew an opportunity when he saw one. He purchased a huge block of tickets—perhaps as many as a thousand. It certainly increased his odds of winning, and win he did. Whatever concerns his success may have triggered about conflict of interest and overspending, a "loud and hearty cheer" reportedly greeted the announcement that the old anti-slavery hero's name had been drawn from the converted draft wheel.[19]

At Gerrit Smith's suggestion the preliminary proclamation remained with Barnes in Albany while Smith searched for another organization to which he might redonate it to generate still more money for the Sanitary Commission. He then feverishly lobbied the New York Assembly and State Senate to acquire it, without initial success. Not until Lincoln's death did the New York Legislature finally pass a bill purchasing the proclamation for $1,000. To this day, the precious document remains in the collections of the New York State Library. And New York deserves additional credit for rescuing the proclamation from the devastating fire that swept through the State Capitol building in 1911. Lincoln gave the handwritten copy of his final proclamation to a similar charity fair that year in Chicago. The fire that struck that city a decade and a half later was far more devastating: the proclamation was destroyed, leaving New York with the only surviving copy in Lincoln's hand.

The year 1864 was not easy for Lincoln—in New York or nationally. No president had sought, much less won, reelection since Andrew Jackson, and Jackson had not had to confront an electorate embittered by the casualties of a three-year-old Civil War that was supposed to have been suppressed in three weeks. No leader anywhere had ever submitted himself to an election during civil war.

New York remained crucial to Lincoln's electoral success, and his support in New York—to borrow a modern term—was soft. One New

Yorker named George Chopat did propose creating a Lincoln Club in an unfriendly ward in Manhattan. He would plant a "Union Flag in the midst of Irish Copperheadism," he promised, but only on one condition: that Lincoln allow the seceding states to return as slave states.[20] Lincoln had no intention of reversing Emancipation, and he never wrote back to Chopat. Yet New York remained, again using modern political parlance, "in play" throughout the 1864 campaign. Lincoln himself stayed far away from the state. He declined an August 1864 invitation to speak in Buffalo, though once again Lincoln provided remarks to be read aloud, in which he declared: "No man desires peace more ardently than I. Still, I am yet unprepared to give up the Union for a peace, which, so achieved, could not be of much duration." As for Emancipation, he added: "Throw [it] away, and the Union goes with it." "It can not be; and it ought not to be."[21] It is not difficult to understand why Lincoln chose not to travel to Buffalo. National candidates of his era simply did not campaign on their own behalf; it was unseemly. Stephen A. Douglas had tried it four years earlier and had been humiliated by the response. As Lincoln explained in a letter to his Buffalo hosts: "I believe it is *not* customary for one holding the office, and being a candidate for re-election, to do so."[22]

Still, it is hard to understand how he could have resisted an earlier New York invitation, this one to speak at a *non*political "Mass Assemblage" honoring General Ulysses S. Grant at Manhattan's Union Square in June 1864. Lincoln would only say: "It is impossible for me to attend." Here was a true lost New York opportunity: a chance for Lincoln to appear in a symbolic setting, the same Union Square where New Yorkers had staged the first mass loyalty rally after the attack on Fort Sumter. He could have linked himself to an immensely popular general, in a vital state that Lincoln, just renominated, needed desperately to carry in November. Imagine a photograph of Lincoln standing before the famous equestrian statue of George Washington! But once again, he declined. Presidents simply did not make such appearances—yet. That old rabble-rouser, Clement Vallandigham, did campaign in New York, by the way—on behalf of

Lincoln's opponent, General McClellan—in Syracuse, where he attracted thousands.[23]

Lincoln won New York State on Election Day 1864, but just barely. And not before Grant ordered General Benjamin Butler and six thousand soldiers to all but occupy New York City and thwart a reported secret plot to start an uprising in town and disrupt the voting. In the end, Lincoln's Empire State majority actually declined, from 53.7 percent in 1860 to 50.4 percent in 1864 (not including the soldiers' vote). But polling was peaceful, and Butler, his men, and his gunboats withdrew.

In the end, Lincoln may have underestimated the growing affection and loyalty of New York and New Yorkers. A few weeks before delivering the Gettysburg Address, he heard from 118 "poor boys of the Charity School" located in the Five Points slum in Manhattan—the school he had visited three years earlier. Now they wrote to say how impressed they were that this same unassuming, western stranger who had come through their doors only a few years earlier had now become one of the best-known men in the world. They praised him for working to end slavery and leading his country through war, "to righteousness, peace, and prosperity." As they put it: "Your own life history illustrates the truth of the words you then addressed to us. May [God] ever own and bless you and yours." Lincoln kept the letter in his files.[24]

Not everyone in the city agreed. Just three weeks after the election, Confederate secret service agents hatched a plan to take advantage of the citywide celebration of Evacuation Day on November 25—the anniversary of the day the British abandoned New York back in 1783—to set fire to a dozen hotels and public buildings, triggering a conflagration that would engulf the city.

The general Lincoln had installed to oversee the city after the draft riots—John A. Dix—called the plot "one of the great atrocities of the age." In all, fourteen major buildings were targeted for arson, to be accomplished by planting ingeniously created four-ounce bottles

of phosphorus that would ignite spontaneously. The terrorists simply
checked into hotels, placed their carpetbags filled with the incendiary
devices, scrap paper, and rosin, and brazenly walked out, believing
the suitcases would soon blow up. One fire did break out in the St.
James Hotel on Broadway and Twenty-Sixth Street at 8:45 pm. But
guards alerted to reports of smoke broke down a locked hotel room
and snuffed it out. At about the same time, a man in a wig and fake
beard set fire to his room in the U.S. Hotel, and it too was put out.
One by one, fires broke out at the Fifth Avenue Hotel, and at 8:55 in
four different rooms at the St. Nicholas. Then another building, then
another—all put out by security men. At 9 pm a fire broke out in the
Barnum's Museum stairwell, and the museum's famous giantess was
seen fleeing into the street. At 9:20 fire struck the La Farge House
next to the Winter Garden Theatre, where the actor who was on stage
calmed the crowd: his future assassin's brother Edwin Booth. Soon
thereafter, flames and smoke were discovered at the Astor House,
where just three years before, one of its guests had been President-
elect Abraham Lincoln. Remarkably, the city survived undamaged,
and the arsonists were later captured in Canada.[25]

Not all the news from New York State was bad. Just two months
before his death, Lincoln received a deeply moving tribute to "our
beloved and honored President" from an admirer in Troy. Thrilled by
the news of Lincoln's reelection, Sarah T. Barnes wrote:

> I do so thank God for it all; and for making you our Presi-
> dent the second time. God has helped you or you never
> could have lived through what you have; of course, He will,
> stand by, and uphold you; and be assured there are thou-
> sands of warm and true hearts all over this noble country,
> who love and honor you, and pray for you, too, every single
> day. Ah! Mr. Lincoln, the nation's hopes are centered in
> you; the national heart beats loyally for you. God bless you
> fully and richly.[26]

Mrs. Barnes may have been correct in her belief that the tide of public opinion had finally turned. But Lincoln did not live to appreciate fully his own transfiguration. After his assassination, New York paid tribute at a series of funerals that retraced in reverse, but far more emotionally, the route of the inaugural journey four years earlier.

Funerals for the president in New York City, and later in Albany, Buffalo, drew hundreds of thousands of mourners. In Manhattan, a long procession marched solemnly down Broadway. One of the wealthy children who watched from the upper floors of their mansions was seven-year-old Theodore Roosevelt.

A less-privileged youngster who waited along with tens of thousands of others to view Lincoln as he lay in state on the second floor landing of the City Hall Rotunda unexpectedly placed a floral wreath with Lincoln's initials, "AL," on the body—and perplexed guards simply left it there. When Jeremiah Gurney took the only known photograph of Lincoln's earthly remains in his coffin, those made-in–New York initials were still visible on his chest. African Americans marched at the rear of the New York City procession—but at least they marched.[27]

Tributes came from the pulpits of every church and synagogue in the city, including Beecher's in Brooklyn, where Lincoln had worshipped just five years earlier. Albany was getting ready to welcome a traveling menagerie that April—a parade of giraffes, bears, tigers, leopards, lions, and an ostrich. At the last minute, it was postponed—reluctantly—and the Lincoln funeral substituted.

Bells tolled throughout Albany, and the streets filled with mourners as Lincoln's body was transported through the streets. But as soon as the train had moved on, the lions, tigers, and bears moved in—one day late. Still, comparing the frigid Manhattan welcome of 1861—when Lincoln was both "scoffed and scowled" upon—to the "love and veneration" that greeted his return in death, the *New York Herald* said of that grand Manhattan funeral: "Yesterday witnessed the *real* triumphal march of Abraham Lincoln; for he had conquered the prejudices of all hordes and classes. . . . Better for his fame that it should come thus late than too soon."[28]

"New York never before saw such a day," the *Herald* concluded. Neither had Abraham Lincoln. One senses that if he had given New York a second chance, he might have.[29]

Lincoln and McClellan
A Reappraisal
John C. Waugh

GEORGE B. MCCLELLAN WAS A CHARMING MAN, A BRILLIANT man, a courageous soldier, a military comet. However, as scores of historians have delighted in pointing out, he bore a fatal flaw, and that was his unbridled hubris. McClellan was what the British nineteenth-century radical John Blight called a self-made man who worshipped his creator.[1]

McClellan was encouraged in his enormous self-regard by an early life unmarked by failure or disappointment of any kind. Born to a renowned surgeon and raised in Philadelphia society, he enjoyed the most privileged of classical educations before marching off to the beat of the military drum in his soul to matriculate at West Point in 1842. He was a star there, too, graduating second out of fifty-nine in the class of 1846 and greatly resenting that he was not first.

All of his classmates, including the one who did finish first, a now mostly forgotten cadet named Charles Seaforth Stewart, believed McClellan to be the most prepossessing of them all—headed for military glory, if any of them were.

Like most of his classmates, McClellan went to the Mexican–American War, which was declared the very month they graduated,

May 1846. He became an engineer on Winfield Scott's staff in that great general's conquest of Mexico City. McClellan was a courageous and resourceful young officer twice brevetted for bravery, having horses shot from under him.

In the 1850s following the war with Mexico, McClellan became a favorite of Secretary of War Jefferson Davis, who favored him with prized and prestigious assignments, which he performed brilliantly. And then, although on a fast track in the Old Army—as fast as tracks got in the Old Army—he left the army to work on the railroad, where he also performed brilliantly—and became acquainted with Abraham Lincoln.

When McClellan left the army he became superintendent, then a vice president, of the Illinois Central Railroad—a higher-paying job. Lincoln was a sometime attorney for the same company, and McClellan remembered Lincoln well—and not necessarily favorably. McClellan came to believe that this hick of a giant from the Illinois frontier may have been an adequate lawyer but that he was certainly not his (McClellan's) social, intellectual, and moral equal. And this opinion, unfortunately, was an opinion that he would never change.

When the Civil War came, the young McClellan, not yet thirty-five years old, became the most sought after West Pointer of them all—coveted by the biggest, most important Northern states—New York, Pennsylvania, and Ohio—to command their volunteer armies. He went with Ohio and was catapulted overnight to major general of its volunteers, and he very soon jumped five grades from captain to major general in the regular army, ranking second only to the general-in-chief himself, Winfield Scott.

Troops under McClellan's command won four small skirmishes in western Virginia in the first months of the war, while the main Union army at Washington was taking a beating from a Confederate army in the first big battle of the war—at Bull Run on the field at Manassas. Following that, McClellan, the hero of the Alleghenies, was urgently called to Washington to take command of the defeated and dispirited army in the East and salvage it for future operations.

And so Lincoln and McClellan met again: Lincoln as the newly inaugurated president and McClellan as his young general. Their relationship powerfully influenced the trajectory, and very likely the length, of the bloody war threatening the Union.

McClellan arrived in Washington on July 27, 1861, swept in on a wave of national acclaim. He came as the "Young Napoleon of the West," in full command of Union hopes, hearts, and hype. William Howard Russell, of the London *Times*, wrote, "He is 'the man on horseback' just now, and the Americans must ride in his saddle, or in anything he likes. Every one . . . is willing to do as he bids: the President confides in him, and 'Georges' him; the press fawn upon him, the people trust him."[2]

Russell, however, was a skeptic. He didn't believe McClellan's small victories in western Virginia deserved all the fuss. Russell called him "'the little corporal' of unfought fields." There was something to that. Although in overall command in the four skirmishes in western Virginia, McClellan had nothing directly to do with any of them, nor was he present on the battlefield for any of them. The noted American satirist James Russell Lowell, also something of a skeptic, wrote, "There is nothing more touching than the sight of a nation in search of its great man, nothing more beautiful than its readiness to accept a hero on trust." No commander, Lowell wrote, "ever had more paid-up capital of fortune, this fame in advance, this success before succeeding, than General McClellan."[3]

Having become in the public mind—and in his own—the man who would save the Union, McClellan was not himself among the skeptics. Early in the war he wrote proudly to his bride of but one year, the beautiful Mary Ellen Marcy of Hartford, Connecticut, "Who would have thought when we were married, that I should so soon be called upon to save my country?"[4] McClellan wrote Nelly— to "*you*, who share all my thoughts"—almost daily when they were apart, and many of those thoughts should never have been committed to paper. In his messianic mission to save his country in late 1861, he wrote, "I find myself in a new & strange position here. Presdt, Cabinet, Genl Scott & all deferring to me—by some strange operation of magic I seem to have become *the* power of the land. I almost think that were I to win some small success now I could become Dictator or anything else that might please me." He did not intend to become dictator, but he was riding that high horse of hubris.[5]

At that moment, it seemed that there could hardly have been a better choice to do what had to be done—drag a dispirited, scattered, defeated rabble of an army up from despair, reorganize it, and hammer it into a great fighting machine. In this McClellan had no peer. No officer in the army was better informed about military organization, strategy, and tactics—the science of war—than George McClellan. He soon proved to be a genius at the job. Within a few short months he would build the biggest, greatest, and best-disciplined army on the planet.

He had big plans for the great army he was shaping on his stern anvil of discipline. The plan, he told Lincoln at the outset, was to build an army so powerful that it could "crush the rebellion at one blow," terminate the war in one campaign, in one great Armageddon of a battle, crush "it at its very heart"—to display "such overwhelming strength, as will convince all our antagonists . . . of the utter impossibility of resistance"—to convince the South it was a war it could not win.[6]

But after less than a month in Washington, the paranoia set in. McClellan began imagining a Confederate juggernaut encamped across the Potomac that was at least one hundred thousand men strong—an army that was well trained, well led, and twice his army's size. By mid-August he would be estimating it at 150,000. It hovered at Manassas Junction and Centreville, vibrating not twenty miles away, and about to strike a blow against Washington at any moment. In reality the Confederate army across the river under General Joseph E. Johnston numbered no more than forty thousand men, and its commander had no intention of attacking Washington or any-place else. It was in a defensive wait-and-see mode.

In a virtual panic, McClellan wrote an urgent letter to Winfield Scott, still the army's general-in-chief, though now aged and over-weight. McClellan told Scott that he had information from various intelligence sources that a Confederate horde far outnumbering his own lay just across the river and that Washington was in imminent danger of an immediate attack. Scott was not buying any of it. "Rely-ing on our numbers, our forts, and the Potomac River, I am confident in the opposite opinion," Scott wrote Secretary of War Simon Cam-eron. "I have not the slightest apprehension for the safety of the Gov-ernment here."[7]

This, of course, meant that McClellan had to add one more enemy to his lengthy list—Scott himself. This list of enemies in the rear would continue to build in his mind, just as the enemy did in his front, and would soon include Lincoln, the entire cabinet, much of the Congress, and, indeed, anybody in the country who didn't see the situation as he did.

This reaction by McClellan to Scott's perceived enmity reveals some important aspects of the McClellan persona. He was a compel-ling personality, a likeable man who made steadfast friends who never wavered in their allegiance and affection for him. Lincoln liked him personally. But his was a charm with limits. He was consti-tutionally unable to avoid making open demonstrations of his hubris. As one critic said, and many would later believe, he was "the only man ever born who could strut sitting down."[8]

He had shown in his young career that he was impatient under another's command, irritated by any interference from above. This was particularly true of interference from people he felt unqualified in military matters—civilians in particular and politicians most of all, including the president. He once compared Congress in session to "animal performances in a bear garden."[9]

Lincoln in his view was the worst sort of politician to be running the country. McClellan saw Lincoln as lacking personal refinement and the desirable trappings of "polite culture," a jokester with the lack of discipline necessary for reasoned action in these desperate times, prone to cave to political pressure and fail to do the right thing. McClellan would soon be calling Lincoln what his outspoken friend Edwin Stanton was calling the president—"the original gorilla." That was before Lincoln, amazingly, named Stanton his secretary of war in early 1862.[10]

When Scott would not buy McClellan's view of the situation, the young general began veering outside the chain of command, promising the more radical congressmen that he would soon attack the enemy, despite the disparity in numbers, if they would help get rid of the old man. Describing Scott to Nelly, McClellan wrote, "I do not know whether he is a *dotard* or a *traitor.* I can't tell which. He *cannot* or *will* not comprehend the condition in which we are placed & is entirely unequal to the emergency . . . that confounded old genl . . . is a perfect imbecile. He understands nothing, appreciates nothing & is ever in my way."[11]

Although Scott did not see this letter, he heard echoes of McClellan's grumbling from several sources. Scott soon tired of it all. He had been wanting to retire after forty years in the army, half of it as general-in-chief, its star of stars, the greatest commander of the age—indeed of any age. At first, Lincoln didn't want to lose the great general and had refused to let him go. But now he relented, and on November 1, 1861, Scott retired. Lincoln soon elevated McClellan to general-in-chief of all the Union armies and told him, "Draw on me for all the sense I have, and all the information. In addition to your present command, the supreme command of the army will entail a vast labor upon you." McClellan was delighted to get this roadblock out of his way and to be in charge of everything. "I can do it all," McClellan told the president.[12]

Doubts that he intended to do *anything* at all soon began to permeate Washington and the entire country. The wave of adulation that had carried him into Washington had greatly ebbed, and as week after week passed and his great army grew, he showed no sign or inclination to attack the enemy with it. Instead of taking it into battle, McClellan continued building it, riding omnipresently among his soldiers and holding spectacular parades and reviews. None of this satisfied the Radical Republicans in Congress, who in their frustration had formed a Joint Committee on the Conduct of the War to, among other things, prod the general to fight. When in December 1861 McClellan came down with typhoid, even the patient Lincoln became disheartened. The president was beginning to believe, as others long since had, that McClellan was "an admirable engineer, but with a special talent for a stationary engine."[13]

Earlier, in a famous incident, McClellan had shown the ultimate disdain for the president. One evening, with his personal secretary, John Hay, and Secretary of State William Seward, Lincoln called on McClellan in his quarters. They learned the general was at a wedding but would soon return. For half an hour they cooled their heels in McClellan's parlor. Finally the general arrived home, was told the president waited, but instead of greeting him, he went upstairs to bed. Hay raged against "this unparalleled insolence of epaulettes." But Lincoln, that ever-patient and forgiving man, said it was better at this time not to be making points of etiquette and personal dignity.[14]

But now, with the general down with typhoid, Lincoln was at his own wit's end. Advised by Quartermaster General Montgomery Meigs to consult with his other generals while McClellan was incapacitated, Lincoln did so—in a series of meetings during which he said that if McClellan didn't intend to use the army, he would like to borrow it for a few weeks.[15]

Recovered from typhoid by mid-January, McClellan would still not be rushed. Despite the rising public clamor that he do something and do it now, he ignored it and marched instead to the pounding of his own peculiar drum.

Finally, in the early spring of 1862, the time came when McClellan had to do something. Alas, the something he wanted to do was something Lincoln did not favor. Lincoln wanted him to attack the enemy army in his immediate front and drive it back to Richmond, at the same time leaving the capital safely protected. McClellan had in mind a different strategy—shipping his great army by water down to the Virginia Peninsula, landing in the Confederate rear, and marching into Richmond from there—a turning movement on a massive scale, a spectacular run around the Confederate end.

Though dubious, Lincoln eventually agreed to his strategy. At least it was something. But the president attached conditions. McClellan must leave Washington entirely secure. The general agreed.

McClellan went to the peninsula with his army, some one hundred thousand men, in early April, thinking it would be ratcheted up with more troops to about 160,000. And with cover from the U.S. Navy, he would march his legions on to Richmond. But when Lincoln learned how lightly held the capital would remain, he withheld more than a corps of these added troops—which McClellan believed fatally crippled his strategy.

Instead of attacking, McClellan laid siege on a thinly garrisoned Yorktown, when his critics believed that he could have—and should have—swatted the Confederates aside and moved on. After a month-long siege, the rebels evacuated Yorktown voluntarily, pulling back toward Richmond. McClellan slowly, warily, pursued, and by the end of May had fought them in Williamsburg and then at Seven Pines, or Fair Oaks, in front of Richmond—all of it more or less to a draw.

McClellan continued to move cautiously, delaying, raging about troops denied him, and pleading without rest for instant reinforcements, predicting disaster if he did not have them and blaming Washington for anything that went wrong. Lincoln kept urging him to move, to strike with what army he had, which was still the largest on the planet. "You must act," Lincoln wrote.[16]

Finally, after four months on the peninsula without any great rebellion-ending battle having been fought, the general who finally acted was not McClellan but Robert E. Lee, whose troops assailed McClellan's army near the small village of Mechanicsville on June 26. That was followed by seven days of almost continuous fighting, which prompted McClellan to order a retreat—which he called a change of base—southward to the James River, where his army fell under the protection of navy gunboats.

Lee's audacious attacks, however, were generally ill timed and uncoordinated, and all but one—at Gaines's Mill on June 27—was repulsed. McClellan, while not a gifted attacker, showed a knack for waging defensive warfare. When the Seven Days ended and the Army of the Potomac was out of harm's way and under the protective muzzles of the navy's guns at Harrison's Landing, nobody was certain who had won. Both sides got half a loaf. Lee had intended to destroy McClellan's army but had failed; McClellan had not taken Richmond but had saved his army. A correspondent from *Vanity Fair* said, "Yes, my boy, we have had a great victory. And now we want to know who is to blame for it!"[17]

Throughout the Virginia Peninsula campaign McClellan's resentment of those he saw as his enemies in Washington mounted and intensified in bitterness. After the battle at Gaines's Mill, his one defeat during the Seven Days Battles, McClellan wrote perhaps the most incendiary message any general ever wrote his superiors. "I feel too earnestly tonight," he wrote his old friend, Secretary of War Stanton, whom he now considered a Judas. "I have seen too many dead & wounded comrades to feel otherwise than that the Govt has not sustained this Army. If you do not do so now the game is lost. If I save this Army now I tell you plainly that I owe no thanks to you or any other persons in Washington—you have done your best to sacrifice this Army." That blazing wire, afire with insubordination, was entirely too hot for the head of the war department's telegraph office. He scissored out the incendiary indictment, and Lincoln and Stanton did not become aware of it until much later.[18]

Letters that McClellan wrote throughout the campaign to his wife Nelly were just as incendiary or more so—total condemnations of Lincoln, Stanton, the cabinet, and the Radicals in the congress, constantly blaming them for the failed campaign. What he had written Nelly in October 1861, when much of the adulation had faded and impatient hostility replaced it, mirrored his thoughts throughout the campaign on the Virginia Peninsula. "I have a set of scamps to deal with," he wrote her, "unscrupulous & false. If possible they will throw whatever blame there is on my shoulders, & I do not intend to be sacrificed by such people. It is perfectly sickening to have to work with such people & to see the fate of the nation in such hands." As for Lincoln, McClellan dismissed him as "nothing more than a well meaning baboon." "What a specimen to be at the head of our affairs now," he wrote.[19]

After the Seven Days Battles, Lincoln ordered McClellan to abandon the campaign, evacuate the peninsula, and send his army to another new army now mounting a new campaign aimed overland toward Richmond—what Lincoln had wanted in the first place. McClellan was disgusted and angry but complied. When that second campaign, called Second Manassas, under General John Pope utterly failed, Lincoln, over the outraged protest of his cabinet, reinstalled McClellan as head of the army. He did so because he understood, as few did, that what the army most needed again, just then, was a reorganizer. And there were none more skilled at that than McClellan.

McClellan was left with very little time to bring another beaten army out of chaos, for almost immediately, in early September, Lee invaded Maryland, and ready or not, McClellan had to take his army out to check him. What followed was the familiar pattern of the Virginia Peninsula: McClellan moving slowly but finally cornering Lee's army across a little creek in Maryland called the Antietam. There, on September 17, 1862, in the bloodiest single day of the war, McClellan, whose forces outnumbered Lee's three to one but believing the odds were just the reverse, fought the battle piecemeal—to a standoff. Lee withdrew unmolested over the Potomac the next night, and McClellan refused to pursue without first restocking his depleted army. For more than a month he delayed, despite Lincoln's repeated urgings. When he finally did pursue in late October but failed to get himself between Lee and Richmond, Lincoln concluded that his brilliant but hesitant general had the "slows" and that he "had tried long enough to bore with an auger too dull to take hold." And so on November 7, 1862, the president fired the general.[20]

Why did this critical relationship fail? After all, it involved two great patriots, each of whom wanted to win the war. It should have worked. Why didn't it? I believe that the answer is clear. The relationship failed because of George B. McClellan.

Ulysses S. Grant, the general who later succeeded on the Virginia Peninsula where McClellan had failed, said of him after the war, with mitigating kindness:

> McClellan is to me one of the mysteries of the war. As a young man he was always a mystery. He had the way of inspiring you with the idea of immense capacity, if he would only have a chance. . . . But the test which was applied to him would be terrible to any man, being made a major general at the beginning of the war. It has always seemed to me that the critics of McClellan do not consider this vast and cruel responsibility—the war, a new thing to all of us, the army new, everything to do from the outset, with a restless people and Congress. McClellan was a young man when this devolved upon him, and if he did not succeed, it was because the conditions of success were so trying. If McClellan had gone into the war as Sherman, Thomas, or Meade, had fought his way along and up, I have no reason to suppose that he would not have won as high a distinction as any of us.[21]

There were those who believed, as McClellan did, that his failure was not his fault. One of them was Helmuth von Molke, the chief of staff of the Prussian army. In a conversation after the war an American said to him, "some of us in America do not estimate McClellan so highly as we do some of our other generals." Von Molke replied, "It may be so, but let me tell you that, if your Government had supported General McClellan in the field as they should have done, your war would have been ended two years sooner than it was."[22]

Lee might have agreed with von Molke. When asked after the war who he thought was the ablest Union general that he had faced, he allegedly picked McClellan. This was a mystery to many at the time, and it remains so to us now. But to Lee it must have made some sense. Except for a failed campaign in western Virginia early in the war, Lee's repulse at Gettysburg in the summer of 1863, and his surrender to Grant after the long siege at Petersburg, the only general who had frustrated him had been McClellan. McClellan had repulsed him repeatedly in the Seven Days Battles, fought him to a draw at Antietam, and forced him back over the Potomac.[23]

Even so, this young, untried general, thrust so brutally so early into such great responsibility, had flaws that were to prove fatal to success. Years later a biographer said of him, "He was in a way one of the worst subordinates and best superiors that ever lived. As a subordinate he was restless, critical, often ill at ease and seemingly unwilling to cooperate with his colleagues or his superiors. He knew what was best and others were, in his estimation, ignorant or insincere." But "as a commanding officer [he was] always thoughtful, considerate, careful of and deeply sympathetic with the rank and file of his men." They knew this and loved him for it.[24]

When confronted with setbacks, as he often was in his dealings with Lincoln and his superiors and detractors in Washington, McClellan overstated the difficulties and overreacted to them, and he would not for an instant accept blame for things gone wrong. While highly critical of others, he was quick to justify himself. This lofty view of himself, sadly, was in the end without accompanying achievement, and he tended to convert minor successes or even failures into positive accomplishments.

McClellan was a unique man and a talented man. He organized a great army—the greatest on the planet—as perhaps no other man could have. He radiated, one of his officers said, "personal magnetism which was a potent, if not an irresistible force." His ability to stir the love of his army was remarkable. One of his officers said of him, "No other commander ever aroused the same enthusiasm in the troops, whether in degree or in kind . . . he could so move upon the hearts of a great army, as the wind sways long rows of standing corn."[25]

But if McClellan "created an army," as one of his aides at Antietam later admitted, it was an army "which he failed to handle." Moreover, he "conceived plans which he failed to carry out." Lincoln's own assessment was that McClellan was "well versed in military matters and has had opportunities of experience and observation. Still, there must be something wrong somewhere, and I'll tell you what it is. He never embraces his opportunities. That's where the trouble is. He always puts off the hour for embracing his opportunities."[26]

One reporter covering the war wrote of McClellan, "He was assuredly not a great general; for he had the pedantry of war rather than the inspiration of war . . . his power as a tactician was much inferior to his talent as a strategist, and he executed less boldly than he conceived: not appearing to know well those counters with which a commander must work—time, place, and circumstance." He appeared unable to "pluck the passing day."[27]

Finally, McClellan made the unfortunate mistake of misjudging—indeed, ignoring—the will of the people of the North, who were impatient for action, for victory, for a quick end of the war. "On to Richmond!" was the cry of the country. McClellan, however, marched instead to his own more muffled drum, set to a more measured beat, and unmindful of the more urgent pounding. It was a fatal fault.

But perhaps his greatest mistake of all was not bonding with Abraham Lincoln, his president and commander-in-chief, not drawing on him for all the sense and information he had—as Lincoln had urged him to do. Instead McClellan saw Lincoln as another enemy. Believing the president his intellectual, social, and moral inferior blinded McClellan to Lincoln's brilliance. He could not bring himself to believe that a man born so low, so common, so political, could have a mind for the ages. A brilliant man himself, he could not see true brilliance in others. His inability to see the greatness in Lincoln, as Grant could, made all the difference—in effect it destroyed McClellan's career and glorified Grant's. Lincoln had held out his hand to McClellan for as long as he could, and McClellan refused to grasp it, refused to confide in the president, refused to make him his partner. Above everything else, that had been his Achilles heel.

In the end, all of these traits and misjudgments contributed to McClellan's failure and kept him from the pantheon of great commanders, while Lincoln is firmly enshrined in the pantheon of great presidents—in the mind of many, the greatest.

Judging Lincoln as Judge

Frank J. Williams

WHILE SCHOLARS, HISTORIANS, AND STUDENTS HAVE ANA-
lyzed nearly every aspect of our sixteenth president's life, including his
childhood, his years as a lawyer, his too-short term as president and
commander-in-chief, and, of course, his assassination, relatively little
attention has been paid to the type of judge Lincoln would have been
and how well he would have served as a member of the judiciary.

Despite that, the very attributes that have made Lincoln a global
icon—his character, leadership, sense of justice, and his commitment
to excellence—suggest that he would have made not only a good judge
but a great one.

What are the attributes of a "great judge"? A great judge requires
hope, confidence, integrity, and unshakable moral and political courage. He or she needs the ability to stay the course even when he or
she stands it alone, as Lincoln so often did. Judges must exercise
scholarship and commonsense in making daily decisions. They have
a duty to articulate their decisions clearly—decisions that help shape
and define how people in our communities live, how they interact
with one another, and how they should conduct themselves in their
transactions and in their daily lives.

John Voelker, himself a wise and much-honored judge on the Michigan State Supreme Court, wrote a successful novel called *Anatomy of a Murder* under the nom de plume Robert Travers. In it, Voelker wrote that "Judges, like people, may be divided . . . roughly into four classes: judges with neither head nor heart—they are to be avoided at all costs; judges with head but no heart—they are almost as bad; then judges with heart but no head—risky, but better than the first two; and finally, those rare judges who possess both head and heart." That last category of judges describes the kind of judge Lincoln might have been—one with great intellectual ability and a strong sense of moral justice.[1]

John J. Duff, one of the few lawyers to consider Lincoln as a judge, noted in *A. Lincoln: Prairie Lawyer*:

> [Lincoln's] intellectual integrity; his capacity for analysis and balanced decision; his practical, hardheaded approach to legal problems; his ability to strip away trivia and get to the heart of a matter; his sensitive consideration of others and his profound insight into the deep recesses of the human mind and heart, coupled with the gift of expressing himself in plain and pointed and unequivocal language, were precisely the essentials for success on the bench—in Lincoln's day or any other day. And if ever the expression "judicial temperament" applied to anyone, it was Lincoln, whose simple dignity and infinite patience, even under great provocation, were impressive credentials. Judges like this don't grow on trees.[2]

Lincoln embodied political courage. He was clear and self-confident in his beliefs. He learned to trust his own judgment, and although he made mistakes, they were not mistakes of self-doubt. A prerequisite for this brand of courage is to be steady amid a barrage of criticism. And certainly Lincoln was no stranger to criticism. During his presidency, Lincoln suffered continuous assaults on his character from nearly every direction: the North, the South, and abroad. Lincoln's height and his long arms led newspapermen to label him a "baboon," a "gorilla," and the "Illinois beast." Northern newspaper editors referred to him as "that wooden head in Washington," "two-faced," to which Lincoln replied: "if I had another face, do you think I would wear this one?" For signing the Emancipation Proclamation he was dubbed "Abraham Africanus I."[3]

Lincoln also showed great political courage as an attorney when he was called upon to defend progress in 1857. At that time, the future of transportation innovation was at stake—old riverboat technology was pitted against new railroad bridge technology. The Rock Island Railroad Company hired Lincoln as lead counsel to defend it in the case of *Hurd v. Rock Island Railroad Company*. The riverboat *Effie Afton*, heading south on the Mississippi, had smacked into an abutment of the railroad bridge that crossed the river, setting it afire. Lincoln tried the case before the U.S. Circuit Court in Chicago and rested his case on a central, key point: the steamboat's crew was to blame for the accident, not the Rock Island Bridge Company—and surely not railroads in general. Ultimately, Lincoln won the case by having a hung jury—the case was never retried. A defeat in this case could well have retarded railroad expansion for decades. Lincoln's victory effectively advanced the cause of commerce in the United States, allowing railroads to emerge as the country's prevailing mode of transportation.[4]

Throughout his presidency, Lincoln had to grapple with the numerous novel, important, and difficult questions of constitutional interpretation and law that came with the Civil War—questions relating to the president's war powers. It is a long list that includes conscription, treason, suspension of the writ of habeas corpus, military rule and arbitrary arrest, martial law and military commissions, ordinances applicable to a regime of conquest and occupied districts of the South, confiscation, emancipation, compensation to slave holders, the partition of Virginia and creation of the new state of West Virginia, and questions concerning the relations between federal and state governments that had not arisen since the adoption of the Constitution. Thus it could be said that he was both the lawyer and judge of his administration.[5]

During his time as an attorney, Lincoln developed a close relationship with Judge David Davis. It was common then for circuit judges to designate attorneys to take their seats on the bench if they were called away. Judge Davis, who held Lincoln in high regard, chose him to take his place whenever he could not attend to his judicial labors. William H. Somers, a clerk of the Champaign Circuit Court, stated that he "[didn't] remember seeing [Judge Davis] extend to any other Attorney, of twenty or more in attendance" the privilege of assuming the judge's seat on the bench.[6]

Although court records do not reveal when an attorney sat in place of a judge, one can determine when Lincoln heard a case based upon an examination of the different handwriting styles entered in the judges' dockets. A thorough assessment of the judges' dockets discloses that Lincoln sat for almost three hundred cases in Davis's stead. Having successfully heard approximately three hundred cases as judge, it is quite clear that not only could Lincoln make a good judge but that he was indeed a good judge.[7]

Lincoln sought to ensure that the people had confidence and respect for the institution of the law. He was able to strike a balance between zealous advocacy for his clients and a strong sense of civility and professional courtesy. One of Lincoln's colleagues, when discussing Lincoln's courtroom demeanor, stated that "[Lincoln] never misstated evidence, but stated clearly and fairly and squarely his opponent's case." As the author Brian Dirck noted in *Lincoln the Lawyer*, "no one seems to have ever accused [Lincoln] of being an unethical attorney."[8]

In one case, Lincoln met with a potential client who had solicited Lincoln's legal expertise. After hearing the facts of the case, Lincoln replied:

> Yes, there is no reasonable doubt but that I can gain your case for you; I can set a whole neighborhood at loggerheads;

I can distress a widowed mother and her six fatherless children, and thereby get for you six hundred dollars which you seem to have a legal claim to; but which rightfully belongs, it appears to me, as much to the woman and her children as it does to you. You must remember some things that are legally right are not morally right. I shall not take your case—but I will give you a little advice for which I will charge you nothing. You seem to be a sprightly, energetic man, I would advise you to try your hand at making six hundred dollars in some other way.[9]

Lincoln was well known for his honesty and integrity, as evidenced by his reputation as "Honest Abe." As he said in one of his famous debates with Stephen Douglas in 1858: "I do not state a thing and say I know it, when I do not . . . I mean to put a case no stronger than the truth will allow."[10]

On one occasion, Judge David Davis appointed Lincoln and another attorney, Leonard Swett, to defend a man indicted for murder. Although this defendant did not have the means to retain a lawyer, he had friends who managed to raise one hundred dollars for his defense. Swett accepted the money and handed half of it to Lincoln. When Lincoln and Swett consulted the defendant, Lincoln became convinced that the defendant was guilty. Lincoln tried to convince Swett that the only way to save the defendant was to have him plead guilty and appeal to the court for leniency. Swett, a rather talented criminal lawyer, would not agree to Lincoln's suggestion, so the case came to trial.[11]

Lincoln did not participate in the trial other than to make an occasional suggestion to Swett in the course of the examination of witnesses. Ultimately, the defendant was acquitted thanks to a number of technicalities that Swett cited. When the jury rendered its verdict, Lincoln reached over Swett's shoulder, with the fifty dollars in hand, and said: "Here, Swett, take this money. It is yours. You earned it, not I."[12]

Lincoln's integrity is perhaps best illustrated by a story Lincoln told when explaining what influenced him in choosing the law as his profession. Lincoln told how a widow had lost her cow when it was killed by a railroad train. She hired Lincoln to represent her and sue the company for damages. Before bringing suit, the railroad company approached Lincoln with the proposition that if he would throw over the widow it would remunerate him handsomely and give him legal work connected with the railroad. Lincoln refused. Instead, not only did Lincoln take the case, but he won it for her.[13]

Yet Lincoln was no innocent simpleton. In the words of Leonard Swett, "Any man who took Lincoln for a simple-minded man would very soon wake up with his back in a ditch." Certainly, Lincoln's honesty and integrity permeated the courtroom when Lincoln filled in for Judge Davis. While sitting as a judge, he heard two motions argued by his law partner, William Herndon. In one case, Lincoln decided a motion against his own client; in another, he sternly ordered his clients "to answer by the 1st of [February] next." While other judges have been chastised for presiding over such cases, to Lincoln's credit, his colleagues had confidence in his veracity and fairness on the bench. Even Herndon's adversary did not object when Lincoln sat in place of Judge Davis on the bench. Instead, his opponent argued the motion before Lincoln without protest. Not only do these illustrations demonstrate that Lincoln had the ability to sit as a fair and impartial judge; they show that Lincoln could maintain such neutrality even when faced with a motion by his own law partner on behalf of his own client.[14]

At about the same time, Lincoln was defending a woman by the name of Melissa Goings against a charge of murdering her husband. The trial was proceeding poorly for Mrs. Goings, and Lincoln requested a recess to confer with his client, leading her from the courtroom. When the court reconvened and Mrs. Goings could not be found, Lincoln was accused of advising her to flee, a charge he vehemently denied. He did acknowledge, however, that the defendant had asked him where she could get a drink of water, and he had pointed out that Tennessee had darn good water. She was never seen again in Illinois![15]

These cases illustrate that ethics, like sand, keeps shifting over time. Today, Lincoln could not have done what he did with Mrs. Goings, nor could he sit as judge while his partner appeared before him. When we judge history or historic individuals, we need to consider events within the context of the times and not through the wrong end of the telescope. Lincoln was not oblivious to ethics. As he so eloquently stated, "resolve to be honest at all events; and if in your own judgment you cannot be an honest lawyer, resolve to be honest without being a lawyer." As it turned out, the charge against Mrs. Goings was dismissed nearly one year later on the state's attorney's motion.[16]

Another story that illuminates Lincoln's puckish sense of humor concerns his friend and admirer Ward Hill Lamon, who appeared in court one morning with a large tear on the seat of his pants. Before Lamon had time to change, he was called to try a case. As a joke, some of the other attorneys in the courtroom passed around a subscription paper to buy a pair of pants for Lamon. When the paper reached Lincoln, he quietly glanced over the paper and, immediately taking up his pen, wrote after his name, "I can contribute nothing to the end in view."[17]

In addition to courage, both political and moral, his respect for the law, his empathy for his clients, and his sense of humor, there is an additional unique attribute that would augment Lincoln's ability to serve effectively on any bench, and that is Lincoln's ability to detach himself from the issues and, like every good lawyer and negotiator, seek out a middle ground between adversaries. Lincoln believed in what we now call alternative dispute resolution long before that term was ever coined. He was a great advocate of settlement without litigation, and he tried whenever possible to pursue mediation or negotiated settlements. Lincoln stated, "Discourage litigation. Persuade your neighbors to compromise whenever you can. Point out to them how the nominal winner is often a real loser—in fees, expenses, in waste of time. As a peace-maker the lawyer has a superior opportunity of being a good man."[18]

Lincoln handled several slander suits, many of which contained accusations against women of adultery or fornication. An illustration of one of Lincoln's typical slander cases involved a woman by the name of Eliza Cabot, who complained that Francis Regnier wrongly accused her of fornication. Lincoln represented Ms. Cabot and "delivered a 'denunciation' of Regnier that was 'as bitter a Philippic as ever uttered.'" Lincoln ultimately secured a verdict of $1,600 for Ms. Cabot. In this case, as in many others, Lincoln was involved heavily in maintaining community reputations and relationships; he played the role of mediator in order to restore peace to the neighborhood and keep the charges out of the courtroom.[19]

In thinking of Abraham Lincoln as a judge, it is useful to consider the words of the late U.S. District Judge Frank M. Johnson: "The basic concept that a good judge has to have is to do what's right, regardless of who the litigants are, regardless of how technical, or regardless of how emotional the issues that are presented are. If you are not willing to do what's right, then you need to get yourself another job. So I never did think that I was entitled to any great credit for doing it, because that was my obligation. That's what I signed on to do."[20]

Lincoln embodied all the qualities that make up a great judge. Great judges speak more clearly than the act of any legislature because they are single individuals. They speak more distinctly than other judges because they have more to teach. They speak to us with force and power. Lincoln had the courage to do what was right in the face of adversity; he fought for the unity of our nation, and he freed the slaves in the Confederate states, until the Thirteenth Amendment ended slavery for all time and in all places. Lincoln knew that results mattered. He wasn't afraid to push the envelope. He knew that he had to have courage, be steadfast, and stand up for what he believed in. Surely, Lincoln would have been a judge, but for his first love—politics.

It is not always easy to stick to your principles, especially when you find yourself standing alone. But to paraphrase Lincoln, as long as you remain true to yourself, if at the end of the day you have lost every other friend on earth, you will at least have one friend left, and that friend shall be inside of you. And Lincoln remained true to himself.

In fact, Lincoln did serve as judge while in the White House. One of his responsibilities was to review the courts-martial during the Civil War. Lincoln took this very seriously, especially when it concerned a death sentence for sleeping sentinels, homesick Union soldiers, and deserters, which he called his "leg cases." In all of these instances, Lincoln acted as final judge and pardoned many of these soldiers. While merciful in such cases, he was likely to sustain harsh sentences for slave traders, those convicted of robbery, and those who committed sexual offenses.[21]

In another noteworthy act of judging, Lincoln reviewed the sentences of 303 Sioux Indians involved in an uprising in Minnesota that had resulted in the deaths of hundreds of white settlers in 1862. The military court had sentenced all 303 Sioux to death, and these cases came before Lincoln to review. Despite great pressure to approve the verdicts, Lincoln ordered that the complete records of the trials be sent to him. Working deliberately, Lincoln reviewed each case one by one. Even though he was in the midst of administering the government in the Civil War, Lincoln carefully worked through the transcripts for a month to sort out those who were guilty of serious crimes. Ultimately, Lincoln commuted the sentences of 265 defendants, and only thirty-eight of the original 303 were executed. Although Lincoln was criticized for this act of clemency, he responded: "I could not afford to hang men for votes."[22]

Of the four different kinds of judges described by Travers in *Anatomy of a Murder*, Lincoln was one of those rare individuals "who possesses both head and heart."

The Madness of Mary Lincoln
A New Examination Based on the Discovery of Her Lost Insanity Letters

Jason Emerson

IN AUGUST 1875, AFTER HAVING LIVED AT BELLEVUE PLACE Sanitarium for more than two months, placed there by her oldest son, Robert, and declared insane by a Chicago jury, Mary Lincoln wrote to her friend Myra Bradwell,

> It does not appear that God is good, to have placed me here. I endeavor to read my bible and offer up my petitions three times a day. But my afflicted heart fails me and my voice often falters in prayer. I have worshipped my son and no unpleasant word ever passed between us, yet I cannot understand why I should have been brought out here.[1]

For eighty years and more, historians have wondered if answers to these questions—or at least some insight about them—might be found in the letters that Mary herself allegedly wrote, mostly from Bellevue, to her friend Myra Bradwell between 1872 and 1878. Until recently, however, no one had read or even seen these letters, and many wondered if they existed at all. In the 1930s, W. A. Evans, who wrote the excellent book *Mrs. Abraham Lincoln: A Study of Her Personality and Her Influence on Abraham Lincoln*, declared that there was nothing left of the letters "except the tradition." In the 1950s, the Mary Lincoln biographer Ruth Painter Randall declared the letter had "vanished." In the 1970s, Justin and Linda Levitt Turner, compilers of Mary Lincoln's life and letters, concluded that Robert must have destroyed the Bradwell correspondence because it was so "damning" to him.[2]

The letters do exist. My discovery of them in a proverbial "trunk in the attic" is a reminder that new information can still be found, but the letters are also important for the new light they shed on the elusive aspects of Mary's troubled life. They reveal new information about her health, her mental state, and the active role she played in securing her own release from Bellevue Place Sanitarium.

This article has two stories: one is the search for, and the eventual discovery of, the Mary Lincoln–Myra Bradwell correspondence. The other is the effect those letters have on our understanding of Mary Lincoln as a historical figure, of her son Robert, and of the culture in which they both lived.

First the discovery. That story begins in March 2005 when I was doing research for a biography of Robert Lincoln. While going through Robert's papers at his home of Hildene in Manchester, Vermont, I discovered a letter written by his attorney, Frederic Towers, in 1927 that described a visit by Myra Pritchard to Mary Harlan Lincoln, Robert's widow. Pritchard was the granddaughter of Myra Bradwell, and in this letter she wrote that she had thirty-five letters written by Mary Lincoln to Myra Bradwell and also that she had written a book about Mary Lincoln based on those letters. She had a publishing contract for the book and had called on Mary Harlan Lincoln as a courtesy to inform her of the upcoming publication. Since no such letters and no such book were known to exist, I was naturally very excited. Moreover, I found a second letter from Frederic Towers to Mrs. Pritchard suggesting that the two women had met in Washington, D.C., to discuss the book.[3]

I made photocopies of both of these letters and took them home with me for further research. I soon discovered that neither letter had ever been quoted or even mentioned in any existing work about Mary Lincoln. I decided to follow the trail to see if there was more to find. I had been to every Lincoln archive in America and knew there were no Myra Bradwell letters at any of them, so I decided to try to track them down through Myra Bradwell's family.

I found a biography of Myra Bradwell called *America's First Woman Lawyer* by Jane M. Friedman. It contained an entire chapter describing the sale of the "insanity letters" based on Pritchard family information. Friedman described how she had tracked down Myra Pritchard's distant relative James Gordon, who had legal documents concerning the sale of the letters. Mr. Gordon did not have the insanity letters or the book manuscript based on them, but he did have the legal correspondence relating to their sale.[4]

I now began to pursue the legal trail through those papers, seeking the record of sale through Robert Lincoln's attorneys. Five months after I found the two letters at Hildene, after much archival digging, online searching, and cold telephone calls to complete strangers who probably thought I was crazy, I finally spoke on the telephone with Frederic Tower's son, also named Frederic, in early August 2005. I told him I was writing a biography of Robert Lincoln, and he said, "Oh, daddy used to talk about Robert all the time!" We had a wonderful chat for ten or fifteen minutes about Robert Lincoln. Just as I was opening my mouth to say, "The reason that I called was . . . " Mr. Towers said, "You know, we just found daddy's old steamer trunk in the attic that has a bunch of papers in it, including some letters from Mary Lincoln when she was in the insane asylum. Do you think they're worth anything?" Of course I was astounded, and I nearly screamed in excitement, "That's why I was calling you!"

The trunk contained hundreds of Lincoln family documents, including Mary Lincoln's letters, as well as Myra Pritchard's unpublished manuscript and all the legal documentation concerning the sale of the letters to Mary Harlan Lincoln. Mr. Towers and his two sisters had only just uncovered the trunk and so were in the midst of deciding what to do with it all: keep it, sell it, donate it to a library or museum, or destroy it all. I sent them every article I had ever written—including one on Mary Lincoln's insanity case—as well as my resume, finally convincing them that I was the right person to entrust with their amazing cache of historical documents. It was every historian's dream: to find an old trunk filled with hundreds of previously undiscovered documents in someone's attic.

The second story is what this discovery reveals about Mary Lincoln and her era. The letters dramatically changed my own view of Mary Lincoln. When I began my research, I did not think Mary was "crazy"—an unhelpful term that I do not like. I believed that she was an overly emotional woman who had been rendered prostrate by her husband's assassination. As I pieced together the evidence, however, I came to conclude that Mary Lincoln had genuine and serious mental problems. The letters she wrote to Myra Bradwell from Bellevue revealed a woman who was not firmly grounded in the real world. She believed things that were not true and reported events that did not happen. The letters are heartbreaking to read.[5]

To date, there have been two main theories about Mary's mental state. The dominant theory, popularized by Jean Baker in her 1987 book *Mary Todd Lincoln: A Biography*, is that Mary was a perfectly sane woman whose troubles were the fault of others, a woman who was the victim of a male chauvinist society and a cold-hearted, rapacious son who wanted to steal her money. The other less prominent theory is that Mary was indeed insane and that Robert did what he had to do to protect her. This view is best summarized in *The Insanity File: The Case of Mary Todd Lincoln*, by Mark E. Neely and R. Gerald McMurtry, published in 1986. Both books utilized Robert Lincoln's personal "Insanity File"—a collection of documents involving Mary's commitment—yet both came up with radically antithetical conclusions, causing one historian to wonder, as one scholar does, "whether evidence matters in matters of historical importance."[6]

Mary Lincoln's mental illness is historically interesting because it is not confined solely to her life and personality. It also has much to do with her family and especially her husband, Abraham Lincoln. It also necessitates understanding aspects of the Civil War, Reconstruction, the Gilded Age, legal, medical and social history, gender issues, the history of psychiatry, and, perhaps most important, understanding the personality and motivations of the oldest Lincoln son, Robert.[7]

To understand Mary's institutionalization, one must appreciate that Robert was a quintessential Gilded Age, Victorian-era gentleman, schooled and groomed for five years in New England, who believed deeply in the dominant cultural tenets of manly honor, duty, and privacy. In accordance with this code, as the last male Lincoln and head of the family, it was Robert's duty to care for and protect his mother. If he failed in that duty, it would bring dishonor upon him. Robert's letters from this time are replete with these notions of honor and duty, as are the contemporary newspaper accounts that discuss Robert and, for the most part, support his actions. Robert took this charge seriously, and he was so intent to protect his mother that he even wrote that he would do what he must to care for her, "even if necessary against her will." One also must look objectively at his mother's symptoms and what medical experts and family friends were advising Robert to do in the face of his mother's behavior.[8]

The burden of evidence is that Mary Lincoln suffered very serious mental illness. Looking at her early life, one can discern early manifestations of manic-depressive illness (now called bipolar disorder), with symptoms of depression, delusions (of persecution, poverty, and various somatic ailments), hallucinations, inflated self-esteem (narcissism), decreased or interrupted sleep (insomnia), mood swings, and extravagant spending (monomania). These early manifestations later developed into full-blown psychotic episodes, with the above symptoms, usually magnified, as well as threats of physical violence against others and attempts at suicide. This multiplicity of psychotic episodes show that she did not suffer simply from one psychotic episode that led to her commitment in 1875—which is the general understanding—but rather that she suffered numerous episodes throughout her life that led to the inevitable denouement.

Of course, Mary Lincoln lived a life full of trauma and tragedy, and this must also be taken into account. She suffered the early deaths of her parents, of three of her four sons, the murder of her husband, the death of numerous relatives in the war, the estrangement of her family and friends during the White House years, the relentless criticism of the press, the apathy of the American people once she left the White House, and the disdain of a Congress that refused for years to give her a pension. Indeed, her life was dominated by traumatic events that almost certainly contributed to Mary's psychotic episodes.

In a span of six months in 1849 and 1850, Mary lost her father, grandmother, and four-year-old son, Eddie. She was so distraught she refused to eat, bathe, or leave her bed, forcing her husband finally to plead, "Mary, you must eat, for we must live." Her condition improved gradually until the next blow, the death of her eleven-year-old son, Willie, in 1862. Again, she was inconsolable and refused all ministrations, forcing her husband, once again, to intervene and warn her that if she did not get over her grief it would drive her mad, and he would be forced to commit her to an insane asylum. Of course Mary then suffered the murder of her husband in 1865 and the death of her seventeen-year-old son, Tad, in 1871.[9]

Some people—including Robert Lincoln—thought Mary's mental troubles began with the assassination; some thought it was the death of Tad in 1871. Without doubt, the later event was one from which she never really recovered. Abraham had been her anchor to sanity for the duration of their marriage, the buffer that she sorely needed between her and the rest of society. As she wrote in 1869, "He was . . . from my eighteenth year—Always—lover—husband—father & all all to me—Truly my all." She also said that during the war that if she did not feel the need to cheer her husband's grief, she would "never have smiled again." When Abraham died, Tad became

Mary's new anchor, and she barely let the poor boy out of her sight for the next six years. Once Tad died, Mary had no one left. She had alienated nearly all her family and friends during the war, and her oldest son Robert was a grown man, with a wife and two children of his own, as well as a thriving law practice in Chicago. He could not give her the attention she needed and wanted.[10]

After Tad's death, Mary became a homeless wanderer in America, going from one health spa to another. In 1873 Mary sought medical care from Dr. Willis Danforth for "fever and nervous derangement of the head," and Robert hired a personal nurse to be her companion. By then she was claiming that an Indian spirit was pulling wires out of her eyes and bones out of her jaw, that he was removing and replacing her scalp; she spoke to voices in the walls and floor and had a terrible fear and delusion of fire, and her spending extravagance continued.[11]

In 1875, while Mary was wintering in Florida, she suddenly had the intense delusion that Robert was on his deathbed, and nothing anyone said could convince her otherwise. She traveled to Chicago, where she was surprised to find him perfectly healthy. Over the next few months, her condition deteriorated at an alarming rate. Robert consulted with seven medical experts as well as three of his father's closest friends and advisors—David Davis, Leonard Swett, and John Todd Stuart, all three of whom had known Mary Lincoln for more than twenty years—about what should be done. Based on all this consultation, Robert decided to commit his mother to a sanitarium, which, under Illinois law, required a jury trial to declare her insane. After three hours of testimony, the jury took ten minutes to convict her, and she was sent to Bellevue Place Sanitarium.[12]

The twenty letters Mary Lincoln wrote to Myra Bradwell in the 1870s do much to illuminate the missing pieces of Mary's life. They discuss her physical health, about which she had lifelong troubles, and of course they reveal instances of her mental state. More than half of the letters show how Mary got herself released from the asylum eight months early. Historians have long assumed that Myra

Bradwell was the catalyst for Mary wanting to leave the sanitarium and that she directed Mary's release. Their correspondence shows that it was Mary Lincoln who orchestrated her own release and that Myra Bradwell was merely her accomplice, however willing and able she may have been.

The letters written after Mary's release from Bellevue Place are among the most interesting. Mary went into a self-imposed exile in Europe from 1876 until 1880, and very little is actually known about that time. The few letters of hers that still exist are mostly about financial matters. Her letters to Myra Bradwell, however, show where she was, what she saw, whom she was with, and how she was feeling.[13]

Perhaps the most interesting letter of the entire cache was Mary's letter dated June 18, 1876, one day before Mary's infamous letter to Robert in which she decried him as a scoundrel and a thief, writing, "You have tried your game of robbery long enough." Mary's letter to Myra Bradwell reads almost like a rough draft of her letter to Robert, denouncing him and his "most villainous plot" against her. She also asks Myra to help her get revenge against Robert by writing articles about him for the *Chicago Times* newspaper. "I have been a deeply wronged woman by one, for whom, I would have poured out my life's blood," she wrote.[14]

I mentioned that the discovery of these letters changed my views of Mary Lincoln. One thing that did not change for me was my belief that she was a person who deserved sympathy—and not a little pity— for the many trials she suffered. On top of her mental illnesses, she endured a life filled with trauma and tragedy. We should not blame her for her unhappiness. Nor, however, should we blame Robert Lincoln for acting as he thought best to protect his mother. Picking sides has been a roadblock to understanding Mary's institutionalization. In trying to explain or understand one of the Lincolns, either Mary or Robert, it should not require vilification of the other. Only by objectively examining the events and the historical record can we finally understand what happened and why.

Notes

Lincoln's Role in the 1860 Presidential Campaign

William C. Harris

1. Christopher C. Brown interview, 1865–1866, in *Herndon's Informants: Letters, Interviews, and Statements About Abraham Lincoln*, ed. Douglas L. Wilson and Rodney O. Davis (Urbana: University of Illinois Press, 1998), 438.

2. Charles S. Zane statement, 1865–1866, in ibid., 490–491.

3. Elihu B. Washburne to Abraham Lincoln (May 19, 1860); Lyman Trumbull to Lincoln (May 18, 20, 1860). Papers of Abraham Lincoln, Manuscript Division, Library of Congress, Washington, D.C. Hereafter Lincoln Papers.

4. As reported in Robert S. Harper, *Lincoln and the Press* (New York: McGraw-Hill, 1951), 54.

5. Fisher's diary entry for May 18, 1860, in *A Philadelphia Perspective: The Diary of Sidney George Fisher Covering the Years 1834–1871*, ed. Nicholas B. Wainwright (Philadelphia: Historical Society of Pennsylvania, 1967), 353.

6. These newspaper quotes appear in Harper, *Lincoln and the Press*, 56–58.

7. *The Liberator* (May 25, 1860).

8. *The Liberator* (June 8, 1860).

9. Abraham Lincoln to Samuel Galloway (June 19, 1860), in *The Collected Works of Abraham Lincoln*, ed. Roy P. Basler, 8 vols. (New Brunswick, N.J.: Rutgers University Press, 1953–1955), 4:80. Hereinafter cited as *Collected Works*.

10. (Springfield) *Illinois State Register* (June 2, 5, August 7, 1860).

11. John G. Nicolay, "Lincoln in the Campaign of 1860," in *An Oral History of Abraham Lincoln: John G. Nicolay's Interviews and Essays*, ed. Michael Burlingame (Carbondale: Southern Illinois University Press, 1996), 91–92.

12. Memorandum (October 16, 1860), in *With Lincoln in the White House: Letters, Memoranda, and Other Writings of John G. Nicolay, 1860–1865*, ed. Michael Burlingame (Carbondale: Southern Illinois University Press, 2000), 6–7.

13. Lowell H. Harrison, *Lincoln of Kentucky* (Lexington: University Press of Kentucky, 2000), 122.

14. Lincoln to Leonard Swett (May 30, 1860); Lincoln to Lyman Trumbull (June 5, 1860), in *Collected Works*, 4:57, 71. For Weed's reaction to Lincoln, see Glyndon G. Van Deusen, *Thurlow Weed: Wizard of the Lobby* (Boston: Little, Brown, 1947), 256.

15. The *Chicago Press and Tribune* (August 15, 1860) printed the correspondent's account that appeared in the *New York Herald* on August 13.

16. Lincoln to John B. Fry (August 15, 1860), in *Collected Works*, 4:95.

17. Lincoln to Edwin D. Morgan (September 20, 1860), in ibid., 4:116.

18. Instructions for John G. Nicolay [c. July 16, 1860], in ibid., 4:83.

19. Lincoln to Caleb B. Smith ([July 23], 1860), in ibid., 4:87–88.

20. John P. Usher to Abraham Lincoln (August 18, 1860), Lincoln Papers. A report of Crittenden's August 2 speech can be found in the *Illinois State Register* (August 23, 1860).

21. James H. McNeely to Joseph Medill (September 1, 1860), Lincoln Papers.

22. James E. Harvey to Abraham Lincoln (May 21, 1860); Schuyler Colfax to Lincoln (May 26, 1860); Elihu B. Washburne to Lincoln (May 20, 1860); David Davis to Lincoln (June 7, 1860), Lincoln Papers. For the Know Nothing vote for Pennsylvania Republicans in 1858 and 1859 and the Republican fear of losing it in 1860, see Russell Errett to David Davis (August 27, 1860), Lincoln Papers.

23. Lincoln to Leonard Swett (July 16, 1860), in *Collected Works*, 4:83–84, 84n; David Davis to Lincoln (August 5, 12, 1860); Thurlow Weed to Lincoln (August 13, 1860), Lincoln Papers.

24. Abraham Lincoln to A. K. McClure (August 30, 1860), Henry Horner Lincoln Collection, Abraham Lincoln Presidential Library and Museum, Springfield, Illinois.

25. As quoted in Doris Kearns Goodwin, *Team of Rivals: The Political Genius of Abraham Lincoln* (New York: Simon and Schuster, 2005), 264.

26. William C. Harris, *Lincoln's Rise to the Presidency* (Lawrence: University Press of Kansas, 2007), 236–237.

27. John G. Nicolay, memorandum, Springfield (October 25, 1860), in *With Lincoln in the White House*, 7.

28. *New York Herald* (October 11, 1860).

29. Abraham Lincoln to Thurlow Weed (August 17, 1860); Lincoln to John Pettit (September 14, 1860), in *Collected Works*, 4:98, 115.

30. Glyndon G. Van Deusen, *William Henry Seward* (New York: Oxford University Press, 1967), 235.

31. *New York Tribune* correspondence as reported in *An Oral History of Abraham Lincoln*, 105–106.

32. Richard N. Current, *The Lincoln Nobody Knows* (1958; repr., New York: Hill and Wang, 1992), 212.

33. William E. Gienapp, "Who Voted for Lincoln?" in *Abraham Lincoln and the American Political Tradition*, ed. John L. Thomas (Amherst: University of Massachusetts Press, 1986), 62. In this essay Gienapp provides a careful analysis of the 1860 election results.

The Baltimore Plot—Fact or Fiction?

Michael J. Kline

1. Isaac N. Arnold, *The History of Abraham Lincoln and the Overthrow of Slavery* (Chicago: Clarke, 1866), 171; Norma B. Cuthbert, *Lincoln and the Baltimore Plot, 1861, from Pinkerton Records and Related Papers* (San Marino, California: Huntington Library, 1949), xvi.

2. Ward Hill Lamon and Chauncy F. Black, *The Life of Abraham Lincoln: From His Birth to His Inauguration as President* (Boston: James R. Osgood and Company, 1872), 513.

3. Worthington G. Snethen to Abraham Lincoln (February 25, 1861), Abraham Lincoln Papers, Library of Congress. Hereafter Lincoln Papers.

4. See George S. Bryan, *The Great American Myth* (New York: Carrick & Evans, 1940), 41n44, citing the *New York Times* (March 5, 1857).

5. Snethen to Lincoln (November 3, 1860), Lincoln Papers.

6. Elihu B. Washburn to Lincoln (January 10, 1861), in *The Lincoln Papers*, ed. David C. Mearns, 2 vols. (New York: Doubleday, 1948), 2:398.

7. George W. Hazzard to Lincoln (January 1861), Lincoln Papers.

8. Ibid.

9. Mearns, *The Lincoln Papers*, 1:296.

10. Horace Greeley to Lincoln (December 22, 1860), in *The Lincoln Papers*, 2:349.

11. Francis Tiffany, *Life of Dorothea Lynde Dix* (Boston: Houghton, Mifflin, 1890), 334.

12. John W. Forney, *Anecdotes of Public Men* (New York: Harper & Brothers, 1873), 250–251.

13. Charles D. C. Williams was probably the alias for one of Price Lewis, John Scully, or Samuel Bridgman. Cuthbert, *Lincoln and the Baltimore Plot*, 20.

14. Lamon and Black, *The Life of Abraham Lincoln*, 513.

15. "Farewell Address, February 11, 1861," in *The Collected Works of Abraham Lincoln*, ed. Roy P. Basler, 8 vols. (New Brunswick, N.J.: Rutgers University Press, 1953–55), 4:190.

16. *Philadelphia Inquirer* (February 23, 1861): 1.

17. Alan Pinkerton report (February 15, 1861), in Cuthbert, *Lincoln and the Baltimore Plot*, 37.

18. Alan Pinkerton report (February 21, 1861), in ibid., 53.

19. George Stearns to S. M. Felton (April 1, 1862), Felton Papers (#1151), box 2, folder 1, Historical Society of Pennsylvania, Philadelphia.

20. Harry W. Davies report (February 23, 1861), in Cuthbert, *Lincoln and the Baltimore Plot*, 91.

21. Harry W. Davies report (February 12, 1861), in ibid., 28–29.

22. Harry W. Davies report (February 19, 1861), in ibid., 46–47.

23. Harry W. Davies report (February 23, 1861), in ibid., 92.

24. George Stearns to Thomas Hicks (February 7, 1861), Maryland Historical Society, Baltimore.

25. Memorandum of Charles P. Stone (February 21, 1861), Lincoln Papers.

26. Statement of Abraham Lincoln in 1864 to Benson J. Lossing, in Benson J. Lossing, *Pictorial History of the Civil War*, 3 vols. (Philadelphia: G. W. Childs, 1866–1868), 1:279–280.

27. Mearns, *The Lincoln Papers*, 2:443.

28. Lucius E. Chittenden, *Recollections of Abraham Lincoln and His Administration* (Harper & Brothers, 1891), 60.

29. Alan Pinkerton report (February 23, 1861), in Cuthbert, *Lincoln and the Baltimore Plot*, 89.

30. *Philadelphia Inquirer* (February 25, 1861): 1.

31. *New York Times* (March 11, 1861): 2.

32. *Philadelphia Inquirer* (February 25, 1861): 1.

33. Harry W. Davies report (February 23, 1861), in Cuthbert, *Lincoln and the Baltimore Plot*, 91.

34. William Louis Schley to Lincoln (February 23, 1861), Lincoln Papers.

35. *New York Evening Post* (March 27, 1862).

36. Cuthbert, *Lincoln and the Baltimore Plot*, 86–87.

37. Ward Hill Lamon, *Recollections of Abraham Lincoln 1847–1865*, ed. Dorothy Lamon Teillard (Washington, D.C.: privately published, 1911), 47.

The Old Army and the Seeds of Change

John F. Marszalek

1. Allan Nevins, *The Ordeal of the Union*, 8 vols. (New York: Charles Scribner's Sons, 1950), 4:335.

2. All statistical information in this essay may be found in *The United States on the Eve of the Civil War as Described in the 1860 Census* (Washington, D.C.: U.S. Civil War Centennial Commission, 1963), 1–7.

3. For a quick overview of happenings during the 1850s, see "1850s Guide Book," at www.housemouse.net/tt1850.htm; and "America's Best History, U.S. Timeline—1850s," at www.americasbesthistory.com/abhtimeline1850.html.

4. Marvin A. Kreidberg and Merton G. Henry, "Raising the Armies," *American Army Information Digest* (August 1961): 52–53.

5. John Y. Simon, "The Union Military Effort in the West, Grant Emerges," in *The Civil War in the West*, ed. John F. Marszalek (Mississippi State: Mississippi State University Department of History, 2001), 50–51. There are numerous books that discuss the pre–Civil War United States Military Academy. See, especially, James L. Morrison Jr., *"The Best School in the World": West Point, the Pre–Civil War Years* (Kent, Ohio: Kent State University Press, 1986).

6. John Keegan, *The Mask of Command* (New York: Penguin, 1987), 187; Wayne Wei-siang Hsieh, *West Pointers and the Civil War: The Old Army in War and Peace* (Chapel Hill: University of North Carolina Press, 2009), 101.

7. Hsieh, *West Pointers and the Civil War*, 1–35, is an excellent synopsis of the condition of the United States Army before the Civil War. Professor Nsieh's book has been very helpful in my discussion of the army during those years.

8. Russell Weigley, *Towards an American Army: Military Thought from Washington to Marshall* (New York: Columbia University Press, 1962), 42.

9. T. Harry Williams, *Americans at War: The Development of the American Military System* (Baton Rouge: Louisiana State University Press, 1960), 48.

10. T. Harry Williams, *Lincoln and His Generals* (New York: Knopf, 1952), 3.

11. Ibid., 5–7.

12. John F. Marszalek, "Where Did Winfield Scott Find His Anaconda?" *Lincoln Herald* 89 (June 1987): 77–81.

13. Stephen W. Sears, *George B. McClellan, The Young Napoleon* (New York: Ticknor and Fields, 1988), 125.

14. David Work, *Lincoln's Political Generals* (Champaign, Ill.: University of Illinois Press, 2009).

15. Biographies of these men include Jean Edward Smith, *Grant* (New York: Simon and Schuster, 2001); John F. Marszalek, *Sherman, A Soldier's Passion for Order* (New York: Free Press, 1993), John F. Marszalek, *Commander of All Lincoln's Armies: A Life of General Henry W. Halleck* (Cambridge, Mass.: Belknap Press of Harvard University Press, 2004). Grant and Sherman both have outstanding memoirs. The first annotated scholarly edition of the Grant memoirs are being prepared by the Ulysses S. Grant Association.

16. The standard biography of William Tecumseh Sherman is John F. Marszalek, *Sherman, A Soldier's Passion for Order* (New York: Free Press, 1993).

17. The standard biography of Ulysses S. Grant is Jean Edward Smith, *Grant* (New York: Simon and Schuster, 2001). A recent study of the Grant-Sherman relationship is Charles Bracelon Flood, *Grant and Sherman, The Friendship That Won the War* (New York: Harper, 2006).

18. The standard biography of Henry W. Halleck is John F. Marszalek, *Commander of All Lincoln's Armies: A Life of Henry W. Halleck* (Cambridge, Mass.: Belknap Press of Harvard University Press, 2001).

19. Ibid., 116, 120.

20. Marszalek, *Sherman*, 180.

21. John F. Marszalek, *Sherman's Other War, the General, and the Civil War Press* (Kent, Ohio: Kent State University Press, 1999), 108–130.

22. Marszalek, *Commander of All Lincoln's Armies*, 122–126.

23. William T. Sherman, *The Memoirs of General W. T. Sherman*, 2 vols. (New York: Library of America, 1990), 1:3:2–16.

24. John A. Logan, *The Volunteer Soldiers in America* (Chicago: R. S. Peale, 1877).

Seward and Lincoln: A Second Look

Walter Stahr

1. See David Herbert Donald, *Lincoln* (New York: Simon & Schuster, 1995), 129–132; Walter Stahr, *Seward: Lincoln's Indispensable Man* (New York: Simon & Schuster, 2013), 105–110.

2. Seward to Frances Seward (September 24, 1848), in Frederick W. Seward, *Seward at Washington . . . 1846–1861* (New York: Derby & Miller, 1891), 79; *Boston Daily Atlas* (September 23, 1848); *New York Tribune* (September 25, 1848); *Albany Evening Journal* (September 26, 1848).

3. The original source is Frances Carpenter, "A Day with Governor Seward at Auburn," July 1870, Seward Papers, University of Rochester, reel 198. Secondary accounts based on this section of Carpenter include Doris Kearns Goodwin, *Team of Rivals: The Political Genius of Abraham Lincoln* (New York: Simon & Schuster, 2005), 127. For reports of Seward's speech, see *Springfield Republican* (September 22, 23, 25, 1848). For Lincoln's departure on the morning train from Boston, see *Boston Daily Atlas* (September 25, 1848). I cannot find anything in the Albany papers to report his arrival, but the train schedule would put him in Albany in the evening.

4. Herndon to Seward (March 21, 1854), Seward Papers, reel 48; Herndon to Seward (December 28, 1858), Seward Papers, reel 57; Seward to Herndon (December 31, 1858), Herndon Papers, Library of Congress. For Seward's Rochester speech, see *New York Times* (October 28, 1858), *New York Tribune* (October 28, 1858).

5. For the election of 1860, see Gary Ecelbarger, *The Great Comeback: How Abraham Lincoln Beat the Odds to Win the 1860 Republican Nomination* (New York: Thomas Dunne Books, 2008); Michael Green, *Lincoln and the Election of 1860* (Carbondale: Southern Illinois University Press, 2011).

6. See Stahr, *Seward*, 70–73, 80–81, 146–153. On the Know Nothings, see Tyler Anbinder, *Nativism and Slavery: The Northern Know Nothings and the Politics of the 1850s* (New York: Oxford University Press, 1992).

7. Lincoln to Joshua Speed (August 24, 1855), in *The Collected Works of Abraham Lincoln*, ed. Roy Basler, 8 vols. (New Brunswick, N.J.: Rutgers University Press, 1953–1955), 2:323; Stahr, *Seward*, 187, 191.

8. James Dixon to Gideon Welles (April 26, 1860), Welles Papers, Library of Congress; Stahr, *Seward*, 186.

9. Lincoln Endorsement (May 17, 1870), in *Collected Works*, 4:50; Joseph Casey to Simon Cameron (May 24, 1860), Cameron Papers, Dauphin County Historical Society; Stahr, *Seward*, 190.

10. John Austin Journal (May 18, 1860), Harvard Divinity School Library; Stahr, *Seward*, 193–208.

11. Charles Adams, *Charles Francis Adams, 1835–1915: An Autobiography* (Boston: Houghton Mifflin, 1916), 64–65; *Chicago Tribune* (October 2, 1860); *Illinois State Journal* (October 2, 1860); *Illinois State Register* (October 2, 1860).

12. *New York Times* (November 24, 1860); Stahr, *Seward*, 210–211.

13. For the text of the speech, see Congressional Globe, 36th Cong., 2d Sess. 341–344. For the context and reaction, see Stahr, *Seward*, 220–227.

14. Seward to Lincoln (March 2, 1861), Abraham Lincoln Papers, Library of Congress; Lincoln to Seward (March 4, 1861), in *Collected Works*, 4:273; Seward draft (February 1861), Lincoln Papers; Lincoln Inaugural Address, in *Collected Works*, 4:271.

15. Seward to Lincoln (April 1, 1861), Lincoln Papers.

16. Lincoln to Seward (April 1, 1861), Lincoln Papers.

17. Electronic counts in the online version of the Lincoln Papers, Library of Congress.

18. Howard Beale, ed., *The Diary of Gideon Welles*, 3 vols. (New York: Norton, 1960), 1:132–133; William Gilman, ed., *The Journals and Miscellaneous Notebooks of Ralph Waldo Emerson*, 16 vols. (Cambridge, Mass: Belknap Press, 1960–1982), 15:194–195; Edward Dicey, *Spectator of America*, ed. Herbert Mitgang (Chicago: Quadrangle, 1971), 93; Frederick Seward, *Seward at Washington . . . 1861–1872* (New York: Derby & Miller, 1891), 197.

19. For Lincoln's remarks, see Stahr, *Seward*, 252–253.

20. General accounts include Norman Ferris, *The Trent Affair: A Diplomatic Crisis* (Knoxville: University of Tennessee Press, 1977); Amanda Foreman, *A World on Fire: Britain's Crucial War in the American Civil War* (New York: Random House, 2010), 175–198; Gordon Warren, *Fountain of Discontent: The Trent Affair and Freedom of the Seas* (Boston: Northeastern University Press, 1981).

21. Lincoln's draft is Lincoln Memorandum on *Trent* (December 1861), Lincoln Papers.

22. C. F. Adams Diary (May 28, 1870), Adams Papers, Massachusetts Historical Society, reel 82. For a more extended version of the *Trent* story, see Stahr, *Seward*, 307–323.

23. *New York Times* (July 2, 1862); Stahr, *Seward*, 299–300, 332–335.

24. Seward to Adams (July 5, 1862), National Archives, publication M77, reel 77; Seward to Frances Seward, in Seward, *Seward at Washington*, 118.

25. Beale, ed., *Welles Diary*, 1:70–71; Gideon Welles, "The History of Emancipation," *The Galaxy* 14 (1872): 843–844.

26. Welles to Edgar Welles (July 13, 1862), Welles Papers, Library of Congress; Welles to Mary Jane Welles (July 13, 1862), Welles Papers; Stahr, *Seward*, 339–340.

27. For the quote, see Francis Carpenter, *Six Months in the White House* (New York: Hurd & Houghton, 1866), 20–22. For general accounts of this cabinet meeting, see Donald, *Lincoln*, 364–366; Goodwin, *Team of Rivals*, 464–468.

28. Stanton's notes are in the Stanton Papers, Library of Congress.

29. For a longer version of this argument, see Stahr, *Seward*, 341–346.

30. See Foreman, *World on Fire*, 63–79, 183, 273–278.

31. Seward to Motley (July 24, 1862), National Archives, publication M77, reel 13; Motley to Seward (August 26, 1862), Seward Papers, reel 70.

32. *New York Times* (July 9, 1863).

33. *New York Times* (September 7, 1864).

34. *Washington Morning Chronicle* (November 21, 1863); Gabor Boritt, *The Gettysburg Gospel: The Lincoln Speech That Nobody Knows* (New York: Simon & Schuster, 1996), 80, 92; Martin Johnson, *Writing the Gettysburg Address* (Lawrence: University Press of Kansas, 2013), 133–138, 145–151.

35. Seward to Frances Seward (August 27, 1864), in Seward, *Seward at Washington*, 241; *New York Times* (September 7, 1864) (speech).

36. Beale, ed., *Welles Diary*, 2:142; *Brooklyn Eagle* (November 2, 1864); Stahr, *Seward*, 409.

37. *Daily National Republican* (November 11, 1864); *Washington Morning Chronicle* (November 11, 1864).

38. For background, see Michael Vorenberg, *Final Freedom: The Civil War, the Abolition of Slavery, and the Thirteenth Amendment* (Cambridge: Cambridge University Press, 2001).

39. William Bilbo to Seward (February 1, 1865), Seward Papers, reel 87; Stahr, *Seward*, 418–420.

40. Stahr, *Seward*, 431–432.

41. Stanton to Lincoln (April 5, 6, 1865), Lincoln Papers.

42. Fanny Seward Diary (April 9, 1865), Seward Papers, reel 198; Seward, *Seward at Washington*, 271–272; Grant to Stanton (April 9, 1865), in *New York Times* (April 10, 1865).

43. Stahr, *Seward*, 433–434.

44. Ibid., 1–3, 435–436.

45. *Sacramento Daily Union* (May 19, 1865; report dated April 20).

Mourning in America: Death Comes to the Civil War White Houses

Catherine Clinton

1. It is well known that Mary Lincoln had Todd brothers and brothers-in-law serving in the Confederate Army. But perhaps not as well known is that Varina Davis had Yankee connections: she was the granddaughter of Richard Howell, governor of New Jersey (1793–1801), thus indicted as someone with "Northern blood" just as Mary had been tainted by her Confederate ties.

2. See Richard Carwardine, "Lincoln's Religion," in *Our Lincoln: New Perspectives on Lincoln and His World*, ed. Eric Foner (New York: Norton, 2008), 223–248.

3. Thomas J. Schlereth, *Victorian America: Transformations in Everyday Life* (New York: Harpers, 1991), 274.

4. Lou Taylor, *Mourning Dress* (London: George Unwin, 1983), 165. See also Sarah Nehama, *In Death Lamented: The Tradition of Anglo-American Mourning Jewelry* (Boston: Massachusetts Historical Society, 2012).

5. Among Catholic peasants in the uplands of Hungary, many feared the restless spirit of the soul of a dead child unbaptized. Legend portrayed that they would wander but appear every seven years at the same bush. When this spirit appeared, any pitying soul should throw a white cloth at it and repeat: "I christen you in the name of the Father, the Son and the Holy Spirit; if you are a boy your name shall be Adam, if you are a girl it shall be Eve." This allegedly freed the soul to make its way into Heaven as an angel. Lou Taylor, *Mourning Dress* (London: George Unwin, 1983), 167.

6. Drew Gilpin Faust, *This Republic of Suffering: Death and the American Civil War* (New York: Knopf, 2008). Faust argues that the Civil War can be called the first modern war in part because it created accountability—for those who served their country. The government henceforth would be required to undertake notifications of next of kin, proper burial, and fitting commemorations. Eventually the state would donate benefits to families of dead Union veterans.

7. Ibid., 65.

8. Ibid., 70.

9. The young German wife of the caretaker of the Evergreen Cemetery in Gettysburg, Pennsylvania, was overwhelmed by the forces that caused her to evacuate her home during the first few days of July 1863. Her husband off in the army, left behind with three young children, Elizabeth Thorn was not prepared for the battle that erupted in her backyard. The aftermath was even more wrenching, as dead soldiers outnumbered the living left behind in the town ten to one. More than a dozen dead horses ringed Thorn's bullet-ridden house—with shattered windows and blood-stained linens. She tried to clean up her home but was called upon to do more. Instructed to fill her graveyard with Union dead, Elizabeth Thorn put an herb-soaked kerchief round her face and braved the foul air to mark off plots. Washing down the corpses, removing identification, and crudely wrapping the dead soldiers in shrouds, she worked steadily for days on end. Despite the unbearable stench, Thorn personally buried over a hundred soldiers, assisted only by her aged father. As late as August 11, she interred thirteen bloated and disfigured bodies in one day. She faced these ghastly conditions while six months pregnant with her fourth child. Thorn claimed that for years after, "those hard days had always told on my life." See Ellen Conklin, *Women at Gettysburg* (Gettysburg: Thomas, 1993).

10. Faust, *This Republic of Suffering*, 112.

11. See Stephen B. Oates, *A Woman of Valor: Clara Barton and the Civil War* (New York: Macmillan, 1994).

12. Faust, *This Republic of Suffering*, 166.

13. Ibid., 148.

14. Ibid., 150.

15. Ibid., 152–153.

16. Taylor, *Mourning Dress*, 204.

17. Ibid., 240.

18. Ibid., 242.

19. Sarah Nehama, *In Death Lamented: The Tradition of Anglo-American Mourning Jewelry* (Boston: Massachusetts Historical Society: 2012). See esp. 70–73, 104–107.

20. Ibid., 243.

21. David Herbert Donald, *Lincoln* (New York: Simon & Schuster, 1995), 153.

22. William Townsend, *Lincoln and the Bluegrass: Slavery and the Civil War in Kentucky* (Lexington: University of Kentucky Press, 1955), 193.

23. Jennifer Fleischner, *Mrs. Lincoln and Mrs. Keckly: The Remarkable Story of the Friendship Between a First Lady and a Former Slave* (New York: Broadway, 2003), 169.

24. *Minutes of the Session of the First Presbyterian Church* (1828–1862), 82, Illinois State Historical Library.

25. Donald, *Lincoln*, 154.

26. With thanks to Donna McCreary for her corrections on the Smith family children.

27. Justin G. Turner and Linda Levitt Turner, *Mary Todd Lincoln: Her Life and Letters* (New York: Knopf, 1972), 64.

28. Michael Burlingame and John Ettlinger, eds., *Inside Lincoln's White House: The Complete Civil War Diary of John Hay* (Carbondale: Southern Illinois University Press, 1997), 176.

29. C. A. Tripp, *The Intimate World of Abraham Lincoln* (New York: Free Press, 2005), 120–121.

30. Doris Kearns Goodwin, *Team of Rivals: The Political Genius of Abraham Lincoln* (New York: Simon and Schuster, 2005), 381.

31. The diary of Fanny Seward (September 9, 1861) records that the Seward women came to pay a call on Mrs. Lincoln at the White House. The group were seated, then told Mrs. L. was "very much engaged" so they filed out—"the truth of Mrs. L.'s engagement was probably that she did not want to see Mother—else

why not give general direction to the doorkeeper to let no one in? It was certainly very rude to have us all seated first." Fanny was extremely annoyed but goes on to compliment Mrs. Lincoln for begging for the life of a soldier. Perhaps Mrs. Lincoln was engaged with trying to deal with all the rumors of scandal and corruption that were raging around her renovations of the White House, which she discovered upon her arrival back in Washington on September 5. It is also true that she blamed Seward, repeatedly, for circulating stories against her. Additionally, missed calls was a common hazard, as Mrs. Seward reported the same week: September 8, 1861, "Mrs. Bates Called last week—I did not see her." Frances Seward to Lazette Worden. See Patricia Carley Johnson, "Sensitivity and the Civil War: The Selected Diaries and Papers, 1858–1866, of Frances Adeline (Fanny) Seward," Ph.D. thesis, University of Rochester, 1974.

32. Fleischner, *Mrs. Lincoln and Mrs. Keckly*, 228.

33. Michael Burlingame, *With Lincoln in the White House: Letters, Memoranda, and Other Writings of John G. Nicolay, 1860–1865* (Carbondale: Southern Illinois University Press, 2000), 67. See also Elizabeth Keckley, *Behind the Scenes; or, Thirty Years a Slave, and Four Years in the White House* (1868; repr. New York: Oxford University Press, 1988), 96–97.

34. Turner and Turner, *Mary Todd Lincoln*, 218.

35. The ball's guest list caused quite a ruckus within Washington society: "Half the city is jubilant at being invited while the other half is furious at being left out in the cold." Fleischner, *Mrs. Lincoln and Mrs. Keckly*, 229. William Stoddard, Lincoln's secretary, was put in charge of the list and had to disabuse several dignitaries that they might impose on Mrs. Lincoln for some extra tickets for gentlemen of the press. See Burlingame, *Inside the White House*, xiv–xv.

36. Flesichner, *Mrs. Lincoln and Mrs. Keckly*, 230.

37. Keckley, *Behind the Scenes*, 106–107.

38. Later, she would reflect: "how much comfort he always was to me, and how fearfully, I always found my hopes concentrating on so good a boy as he was." See Turner and Turner, *Mary Todd Lincoln*, 128.

39. Keckley, *Behind the Scenes*, 100.

40. Ibid., 100–102.

41. Howard K. Beale, ed., *The Diary of Edward Bates, 1859–1866* (Washington: U.S. Govt. Print. Off., 1933), 233.

42. Julia Taft Bayne, *Tad Lincoln's Father* (Lincoln: University of Nebraska Press, 2001), 199–200.

43. Ida Tarbell, *The Life of Abraham Lincoln*, 2 vols. (New York: Doubleday, Page & Co., 1895), 2:89.

44. Keckley, *Behind the Scenes*, 103. See also Burlingame, *With Lincoln in the White House*, 71.

45. Keckley, *Behind the Scenes*, 103–104.

46. Anna Boyden, *Echoes from the Hospital and the White House* (Boston: D. Lathrop & Co., 1884), 51, 53–55.

47. See Milton Shutes, "Mortality of the Five Lincoln Boys," *Lincoln Herald* 57 (Spring/Summer 1955): 6. See also *New York Herald* (February 21, 1862): "His disease was pneumonia."

48. She sent specific directives to New York to order new wardrobe items, such as a "mourning bonnet—which must be exceedingly plain & genteel." Mary Lincoln to Ruth Harris (May 17, 1862), in Turner and Turner, *Mary Todd Lincoln*, 125.

49. Keckley, *Behind the Scenes*, 104.

50. Elizabeth Edwards to Julia Baker (March 2, 1862), SC 445, Abraham Lincoln Presidential Library, Springfield, Illinois. She ended up sleeping in the same room in which Willie died and pronounced it the "Death Chamber."

51. Turner and Turner, *Mary Todd Lincoln*, 129–130.

52. *New York Herald* (July 17, 1862).

53. "Donation for the Sick," *New York Tribune* (August 13, 1862).

54. Mrs. E. F. Ellet, *The Court Circles of the Republic* (Hartford, Ct.: Hartford Publishing Company, 1869), 526.

55. Matthew Pinsker, *Lincoln's Sanctuary: Abraham Lincoln and the Soldiers' Home* (New York: Oxford University Press, 2005), 30.

56. Robert Cox, *Body and Soul: A Sympathetic History of American Spiritualism* (Charlottesville: University of Virginia Press, 2003), 71.

57. Cox, *Body and Soul*, 71–72.

58. Earl Wesley Fornell, *Unhappy Medium: Spiritualism and the life of Margaret Fox* (Austin: University of Texas Press, 1964), 79.

59. George Templeton Strong marveled in 1855: "What would I have said six years ago to anybody who predicted that before the enlightened nineteenth century ended that hundreds of thousands of people in this country would believe themselves able to communicate with the ghosts of their grandfathers?" Allan Nevins and Milton Halsey Thomas, eds., *Diary of George Templeton Strong*, 4 vols. (New York, Macmillan, 1952), 2:244–245.

60. Ann Braude, *Radical Spirits: Spiritualism ad Women's Rights in Nineteenth-Century America* (Boston: Beacon, 1989), 53.

61. Barbara White, *The Beecher Sisters* (New Haven, Conn.: Yale University Press, 2003), 233.

62. Earl Schenck Miers, ed. *Lincoln Day by Day: A Chronology, 1809: 1865*, 3 vols. (Washington, D.C.: Lincoln Sesquicentennial Association, 1960), 3:139.

63. Her niece Katherine Helm cited it as evidence of her famous aunt's mental imbalance in her biographical reminiscences about Mrs. Lincoln. Katherine Helm, *The True Story of Mary: Wife of Lincoln* (New York: Harper & Brothers, 1923), 226–227.

64. Later in life, she commented on wedding an older man to a friend whose daughter was contemplating such a marriage: "I gave the best & all of my life to a girdled tree, it was live oak & was good for any purpose except for blossom & fruit, and I am not willing for Belle to be content with anything less than the whole of a man's heart." For these and other insights, see Joan Cashin's *First Lady of the Confederacy: Varina Davis's Civil War* (Cambridge, Mass.: Harvard University Press, 2006).

65. Ishbel Ross, *First Lady of the South: The Life of Mrs. Jefferson Davis* (New York: Harper & Bros., 1958), 70.

66. Taylor, *Mourning Dress*, 145.

67. William Cooper, *Jefferson Davis, American* (New York: Knopf, 2000), 298.

68. Ibid., 300.

69. Hudson Strode, *Jefferson Davis, Confederate President* (New York: Harcourt, 1959), 2:187.

70. C. Vann Woodward, ed. *Mary Chesnut's Civil War* (New Haven, Conn.: Yale University Press, 1981), 526.

71. Ibid.

72. Strode, *Jefferson Davis*, 2:31.

73. William Cooper, *Jefferson Davis, American*, 480.

74. Cass Canfield, *The Iron Will of Jefferson Davis*, (New York: Harcourt Brace, Jovanavich, 1978), 119.

75. Strode, *Jefferson Davis*, 2:34.

76. Ibid.

77. Cooper, *Jefferson Davis, American*, 569.

78. Allen Tate, *Jefferson Davis, His Rise and Fall* (New York: Minton, Balch & Company, 1929), 225. And we know that Mrs. Davis wore a lavender calico during this period, still in the hands of the White House of the Confederacy.

79. Felicity Allen, *Jefferson Davis: Unconquerable Heart* (Columbia: University of Missouri Press, 1999), 373.

80. She only removed her widow's weeds once, for Tad's eighteenth birthday. And he died later in that year. Catherine Clinton, *Mrs. Lincoln: A Life* (New York: Harper Collins, 2009), 290.

Abraham Lincoln, Admiral-in-Chief

Craig L. Symonds

1. Doris Kearns Goodwin, *Team of Rivals: The Political Genius of Abraham Lincoln* (New York: Simon & Schuster, 2005).

2. Lincoln to Welles (May 14, 1861), in *The Collected Works of Abraham Lincoln*, ed. Roy P. Basler, 8 vols. (New Brunswick, N.J.: Rutgers University Press, 1953–55), 4:370. Hereafter cited as *Collected Works*.

3. John Hay, *Inside Lincoln's White House: The Complete Civil War Diary of John Hay*, ed. Michael Burlingame and John R. T. Ettinger (Carbondale: Southern Illinois Press, 1997), 11 (entry of April 25, 1861).

4. Lincoln to Buell (January 13, 1862), in *Collected Works*, 5:98. Italics in original. Lincoln sent a nearly identical copy of this letter to Halleck the same day.

5. This statement is from Hay's diary of July 14, 1863, and is quoted in *Collected Works*, 6:329.

6. The "despair" in East Tennessee is in Lincoln to Buell (January 6, 1861), in *Collected Works*, 5:91. Halleck's unhelpful letter, also dated January 6, is in the Lincoln Papers, Library of Congress, Series I (Lincoln's endorsement, but not the letter, is in *Collected Works*, 5:92, 95); Lincoln to Cameron (January 11, 1862), in *Collected Works*, 5:97; *Inside Lincoln's Cabinet: The Civil War Diaries of Salmon P. Chase*, ed. by David Donald (New York: Longmans, Green & Co., 1954), 57 (January 6, 1862); Meigs Diary (January 10, 1862), *American Historical Review* 27(October 1920–July 1921): 302.

7. *The Diary of Edward Bates, 1869–1866*, ed. Howard K. Beale (New York: Da Capo, 1971), 218, 223 (December 31, 1861; January 10, 1862). Hereafter cited as Bates Diary. Meigs Diary (January 10, 1862), *American Historical Review* 27 (Oct 1920–July 1921):292, 302.

8. McDowell's notes on the meeting are in Henry J. Raymond, *The Life and Public Services of Abraham Lincoln* (New York: Derby and Miller, 1865), 772–777; Franklin's notes are in W. B. Franklin, "First Great Crime," in *Annals of the War* (Philadelphia: Times, 1879): 76–77. McClellan's account is in *McClellan's Own Story* (New York: C. L. Webster and Co., 1887), 155–159.

9. Welles to Rodgers (May 16, 1861), and Rodgers to Welles (June 8 and September 7, 1861), both in *Official Records of the Union and Confederate Navies in the War of the Rebellion* (Washington: Government Printing Office, 1894–1917), 22:280, 288, 318–320. Hereafter cited as *ORN*. All references are to Series I.

10. Welles to Rodgers (the telegram is dated June 11 and the letter June 12, 1861), in *ORN*, 22:286, 284–285.

11. Benjamin Franklin Cooling, *Forts Henry and Donelson: The Key to the Confederate Heartland* (Knoxville: University of Tennessee Press, 1987), 23; *The Diary of Gideon Welles*, 3 vols. (Boston: Houghton & Mifflin, 1911), 1:345.

12. Welles to Foote (August 30, 1861), Foote to Welles (September 30, 1861), Foote to Meigs (September 30, 1861), and Foote to Cameron (October 2, 1861), all in *ORN*, 22:307, 355, 356; Bates Diary (January 10, 1862), 223. Italics in original.

13. David Dixon Porter, *Incidents and Anecdotes of the Civil War* (New York: D. Appleton, 1885), 64; Chester G. Hearn, *Admiral David Dixon Porter: The Civil War Years* (Annapolis, Md.: Naval Institute Press, 1996), 70–71.

14. Fox to Foote (January 10, 1862), in *ORN*, 22:491.

15. Lincoln to Foote (January 23, 1862), in *Collected Works*, 5:108, 108n.

16. Foote to Symington (January 29, 1862), in *ORN*, 22:525.

17. Foote to Lincoln (January 27, 1862), Abraham Lincoln Papers, Library of Congress; Wise to Ripley (February 8, 1862), Wise Letter Book, National Archives, vol. 1; Wise to Foote (January 27, January 31, March 1, and March 5, 1862), all in *ORN*, 22:523, 526–527, 650, 657.

18. Wise to Ripley (February 28, 1862), Wise to Foote (January 31, 1862), and Fox to Foote (January 27, 1862), all in *ORN*, 22:576, 527, 522.

19. Foote to Welles (February 6, 1862 [received February 7]), in *ORN*, 22:537.

20. Foote to Welles (February 11, 1862), and Welles to Foote (February 13, 1862), both in *ORN*, 22:570, 547.

21. Scott (Asst Secy of War) to Foote (February 8, 1862), and Halleck to Foote (February 9, 1862), both in *ORN*, 22:576, 547.

22. Halleck to Buell (February 12, 1862), in *War of the Rebellion, Official Records of the Union and Confederate Armies in the War of the Rebellion* (Washington: Government Printing Office, 1894–1922), 7:608. Hereafter cited as *OR*; all references are to Series I. There is no indication in *OR* that Halleck sent this information on to Washington, but it would have been irresponsible for him not to have done so. See also Halleck to McClellan (February 15, 1862), in *OR*, 7:616. The telegrams are Halleck to McClellan (February 15, 1862 [3 pm and 8 pm]), in *OR*, 7:616, 617.

23. Foote to Welles (February 15, 1862), in *ORN*, 22:584.

24. Abraham Lincoln to Halleck (February 16, 1862), in *Collected Works*, 5:135 (also in *OR*, 7:624); Cullum to McClellan (February 17, 1862), Lincoln Papers.

25. David Donald, *Lincoln* (New York: Simon & Schuster, 1995), 36.

26. Wise to Halleck (February 28, 1862 [midnight]), in *ORN*, 22:641; Bates Diary (January 10, 1862), 223–224.

27. Bates Diary (March 15, 1862), 242.

28. All these telegrams are in *ORN*, 22:691–95. Wise's cover letters indicating that he took them directly to Lincoln are in the Henry A. Wise Letter Book, National Archives, vol. 1.

29. Foote to Welles (April 5, 1862 [received April 6]), in *ORN*, 22:711; Bates Diary (April 8–9, 1862), 246–247; Foote to Welles (April 7, 1862 [received April 8]), in *ORN*, 22:720; Stager to Stanton (April 8, 1862 [received 6:30 pm]), Lincoln Papers.

30. Fox to Welles (April 29, 1862), Lincoln Papers.

31. Charles L. Dufour, *The Night the War Was Lost* (Garden City, N.Y.: Doubleday, 1960), 265–285; Chester G. Hearn, *The Capture of New Orleans, 1862* (Baton Rouge: Louisiana State University Press, 1995), 209–236.

32. Dufour, *The Night the War Was Lost*, 287–298; Hearn, *The Capture of New Orleans*, 237–248.

Jefferson Davis and Robert E. Lee: Reluctant "Traitors"

William C. Davis

1. Haskell M. Monroe and James T. McIntosh, eds., *The Papers of Jefferson Davis*, vol. 1, *1808–1840* (Baton Rouge: Louisiana State University Press, 1971), lxxix; Lynda Lasswell Crist, ed., "Jefferson Davis Ponders His Future," *Journal of Southern History* 49 (November 1975): 520–521.

2. Stephen R. Mallory Diary (September 27, 1865), Stephen R. Mallory Papers, Southern Historical Collection, University of North Carolina, Chapel Hill.

3. Lynda Lasswell Crist, ed., *The Papers of Jefferson Davis*, vol. 4, *1849–1852* (Baton Rouge: Louisiana State University Press, 1983), 19–20.

4. Dunbar Rowland, comp., *Jefferson Davis, Constitutionalist* (Jackson: Mississippi Department of Archives and History, 1923), 1, 378, 381, 432–433, 509.

5. Crist, *Papers*, 4:300.

6. Lynda Lasswell Crist and Mary Seaton Dix, eds., *The Papers of Jefferson Davis*, vol. 6, *1856–1860* (Baton Rouge: Louisiana State University Press, 1989), 54–55.

7. Rowland, *Jefferson Davis, Constitutionalist*, 3:327.

8. Ibid., 3:285, 287, 329.

9. Ibid., 3:339–360, *passim*.

10. Ibid., 3:6, 86–87; Crist and Dix, *Papers*, 6:154, 228, 618.

11. *Weekly Whig* (Vicksburg) (November 14, 1860).

12. Reuben Davis, *Recollections of Mississippi and Mississippians* (New York: Houghton, Mifflin, 889), 396.

13. United States War Department, *War of the Rebellion: Official Records of the Union and Confederate Armies* (Washington: Government Printing Office, 1880–1901), Series IV, 1:28–29.

14. Jefferson Davis to Clement C. Clay (January 19, 1861), Clement C. Clay Papers, Duke University, Durham, North Carolina.

15. Douglas Southall Freeman, *R. E. Lee* (New York: Scribner's, 1934), 1, [?]. Uncharacteristically, Freeman gives no source for this statement. Presumably it was made prior to the death of the Whig Party in 1854.

16. Michael Fellman, *The Making of Robert E. Lee* (New York: Random House, 2000), 55–56.

17. Elizabeth Brown Pryor, *Reading the Man: A Portrait of Robert E. Lee Through His Private Letters* (New York: Viking, 2007), 158.

18. Thomas L. Connelly, *The Marble Man: Robert E. Lee and His Image in American Society* (Baton Rouge: Louisiana State University Press, 1977), 200.

19. Commonplace Book, Virginia Historical Society, as quoted in Fellman, *Lee*, 79.

20. Fellman, *Lee*, 81.

21. Ibid., 87.

22. Ibid., 84.

23. Ibid., 84–85.

24. Ibid., 87.

25. Anna Maria Mason Lee to Daniel Murray Lee (May 27, 1861), Lee and Ficklin Family Archives, courtesy of Robert K. Krick, Fredericksburg, Virginia.

26. John S. Mosby, *Memoirs of Colonel John S. Mosby* (Boston: Little, Brown, 1917), 379.

27. Freeman, *Lee*, 1:441.

28. *Gazette* (Alexandria, Va.) (April 27, 1861), in *Daily Telegraph* (Macon, Ga.) (April 29, 1861).

29. Jefferson Davis to John Letcher (April 22, 1861), Executive Papers, Virginia State Library, Richmond.

"The Battle Hymn of the Republic": Origins, Influence, Legacies

John Stauffer

1. This chapter is based on John Stauffer and Benjamin Soskis, *The Battle Hymn of the Republic: A Biography of the Song That Marches On* (New York: Oxford University Press, 2013).

2. Steffe was first publicly identified as the song's originator in an 1883 article by Major O. C. Bosbyshell, a Civil War veteran, in an obscure Philadelphia jour-

nal. Steffe's claim was then circulated in an influential 1887 *Century* article on Civil War music. See O. C. Bosbyshell, "Origin of 'John Brown's Body,'" *Grand Army Scout and Soldier's Mail*, typescript copy in the John Brown/Boyd B. Stutler database, West Virginia Memory Project: http://www.wvculture.org/history; Brander Matthews, "The Songs of the Civil War," *Century Illustrated* 34, no. 4 (1887): 622. For a more sustained discussion of Steffe as the originator of the "Battle Hymn" tune, see Stauffer and Soskis, *The Battle Hymn*, 44–46, 313n7, 314n8. According to the *Oxford English Dictionary*, in the 1850s "bummer" referred to an idler or loafer (from the German *bummler*), but it also referred to someone who left his assigned task for another, such as a soldier who went on the prowl for food. After the Civil War, "bummer" became associated with vagrancy (from "bum"), and beginning in the 1960s "bummer" referred to an unpleasant experience, especially one induced by a hallucinatory drug or more generally a disappointment or failure.

3. On camp meetings, see Dickson D. Bruce, *And They All Sang Hallelujah: Plain-Folk Camp Meeting Religion, 1800–1845* (Knoxville: University of Tennessee Press, 1974); Christine Leigh Heyrman, *Southern Cross: The Beginnings of the Bible Belt* (New York: Knopf, 1997); Ellen Jane Lorenz, *Glory, Hallelujah! The Story of the Campmeeting Spiritual* (Nashville, Tenn.: Abingdon, 1980); Charles A. Johnson, "The Frontier Camp Meeting: Contemporary and Historical Appraisals, 1805–1840," *Mississippi Valley Historical Review* 37, no. 1 (1950): 91–110; Charles A. Johnson, "Camp Meeting Hymnody," *American Quarterly* 4, no. 2 (1952): 110–126; Stauffer and Soskis, *The Battle Hymn*, 17–21.

4. Stauffer and Soskis, *The Battle Hymn*, 17–22; Stith Mead, *A General Selection of the Newest and Most Admired Hymns & Spiritual Songs, Now in Use* (Richmond, Va.: Seaton Grantland, 1807), 2:80–81. A fragment of the "Say Brothers" hymn appears in 1806 as the last stanza of an elaborate folk hymn, "Almighty Love Inspire," published in an 1806 North Carolina hymnbook edited by David Mintz. This appearance in Mintz's 1806 hymnbook suggests that the "Say Brothers" hymn was already "orally current" in both states, to quote the folklorist George Pullen Jackson. See George Pullen Jackson, *White and Negro Spirituals: Their Life Span and Kinship* (Locust Valley, N.Y.: J. J. Augustin, 1943), 66; David B. Mintz, ed., *Collection of Hymns, and Spiritual Songs, Mostly New* (New Bern, N.C.: John M'Williams and Christopher D. Neale, 1806), 19–20.

5. Mead, *General Selection of the Newest and Most Admired Hymns*, 80–81; Stauffer and Soskis, *The Battle Hymn*, 23–25, 306n22.

6. Stauffer and Soskis, *The Battle Hymn*, 25; Heyrman, *Southern Cross*, 4; Frederick Douglass, *My Bondage and My Freedom*, ed. John Stauffer (New York: Modern Library, 2003), 159–160.

7. Stauffer and Soskis, *The Battle Hymn*, 26–27; Jackson, *White and Negro Spirituals*, 119–123; Bruce, *And They All Sang Hallelujah*, 56–57; Johnson, "Frontier Camp Meeting," 98–99.

8. John Stauffer and Zoe Trodd, eds., *The Tribunal: Responses to John Brown and the Harpers Ferry Raid* (Cambridge, Mass.: Harvard University Press, 2012), 126–127; Henry Greenleaf Pearson, *The Life of John A. Andrew, Governor of Massachusetts, 1861–1865* (Boston: Houghton, Mifflin and Company, 1904), 1:95–101; James Brewer Stewart, "John Albion Andrew," *American National Biography*, http://www.anb.org.ezpprod1.hul.harvard.edu/articles/04/04-00022.html?a=1&n;eqandrew%20john&d=10&ss=0&q=6.

9. Stauffer and Soskis, *The Battle Hymn*, 47–53; *New York Times* (July 25, 1861); *New York Tribune* (July 28, 1861).

10. James Oakes, *Freedom National: The Destruction of Slavery in the United States, 1861–1865* (New York: Norton, 2013), chap. 4.

11. Stauffer and Soskis, *The Battle Hymn*, 74–81; *The Centenary Edition of the Works of Nathaniel Hawthorne*, vol. 17: *The Letters, 1853–1856*, ed. Thomas Woodson et al. (Columbus: Ohio State University Press, 1987), 177.

When Sumner met Brown, he was recovering from his vicious caning on the Senate floor by the South Carolinian Preston Brooks. As they discussed the caning, Sumner told Brown: "The coat I had on at the time is hanging in that closet. Its collar is stiff with blood." Brown went to the closet, took out the coat, "and looked at it as a devotee would contemplate the relic of a saint." James Freeman Clarke, *Anti-Slavery Days* (1883; repr., New York: Negro Universities Press, 1970), 153–154. See also Clarke's earlier and almost identical but a bit wordier description in *Memorial and Biographical Sketches* (Boston: Houghton, Osgood and Company, 1878), 101–102.

12. Stauffer and Soskis, *The Battle Hymn*, 82–83; Julia Ward Howe, *Reminiscences, 1819–1899* (Boston: Houghton, Mifflin and Company, 1899), 274–275.

13. Stauffer and Soskis, *The Battle Hymn*, 83–84; Howe, *Reminiscences*, 275; Harriet Beecher Stowe, "The Author's Introduction," in *The Writings of Harriet Beecher Stowe*, vol. 1: *Uncle Tom's Cabin* (Boston: Houghton, Mifflin and the Riverside Press, 1896), xxxv–xxxvi; Annie Fields, ed., *Life and Letters of Harriet Beecher Stowe* (Boston: Houghton, Mifflin and Company, 1897), 377; Joan Hedrick, "Harriet Beecher Stowe's Prophetic Engine," *Huffington Post* (January 15, 2013): http://www.huffingtonpost.com/joan-d-hedrick/harriet-beecher-stowes-prophetic-engine_b_2481986.html.

14. Stauffer and Soskis, *The Battle Hymn*, 83–84; Ernest Lee Tuveson, *Redeemer Nation: The Idea of America's Millennial Role* (Chicago: University of Chicago Press, 1968), 187–214; James H. Moorhead, *American Apocalypse:*

Yankee Protestants and the Civil War, 1860–1869 (New Haven, Conn.: Yale University Press, 1978), 79–81. Frederick Douglass borrowed from Revelation 12 to define the war as an "apocalyptic vision," a battle of "Michael and his angels" against "the infernal host of bad passions." See Douglass, "The American Apocalypse," in *The Frederick Douglass Papers*, ed. John W. Blassingame (New Haven, Conn.: Yale University Press, 1985), 1:3:437 (quoted), also 529, 552.

15. Stauffer and Soskis, *The Battle Hymn*, 44, 53–59, 63–71; Henry A. Beers, "Literature and the Civil War," *Atlantic Monthly* 88, no. 530 (December 1901): 759–760; Fred Winslow Adams, "Our National Songs: 'Battle Hymn of the Republic,'" *Zion's Herald* (July 27, 1898): 938; Henry A. Beers, "Literature and the Civil War," *Atlantic Monthly* 88 (December 1901): 759–760; Christian McWhirter, *Battle Hymns: The Power and Popularity of Music in the Civil War* (Chapel Hill: University of North Carolina Press, 2012), 43–44.

16. Stauffer and Soskis, *The Battle Hymn*, 44; Oliver Wendell Holmes, "Lecture—1865," quoted in McWhirter, *Battle Hymns*, 46–47.

17. Stauffer and Soskis, *The Battle Hymn*, 59–62; "'Marching On!': The Fifty-Fifth Massachusetts Colored Regiment Singing John Brown's March in the Streets of Charleston," *Harper's Weekly* (March 18, 1865); Henry Mayer, *All on Fire: William Lloyd Garrison and the Abolition of Slavery* (New York: St. Martin's, 1998), 577.

18. Stauffer and Soskis, *The Battle Hymn*, 92–93; Frank Milton Bristol, *The Life of Chaplain McCabe: Bishop of the Methodist Episcopal Church* (New York: Fleming H. Revell, 1908), 95, 188, 197, 135; William E. Ross, "The Singing Chaplain: Bishop Charles Cardwell McCabe and the Popularization of the 'Battle Hymn of the Republic,'" *Methodist History* 28, no. 1 (1989): 22–32.

19. Stauffer and Soskis, *The Battle Hymn*, 93–94; Bristol, *Life of Chaplain McCabe*, 202, 198–200; George Stuart to Abraham Lincoln (June 18, 1864), in Abraham Lincoln Papers, Library of Congress. Since McCabe recorded the scene of Lincoln's making a vocal request just a few days after the meeting, and others in attendance recalled the scene similarly, it seems likely that Lincoln called for McCabe to sing the "Battle Hymn" again.

20. Stauffer and Soskis, *The Battle Hymn*, 106–139, 144–145.

21. Ibid., 140–143, 145–161, 165–175.

22. Ibid., 11, 162–164.

23. Ibid., 176–207; Melvyn Dubofsky, *We Shall Be All: A History of the Industrial Workers of the World* (Chicago: Quadrangle, 1969), 160 (quoted); "Solidarity Forever," in *I.W.W. Songs: To Fan the Flames of Discontent* ["Little Red Songbook"] (Chicago: Industrial Workers of the World, 1923), 25–26

(quoted); Upton Sinclair, *The Jungle*, ed. Clare Virginia Eby (1906; repr., New York: Norton, 203), 299 (quoted).

24. Stauffer and Soskis, *The Battle Hymn*, 208–212.

25. Ibid., 209–211.

26. Ibid., 227–234; Cliff Barrows, Interview with authors (quoted); Graham, *Hour of Decision*, Billy Graham Center Archives, Wheaton College. Hereafter cited as BGCA.

27. Stauffer and Soskis, *The Battle Hymn*, 128–129; William Martin, *A Prophet with Honor: The Billy Graham Story* (New York: William Morrow, 1991), 52–62; Barrows, interview with authors. Graham's decision to headquarter his Billy Graham Evangelical Association in Minneapolis also reflected his ambition to become known as a national and international revivalist rather than a Southern preacher.

28. Stauffer and Soskis, *The Battle Hymn*, 255–258, 262–271. By standing as a witness to God's justice, King reconciled the song's rhetoric of violence with his dedication to peace.

29. Ibid., 225–226; "Adds to Sunday's 'Hell List,'" *New York Times* (May 7, 1917); Roger A. Bruns, *Preacher: Billy Sunday and Big-Time American Evangelism* (New York: Norton, 1992), 266 (quoted); William G. McLoughlin, *Billy Sunday Was His Real Name* (Chicago: University of Chicago Press, 1955), 276–283.

30. Stauffer and Soskis, *The Battle Hymn*, 282–292.

31. Ibid., 3–8.

32. Some scholars have argued that there is no biblical foundation for Howe's reference to lilies where Christ was born. But Matthew 6:28–30 offers just such a connection, as Francis F. Bodkin noted: "Consider the lilies of the field, how they grow; they toil not, neither do they spin: . . . Wherefore, if God so clothe the grass of the field, which today is, and tomorrow is cast into the oven, shall He not much more clothe you, O ye of little faith?" God clothes and watches over His children as they grow. Francis S. Bodkin, e-mail to the author (December 8, 2013). Edmund Wilson is the best-known critic who challenged Howe's reference to Jesus' birth "in the beauty of the lilies." See Edmund Wilson, *Patriotic Gore: Studies in the Literature of the American Civil War* (1962; repr., New York: Norton, 1994), 96.

33. On American civil religion see especially Robert N. Bellah, "Civil Religion in America," *Daedalus* 96 (Winter 1967): 1–21; and Robert N. Bellah, *The Broken Covenant: American Civil Religion in Time of Trial*, 2nd ed. (Chicago: University of Chicago Press, 1992).

34. Paul Boyer, *When Time Shall Be No More: Prophecy Belief in Modern American Culture* (Cambridge, Mass.: Harvard University Press, 1992), 1–18.

The Emancipation of Abraham Lincoln

Eric Foner

1. Eric Foner, *The Fiery Trial: Abraham Lincoln and American Slavery* (New York: Norton, 2010).

2. Lincoln Speech at Springfield (June 26, 1857), in *The Collected Works of Abraham Lincoln*, 8 vols., ed. Roy P. Basler (New Brunswick, N.J.: Rutgers University Press, 1953–1955), 2: 405. Hereafter *Collected Works*.

3. Lincoln Speech at Chicago (July 10, 1858), ibid., 2:492.

4. Lincoln Speech at Peoria (October 16, 1854), ibid., 2:252, 3:313.

5. Lincoln's Reply to Douglas at Alton (October 15, 1858), ibid., 2:320.

6. Peoria speech, ibid., 2:255–256.

7. Lincoln to James N. Brown (October 18, 1858), ibid., 3:327.

8. From the debate at Charleston (September 18, 1858), ibid., 3:145.

9. Eric Foner, "Lincoln and Colonization," in *Our Lincoln: New Perspectives on Lincoln and His World*, ed. Eric Foner (New York: Norton, 2008), 135–166.

10. James F. Hopkins, ed., *Papers of Henry Clay*, 10 vols. (Lexington: University of Kentucky Press, 1959–1991), 10:844–846.

11. John C. Miller, *Wolf by the Ears: Thomas Jefferson and Slavery* (New York: Norton, 1977), 207.

12. Peoria Speech, *Collected Works*, 2:256.

13. Ibid., 2:453, 2:461, 3:18; Hopkins, ed., *Papers of Henry Clay*, 10:844–846.

14. Foner, *The Fiery Trial*, 181–184, 212–213.

15. Speech by Lincoln (August 14, 1862), in *Collected Works*, 5:371–375.

16. Ibid., 5:337.

17. Ibid., 5:537; Foner, *The Fiery Trial*, 237.

18. Final Emancipation Proclamation (January 1, 1863), in *Collected Works*, 6:30.

19. Ibid., 6:30; Foner, *The Fiery Trial*, 219.

20. Karl Marx and Frederick Engels, *The Civil War in the United States*, 3rd ed., ed. Richard Enmale (New York: International Publishers, 1961), 200.

21. Lincoln interview with Alexander W. Randall and Joseph T. Mills (August 19, 1864), *Collected Works*, 7:507.

22. Ibid., 8:403.

23. Ibid., 8:332–333.

Lincoln and the Struggle to End Slavery

Richard Striner

1. The author's overall interpretation of the Civil War and Lincoln is presented—and documented—in Richard Striner, *Father Abraham Lincoln's Relentless Struggle to End Slavery* (New York: Oxford University Press, 2006).

2. Lincoln, "Speech at Peoria, Illinois" (October 16, 1854), in *The Collected Works of Abraham Lincoln*, 8 vols., ed. Roy P. Basler (New Brunswick, N.J.: Rutgers University Press, 1953), 2:265. Hereafter cited as *Collected Works*.

3. Lincoln to Joshua F. Speed (August 24, 1855), in ibid., 2:320–322.

4. Lincoln, "Speech at Chicago, Illinois" (July 10, 1858), in ibid., 2:501.

5. Lincoln, "Notes for Speeches at Columbus and Cincinnati, Ohio" (September 16, 17, 1859), in ibid., 3:431–432.

6. Lincoln, "Speech at Columbus, Ohio" (September 16, 1859), in ibid., 3:423–424.

7. Stephen A. Douglas, "Mr. Douglas's Speech," in "First Debate with Stephen A. Douglas at Ottawa, Illinois" (August 21, 1858), in ibid., 3:9.

8. Lincoln, "Mr. Lincoln's Reply," in ibid., 3:16.

9. Stephen A. Douglas, "Senator Douglas's Reply," in "Sixth Debate with Stephen A. Douglas at Quincy, Illinois" (October 13, 1858), in ibid., 3:261.

10. Lincoln, "Speech at Springfield, Illinois" (July 17, 1858), in ibid., 2:519–520.

11. Lincoln, "Speech at Chicago, Illinois" (July 10, 1858), in ibid., 2:500–501.

12. Moncure Daniel Conway, *Autobiography, Memories, and Experiences* (New York: Houghton Mifflin Company, 1904), 1:345–346.

13. Lincoln to Nathaniel Banks (December 24, 1863), in *Collected Works*, 7:90.

14. Lincoln to James C. Conkling (August 26, 1863), in ibid., 6:406–410.

15. See Frederick Douglass, *Life and Times of Frederick Douglass, Written by Himself* (Hartford, Conn.: Park, 1881; facsimile ed., Secaucus, N.J.: Citadel, 1983), 363–364.

16. See Lincoln to Michael Hahn (March 13, 1864), in *Collected Works*, 7:243.

17. See Lincoln, "To the Senate and House of Representatives" (February 5, 1865), in ibid., 8:260.

18. Lincoln, "Last Public Address" (April 11, 1865), in ibid., 8:399–405.

19. Ibid.

20. Frederick Douglass, "Draft of Speech" (June 1, 1865), Frederick Douglass Papers, Library of Congress.

Lincoln's Emancipation Proclamation: A Propaganda Tool for the Enemy?

Amanda Foreman

1. Charles Francis Adams to Charles Francis Adams Jr. (June 21, 1861), in *A Cycle of Adams Letters*, ed. Worthington Chauncey Ford (Boston: Houghton Mifflin, 1920), 1:13–15.

2. Yancey to R. Chapman (July 3, 1861), William L. Yancey Papers, Alabama Department of Archives and History.

3. *The Economist* (February 2, 1861). "But far more inflammatory had been Seward's recent note, sent to all foreign governments, asking them to refuse asylum to escaped slaves." *Englishwoman's Journal* (June 1861).

4. Yancey, Rost, and Dudley Mann to Toombs (July 15, 1861), NOR, ser. 2, vol. 3, 202.

5. Yancey to R. Chapman (July 3, 1861), William L. Yancey Papers.

6. Henry Adams to Charles Francis Adams Jr. (October 25, 1861), in *A Cycle of Adams Letters*, 1:61–63.

7. W. D. Jones, "Blyden, Gladstone, and the War," *Journal of Negro History* 49 (1964): 58n.

8. Ibid., 58. Blyden had recently returned from a diplomatic mission to the United States, where he was subjected to the usual treatment meted out to free blacks, such as being denied the right to ride on public buses or eat in white-owned restaurants. He was particularly upset at being denied entry to the House of Representatives. There was no such bar to the Houses of Parliament, which surprised some Northerners. Benjamin Moran laughed at Charles Wilson's annoyance at having to sit beside "the negro representative from Hayti." On February 6 he wrote in his diary: "From what I have been told the black exhibited a good deal better manners than did my fellow secretary. For all his 'black republicanism,' he clearly indicated by his uneasiness a decided antipathy to 'the nigger.'"

9. George Thompson to William Lloyd Garrison (December 25, 1862), in Clare Taylor, *British and American Abolitionists: An Episode in Transatlantic Understanding* (Edinburgh: Edinburgh University Press, 1974), 491.

10. Howard Jones, *Blue and Gray Diplomacy* (Chapel Hill: University of North Carolina Press, 2009), 232.

11. London *Times* (October 7, 1862). Even Liberal newspapers were shocked. The *Morning Advertiser* remarked on October 6: "We can give no credit to President Lincoln . . . the motive was not any abhorrence of Slavery in itself,

but a sordid, selfish motive, nor can we approve the means to which he is prepared to resort." For Britain, the atrocities committed in the Indian Mutiny were still fresh memories. His suggestion that Lincoln was trying to engineer similar mayhem and bloodshed in the South was enough to stir the public against him.

12. Dudley Mann to Judah Benjamin (October 7, 1862), NOR, ser. 2, vol. 3, 549–551.

13. John Morley, *The Life of William Ewart Gladstone: 1809–1872*, 2 vols. (London, 1908), 2:536; Henry Steele Commager, ed., *The Civil War Archive* (New York: Black Dog & Leventhal, 2000), 62–63. The quotation in the footnote below is from *Harper's Magazine* 54 (1877): 111.

14. Virginia Mason, *The Public Life and Diplomatic Correspondence of James M. Mason* (New York, 1906), 387–392.

15. *The Journal of Benjamin Moran, 1857–1865*, 2 vols., ed. Sarah Agnes Wallace and Frances Elma Gillespie (Chicago: University of Chicago Press, 1948–1949), 2:1106 (January 14, 1863).

16. Ibid., 2:1110 (January 21, 1863).

17. Herbert to Jack (January 28, 1863), British Library Add. MS 415670, ff. 242–243.

18. Philip Van Doren Stern, *When the Guns Roared: World Aspects of the American Civil War* (New York: Doubleday, 1965), 177.

19. Hotze to Benjamin (October 24, 1862), NOR, ser. 2, vol. 3, 565–567.

20. James Spence to Mason (June 16, 1863), Library of Congress, Mason Papers.

21. Warren F. Spencer, *The Confederate Navy in Europe* (Tuscaloosa: University of Alabama Press, 1983), 135–136 (January 21, 1863; January 20, 1863).

22. Mason to Benjamin (March 26, 1865), in *A Compilation of the Messages and Papers of the Confederacy*, 2 vols. (Nashville, Tenn., 1905), 2:717.

The Gettysburg Campaign and the New York City Draft Riots: Conspiracy or Coincidence?

Barnet Schecter

1. New York *Daily News* (July 13, 1863); Barnet Schecter, *The Devil's Own Work* (New York: Walker, 2005), 251; Eric Foner, *Reconstruction* (New York: Perennial, 1989), 32.

2. Adrian Cook, *Armies of the Streets* (Lexington: University of Kentucky Press, 1974), 194–198; *Report of the Committee of Merchants for the Relief of Colored People*, 7; *Christian Recorder* (August 1, 1863).

3. Robert E. Lee, *The Wartime Papers of Robert E. Lee* (Boston: Little, Brown, 1961), 507–509; *New York Daily Tribune* (June 30, July 7, 1863); *New York Times* (July 16, 1863).

4. William Osborn Stoddard, *Volcano Under the City* (New York: Fords, Howard and Hulbert, 1887), 33.

5. Oscar Kinchen, *Confederate Operations* (North Quincy, Mass.: Christopher, 1970), 20–21; John William Headley, *Confederate Operations* (New York: Neale, 1906), 133; Philip Van Doren Stern, *Secret Missions* (New York: Bonanza, 1990), 155.

6. *New York Daily Tribune* (July 7, 1863).

7. *New York Times* (July 16, 1863).

8. Edmund Ruffin, *Diary*, 3 vols. (Baton Rouge: Louisiana State University Press, 1989), 3:70; Edmund Ruffin, *Anticipations of the Future* (Richmond: J. W. Randolph, 1861), 285–312.

9. *Detroit Free Press* (March 5, 1863); New York *World* (March 13, 1863); *New York Daily Tribune* (July 14–18, 1863).

10. New York *Herald* (July 12, 1863); James R. Gilmore, *Personal Recollections* (Boston: L. C. Page, 1898), 168–169; Joel Tyler Headley, *Great Riots of New York* (New York: Dover, 1971), 149; *World* (July 14, 1863).

11. *Evening Post* (July 13, 1863); Headley, *Great Riots*, 152–153, 165; *Times* (July 14, 1863); Stoddard, *Volcano Under the City*, 41–43, 52–53.

12. Foner, *Reconstruction*, 32.

13. Association for the Benefit of Colored Orphans, *Twenty-Seventh Annual Report* (New York, 1864), 5–14; Arthur Schlesinger Jr. *The Age of Jackson* (Old Saybrook, Conn.: Konecky and Konecky, 1971), 424–426.

14. Association for the Benefit of Colored Orphans, *Twenty-Seventh Annual Report*, 5–14; *Times* (July 14, 1863), quoted in *African-American History in the Press* (New York: Thomson Gale, 1996), 1:302; *Times* (July 16, 1863).

15. *Harper's Weekly* (August 1, 1863): 494; reprinted in *African-American History in the Press*, 1:302.

16. Maritcha Lyons, "Memories of Yesterdays," Williamson Collection, Schomburg Center, New York Public Library.

17. *World* (July 16, 1863); *Times* (July 16, 1863).

18. "Introduction" by James McCune Smith in Henry Highland Garnet, *A Memorial Discourse* (Philadelphia: J. M. Wilson, 1865), 56; *Proceedings of the National Convention of Colored Men* (Boston: G. C. Avery, 1864), 19.

19. James McPherson, *Ordeal by Fire* (New York: Knopf, 1982), 32–33, 498; Noel Ignatiev, *How the Irish Became White* (New York, Routledge, 1995), 100; Jerome Mushkat, *Fernando Wood* (Kent, Ohio: Kent State University Press, 1990),

922–923; David Quigley, "Southern Slavery in a Free City: Economy, Politics, and Culture," in Ira Berlin, ed., *Slavery in New York* (New York: New Press and New-York Historical Society, 2005), 263.

20. Edward O'Donnell, *1001 Things Everyone Should Know About Irish American History* (New York: Broadway Books, 2002), 128, 204–208.

21. Edward Spann, *Gotham at War* (Wilmington, Del.: Scholarly Resources, 2002), 60.

22. Ibid., 114–119; Seymour's speech in *Daily News* (July 6, 1863); *World* (June 9, 1863).

23. *World* (July 15, 1863).

24. *Times* (July 15, 1863).

25. Iver Bernstein, *The New York City Draft Riots* (New York: Oxford, 1990), 55–56; James Geary, *We Need Men* (Dekalb: Northern Illinois University Press, 1991), 78.

26. Foner, *Reconstruction*, xxv, 585.

Lincoln and New York: A Fraught Relationship

Harold Holzer

1. Harold Holzer, *Lincoln at Cooper Union* (New York: Simon & Schuster, 2005).

2. Grace Bedell to Lincoln (October 15, 1860), in *The Collected Works of Abraham Lincoln*, ed. Roy P. Basler, 8 vols. (New Brunswick, N.J.: Rutgers University Press, 1953–1955), 4:130. Hereafter *Collected Works*.

3. Ibid., 4:129.

4. Speech at Westfield, New York (February 16, 1861), in ibid., 4:219.

5. *Philadelphia Inquirer* (February 20, 1861).

6. *Collected Works*, 4:219–221.

7. Ibid., 4:222–224; *Schenectady Evening Star* (February 19, 1861).

8. Harold G. and Oswald Garrison Villard, eds., *Lincoln on the Eve of '61: A Journalist's Story by Henry Villard* (New York: Knopf, 1941), 92–93; William Kennedy, *O Albany* (New York: Viking, 1983), 11; *New York Herald* (February 19, 1861).

9. Reply to a welcome by New York Governor Edwin D. Morgan, Albany, New York (February 18, 1861), *Collected Works*, 4:225.

10. Address to the New York State Legislature, Albany (February 18, 1861), in ibid., 4:226.

11. Lincoln's visit to New York is described in Harold Holzer, *Lincoln President-Elect* (New York: Simon & Schuster, 2008), 347–350.

12. Walt Whitman, *Specimen Days*, orig. pub. 1883, *Memoranda During the War*, ed. Peter Coviello (New York: Oxford University Press, 2004), 39–40; Reply to New York City Mayor Fernando Wood, City Hall (February 20, 1861), in *Collected Works*, 4:233. Quoted in Harold Holzer, *State of the Union: New York and the Civil War* (New York: Fordham University Press, 2002), 8.

13. From an address to the New York State Legislature (February 18, 1861), in *Collected Works*, 4:226.

14. Letter to George Opdyke and others (December 2, 1863), in *Collected Works*, 7:32.

15. Lincoln to Erastus Corning and others (June 12, 1863), in *Collected Works*, 6:266.

16. Corning and others to Lincoln (June 30, 1863), Abraham Lincoln Papers, Library Congress. Lincoln to Corning and others (June 12, 1863), in *Collected Works*, 6:266.

17. For the complete history of the Albany Sanitary Fair and Lincoln's donation, see Harold Holzer, *Emancipating Lincoln: The Emancipation Proclamation in Text, Context, and Memory* (Cambridge, Mass.: Harvard University Press, 2012), 113–119.

18. Ibid.

19. Ibid.

20. George Chopat to Lincoln (August 24, 1864), Lincoln Papers.

21. Isaac M. Schermerhorn to Lincoln (September 9, 1864) (asking for a reply to his August invitation to Buffalo), in *Collected Works*, 7:546; reply to Schermerhorn (meant to be read aloud in Buffalo) (September 12, 1864), in *Collected Works*, 8:1–2.

22. Cover letter to Isaac Schermerhorn (September 12, 1864), in *Collected Works*, 8:2.

23. Lincoln to Franklin A. Conkling and others, June 3 1864, in *Collected Works*, 7:374.

24. Patrick McCarty and others to Lincoln (October 16, 1863), Lincoln Papers.

25. *New York Times* (November 30, 1864).

26. Sarah T. Barnes to Lincoln (February 7, 1865), Lincoln Papers. Mrs. Barnes enclosed with her heartfelt letter a newspaper clipping reporting that Lincoln had become a Christian when he "went to Gettysburg, and looked upon the graves of our dead heroes who had fallen in defense of their country."

27. The floral tribute is visible on the only photograph of Lincoln's body; see Charles Hamilton and Lloyd Ostendorf, *Lincoln in Photographs: An Album of Every Known Pose* (Norman, Oklahoma: University of Oklahoma Press, 1963), 235. The story of "George Washington Irving Wellington Bishop" and his "AL"

floral arrangement is told in Dorothy Meserve Kunhardt and Philip B. Kunhardt Jr., *Twenty Days . . .* (New York: Harper & Row, 1965), 166.

28. Kunhardt and Kunhardt, *Twenty Days . . .* 172–173.

29. *New York Herald* (April 26, 1865).

Lincoln and McClellan: A Reappraisal

John C. Waugh

1. John Bartlett, *Familiar Quotations: A Collection of Passages, Phrases, and Proverbs Traced to Their Sources in Ancient and Modern Literature*, ed. Justin Kaplin, 16th ed. (Boston: Little, Brown, 1992), 462.

2. William Howard Russell, *My Diary North and South*, ed. Eugene H. Berwanger (Baton Rouge: Louisiana State University Press, 2001), 288.

3. Ibid.; James Russell Lowell, "General McClellan's Report," *North American Review* 98 (April 1864): 551–552.

4. George B. McClellan, *The Civil War Papers of George B. McClellan: Selected Correspondence, 1860–1865*, ed. Stephen W. Sears (New York: Ticknor & Fields, 1989), 71.

5. Ibid., 82, 70.

6. A memorandum from McClellan to Lincoln embodying these statements is in ibid., 71–75.

7. U.S. War Department, *The War of the Rebellion: A Compilation of the Official Records of the Union and Confederate Armies*, 70 vols. in 128 parts (1880; repr., Harrisburg, Penn.: Historical Times, 1985), ser. 1, vol. 11, pt. 3, p. 3; ser. 1, vol. 11, pt. 3, p. 4. Hereafter cited as OR.

8. Andre Maurois, "A Princely Service," *American Heritage* 17 (April 1966): 58.

9. Stephen W. Sears, *George B. McClellan: The Young Napoleon* (New York: Ticknor & Fields, 1988), 56.

10. Ethan S. Rafuse, *McClellan's War: The Failure of Moderation in the Struggle for the Union* (Bloomington: Indiana University Press, 2005), 123; McClellan, Civil War Papers, 135, 136n, 515.

11. McClellan, *Civil War Papers*, 81.

12. John Hay, *Inside Lincoln's White House: The Complete Civil War Diary of John Hay*, ed. Michael Burlingame and John R. Turner Ettlinger (Carbondale: Southern Illinois University Press, 1997), 30.

13. Alexander K. McClure, *Lincoln's Yarns and Stories: A Complete Collection of the Funny and Witty Anecdotes That Made Abraham Lincoln Famous as America's Greatest Story Teller* (Chicago: John C. Winston, n.d.), 31.

14. Hay, *Inside Lincoln's White House*, 32.

15. William B. Franklin, "The First Great Crime of the War," in *The Annals of the War, Written by the Leading Participants North and South* (1878; repr., Dayton, Ohio: Morningside House, 1988), 76.

16. *Collected Works of Abraham Lincoln*, ed. Roy P. Basler, 8 vols. (New Brunswick, N.J.: Rutgers University Press, 1953), 5:185.

17. Frederick W. Seward, *Reminiscences of a War-Time Statesman and Diplomat, 1830–1915* (New York: G. P. Putnam's Sons, 1916), 205.

18. McClellan, *Civil War Papers*, 323.

19. These three opinions are in ibid., 113, 106, 135.

20. George Ticknor Curtis, *McClellan's Last Service to the Republic, Together with a Tribute to His Memory* (New York: D. Appleton, 1886), 96; William Ernest Smith, *The Francis Preston Blair Family in Politics*, 2 vols. (New York: Macmillan, 1933), 2:144.

21. John Russell Young, *Around the World with General Grant: A Narrative of the Visit of General U. S. Grant, Ex-President of the United States, to Various Countries in Europe, Asia, and Africa, in 1877, 1878, 1879*, 2 vols. (New York: American News Company, 1879), 216–217.

22. Curtis, *McClellan's Last Service to the Republic*, 126.

23. Thomas J. Rowland, *George B. McClellan and Civil War History: In the Shadow of Grant and Sherman* (Kent, Ohio: Kent University Press, 1998), 195–196, 196n.

24. William Starr Myers, *General George Brinton McClellan: A Study in Personality* (New York: D. Appleton, 1934), 21.

25. James B. Fry, "McClellan and His Mission," *Century Magazine* 48 (October 1894): 932; Francis A. Walker, *History of the Second Army Corps in the Army of the Potomac* (New York: Charles Scribner's Sons, 1886), 138.

26. David Hunter Strother, "Personal Recollections of the War, by a Virginian," *Harper's New Monthly Magazine* 36 (April 1868): 581; *Cincinnati Gazette* (August 11, 1862), in *Recollected Words of Abraham Lincoln*, ed. Don E. Fehrenbacher and Virginia Fehrenbacher (Stanford, Calif.: Stanford University Press, 1996), 10.

27. William Swinton, *Campaigns of the Army of the Potomac* (1866; repr., Secaucus, N.J.: Blue and Gray Press, 1988), 228; Charles Ellet Jr., *The Army of the Potomac and Its Mismanagement* (Washington, D.C.: L. Towers, 1861), 16.

Judging Lincoln as Judge

Frank J. Williams

1. Robert Travers [John Voelker], *Anatomy of a Murder* (New York: St. Martin's Griffin, 1958), 313–314. The author would like to thank Margaret Vellucci for her research assistance.

2. John J. Duff, *A. Lincoln: Prairie Lawyer* (New York: Bramhall House, 1960), 301.

3. David Herbert Donald, *Lincoln* (New York: Simon & Schuster, 1995), 387; Ronald C. White, *Lincoln's Greatest Speech: The Second Inaugural* (New York: Simon & Schuster, 2002), 55; Philip Henderson, *The Presidency Then and Now* (New York: Rowan & Littlefield, 2000), 149; John C. Waugh, *Reelecting Lincoln* (Cambridge, Mass: DaCapo, 2001), 78.

4. Brian Dirck, *Lincoln the Lawyer* (Urbana: University of Illinois Press, 2007), 96–97; Donald, *Lincoln*, 157.

5. Frank Williams, *Judging Lincoln* (Carbondale: Southern Illinois University Press, 2002), 36–40.

6. Duff, *A. Lincoln*, 188, 167, 297–298.

7. Ibid., 297–299. Duff notes that Lincoln's handwriting appeared on the docket for all three of these cases. In 1856, Lincoln sat for forty-six cases; in 1857 it was for 138 cases.

8. Dirck, *Lincoln the Lawyer*, 43, 146.

9. Ward H. Lamon, *The Life of Abraham Lincoln: From His Birth to His Inauguration as President* (Boston: James R. Osgood & Company, 1872), 317.

10. *The Collected Works of Abraham Lincoln*, ed. Roy P. Basler, 9 vols. (New Brunswick, N.J.: Rutgers University Press, 1952–55), 3:126. Hereafter *Collected Works*.

11. Lambert Tree, "Side-Lights on Lincoln," *Century Illustrated Monthly* (1911), 81:592.

12. Ibid.

13. Ida M. Tarbell, *Boy Scouts' Life of Lincoln* (New York: The Macmillan Co., 1921), 87.

14. Donald, *Lincoln*, 149; Duff, *A. Lincoln*, 298.

15. Duff, *A. Lincoln*, 348–350.

16. *Collected Works*, 2:81–82; Earl S. Miers, *Lincoln Day-by-Day: A Chronology, 1809–1865* (Washington: Lincoln Sesquicentennial Commission, 1960), 202, 231.

17. Ward H. Lamon, *Recollections of Abraham Lincoln* (1911), 16–17.

18. John P. Frank, *Lincoln as Lawyer* (Urbana: University of Illinois Press, 1961), 4; *Collected Works*, 2:81–82.

19. Dirck, *Lincoln the Lawyer*, 113; Mark E. Stiener, *An Honest Calling* (DeKalb: Northern Illinois University Press, 2006), 87.

20. Interview of Frank M. Johnson (March 16, 1991), Montgomery, Alabama.

21. Allen D. Spiegel, *Lincoln, Esquire: A Shrewd, Sophisticated Lawyer in His Time* (Macon: Mercer University Press, 2002), 267; Charles Hubbard, *Lincoln Reshapes the Presidency* (Macon: Mercer University Press, 203), 101, 107.

22. Hubbard, *Lincoln Reshapes the Presidency*, 108–110; Donald, *Lincoln*, 394.

The Madness of Mary Lincoln: A New Examination Based on the Discovery of Her Lost Insanity Letters

Jason Emerson

1. Robert Todd Lincoln Family Papers, Manuscripts Division, Library of Congress.

2. W. A. Evans, *Mrs. Abraham Lincoln: A Study of Her Personality and Her Influence on Abraham Lincoln* (New York: Knopf, 1932), 27; Ruth Painter Randall, *Mary Lincoln: Biography of a Marriage* (Boston: Little Brown, 1953), 434; Justin G. Turner and Linda Levitt Turner, *Mary Todd Lincoln: Her Life and Letters* (New York: Knopf, 1972), 612.

3. Frederic Towers to Katherine Helm, and Frederic Towers to Myra Pritchard (both October 14, 1927), box 94, Friends of Hildene, Inc., Manchester, Vermont.

4. Jane M. Friedman, *America's First Woman Lawyer: The Biography of Myra Bradwell* (Buffalo, N.Y.: Prometheus, 1993), 71–76.

5. The letters discovered in the Towers' attic are printed in Jason Emerson, *The Madness of Mary Lincoln* (Carbondale: Southern Illinois University Press, 2012), Appendix 1: "Unpublished Mary Todd Lincoln Letters," 159–178.

6. Jean Baker, *Mary Todd Lincoln: A Biography* (New York: Norton, 1987). For Baker's discussion of Mary's trial and confinement at Bellevue, see 315–350; Mark E. Neely and R. Gerald McMurtry, *The Insanity File: The Case of Mary Todd Lincoln* (Carbondale: Southern Illinois University Press, 1986); Charles B. Strozier, "The Psychology of Mary Todd Lincoln," *Psychohistory Review* 17 (1988): 15.

7. My main expert was Dr. James S. Brust MD, chair of the department of psychiatry and medical director of the psychiatric unit at San Pedro Peninsula Hospital, San Pedro, California, and coauthor of *Where Custer Fell: Photographs of the Little Bighorn Battlefield Then and Now*. I am indebted to Dr. Brust not only for his counsel but also for the contribution of his original essay, "The Psychiatric Illness of Mary Lincoln," which is his professional opinion of Mary's mental state and which was printed as Appendix 3 in my book, *The Madness of Mary Lincoln*, 185–190. I also consulted with Dr. Eugene Taylor PhD, Harvard Medical School lecturer in psychiatry, senior psychologist at Massachusetts General Hospital, and author of *Shadow Culture: Psychology and Spirituality in America*; and Dr. Dennis Nissim-Sabat PhD, professor of psychology, University of Mary Washington, Fredericksburg, Virginia.

8. Robert Lincoln to Ninian Edwards (December 21, 1875), Mary Todd Lincoln Insanity File, Lincoln Museum, Fort Wayne Indiana.

9. Mrs. John Todd Stuart, interview by *Chicago Tribune*, in "His Early Social Life and Marriage," *Chicago Tribune*, Patriotic Supplement 4, Abraham Lincoln (February 12, 1900): 14, located in Memoranda/Clippings Folder, Research Material, 1860–1942, Box 8, John G. Nicolay Papers, Manuscripts Division, Library of Congress; Octavia Roberts, *Lincoln in Illinois* (Boston: Houghton Mifflin, 1918), 67; Elizabeth Keckley, *Behind the Scenes; Or, Thirty Years a Slave and Four Years in the White House* (1868; repr. New York: Oxford University Press, 1988), 104–105.

10. Mary Lincoln to Sally Orne (December 12, 1869), in Turner and Turner, *Mary Todd Lincoln*, 534. Emily Helm noticed that Mary "has always a cheerful word and a smile for Mr. Lincoln, who seems thin and care-worn and seeing her sorrowful would add to his care." Diary of Emily Todd Helm (October 1863), quoted in Katherine Helm, *The True Story of Mary, Wife of Lincoln* (1928; repr. Manchester, Vt.: Friends of Hildene, 2005), 223, 226.

11. Mary Lincoln sanity trial testimony of Willis Danforth, printed in "Clouded Reason: Trial of Mrs. Abraham Lincoln for Insanity," *Chicago Tribune* (May 20, 1875): 1; "Mrs. Lincoln: The Widow of the Martyred President Adjudged Insane in County Court," *Chicago Inter Ocean* (May 20, 1875): 1.

12. Verdict of Jury Declaring Mary Lincoln Insane (May 19, 1875), Cook County Court Documents, Folder 33, Box 2, Mary Todd Lincoln Insanity File, Lincoln Museum, Fort Wayne, Indiana.

13. See Emerson, *The Madness of Mary Lincoln*, Appendix 1.

14. Mary Lincoln to Robert Lincoln (June 19, 1876), in Turner and Turner, *Mary Todd Lincoln*, 615–616; Mary Lincoln to Myra Bradwell, Springfield (June 18, 1876), Robert Todd Lincoln Family Papers, Library of Congress; also published in Emerson, *The Madness of Mary Lincoln*, 168–170.

Contributors

HAROLD HOLZER is Roger Hertog Fellow at the New-York Historical Society and one of the nation's leading authorities on Lincoln and the political culture of the Civil War era. He is chairman of the Abraham Lincoln Bicentennial Foundation and has written, co-written, or edited forty-seven books, most recently *Lincoln and the Power of the Press.*

CRAIG L. SYMONDS, co-editor, retired in 2005 after nearly thirty years as professor of history at the U.S. Naval Academy at Annapolis; he is now professor of history emeritus at the academy. He is the author or editor of more than twenty books on U.S. naval and military history, including *Lincoln and His Admirals*—for which he received the Lincoln Prize. He is a member of the Executive Committee of the Lincoln Forum.

FRANK J. WILLIAMS, co-editor, is founding chairman of the Lincoln Forum, longtime president of the Ulysses S. Grant Association, and a member of the U.S. Abraham Lincoln Bicentennial Foundation. He retired in 2009 after serving for eight years as chief justice of the Supreme Court of Rhode Island. His many books include *Judging Lincoln*, *Lincoln Lessons*, and *Lincoln as Hero*.

CATHERINE CLINTON is Gilbert Denman Chair of American History at the University of Texas in San Antonio and the author or editor of more than two dozen books, most recently *Mrs. Lincoln: A Life* and the Penguin Classics edition of Mary Chesnut's *Civil War Diary*. She serves on the scholarly advisory boards of Ford's Theatre and the Lincoln Cottage and Soldier's Home.

WILLIAM C. DAVIS has published more than fifty books on Southern history, was a consultant for the television series *Civil War Journal*, and served as executive director of the Virginia Center for Civil War Studies. A three-time winner of the Jefferson Davis Award for Confederate History, he sat on the Advisory Board of the Abraham Lincoln Bicentennial Commission.

JASON EMERSON, an independent historian and journalist, is the author or editor of multiple books about Abraham Lincoln and his family, including *The Madness of Mary Lincoln* and *Giant in the Shadows: The Life of Robert T. Lincoln*.

ERIC FONER is DeWitt Clinton Professor of History at Columbia University and the author of numerous books. *The Fiery Trial: Abraham Lincoln and American Slavery* (2010) was awarded the Pulitzer, Bancroft, and Lincoln prizes. His most recent book is *Gateway to Freedom: The Hidden History of the Underground Railroad*, published in 2015.

AMANDA FOREMAN is the award-winning historian and internationally bestselling author of *Georgiana, Duchess of Devonshire* and *A World on Fire: An Epic History of Two Nations Divided*. She is the recipient of the 1998 Whitbread Award for Biography and the 2011 Fletcher Pratt Award for Civil War History.

WILLIAM C. HARRIS is the author or editor of twelve books, including *With Charity for All: Lincoln and the Restoration of the Union*; *Lincoln's Rise to the Presidency*; *Lincoln and the Border States: Preserving the Union*, which won the Lincoln Prize in 2012; and *Lincoln and the Union Governors*, his most recent book.

MICHAEL J. KLINE is the author of *The Baltimore Plot: The First Conspiracy to Assassinate Abraham Lincoln* and is much in demand as a speaker on the topic of Lincoln's assassination. He graduated *cum laude* from the University of Pittsburgh School of Law, where he was editor-in-chief of the *Journal of Law and Commerce*.

JOHN F. MARSZALEK is executive director and managing editor of the Ulysses S. Grant Association's Ulysses S. Grant Presidential Library, Mississippi State University, where he retired as Giles Distinguished Professor of History in 2002. He is best known for his prize-winning biographies of William T. Sherman and Henry W. Halleck.

BARNET SCHECTER, an independent historian, is the author of *George Washington's America: A Biography Through His Maps*; *The Devil's Own Work: The Civil War Draft Riots and the Fight to Reconstruct America*; and *The Battle for New York: The City at the Heart of the American Revolution*.

WALTER STAHR is the author of biographies of John Jay and William Henry Seward. He practiced law for twenty-five years, including work for private firms in Asia and for the Securities and Exchange Commission in Washington, D.C. He is currently at work on a biography of Edwin Stanton.

JOHN STAUFFER is Professor of English, American Studies, and African American Studies at Harvard University. He is the author or editor of thirteen books and more than 100 articles, including *Giants: The Parallel Lives of Frederick Douglass and Abraham Lincoln* (2008) and *The Battle Hymn of the Republic: A Biography of the Song That Marches On* (2013), which was a Lincoln Prize finalist.

RICHARD STRINER, professor of history at Washington College, is an interdisciplinary scholar, writing from historical and policy perspectives on presidential leadership and economics. He has also published books on architecture and film.

JOHN C. WAUGH, in two earlier careers, was a journalist—a staff correspondent for and bureau chief of the *Christian Science Monitor*—and then served on the senior staffs of two national politicians, Vice President Nelson A. Rockefeller and Senator Jeff Bingaman of New Mexico. In 1989 he turned from writing about the present to writing about the past, since publishing twelve books on the Civil War era, four of them on Abraham Lincoln.

The Lincoln Forum
A History

THE LINCOLN FORUM—NOW IN ITS TWENTIETH YEAR—WAS formed when several historians and students of Abraham Lincoln and the Civil War met in Florida during one of Robert Maher's legendary Civil War Education Association conferences. Among those who attended this first meeting were, in addition to Bob, Frank J. Williams, Harold Holzer, David E. Long, the late Charles D. Platt, and Maynard Schrock. Here the idea was born to create an annual conference in the eastern United States for the presentation of papers and events relating to Abraham Lincoln and the Civil War—with Gettysburg, Pennsylvania, chosen as the venue. With the encouragement of Professor Gabor S. Boritt, director of the Civil War Institute at Gettysburg College, and his administrative assistant, Tina Grim, the Lincoln Forum held its first meeting on November 16–18, 1995. The forum has been meeting annually on these November dates ever since.

The founders believed these dates would be the most logical since November 19 is the anniversary of the Gettysburg Declaration, and three days of Lincoln focus would inevitably ensure more informed celebrations of the oration. The phenomenal growth of the Lincoln

Forum has suggested that this was a wise decision. The first two meetings were held at the Eisenhower Inn at the southern edge of the battlefield, with many subsequent meetings at the Holiday Inn–Gettysburg until the forum outgrew the Holiday Inn. For the last five years, the forum has been held in larger spaces at the nearby Wyndham, with many attendees witnessing the annual observation of the Gettysburg Address that follow in town.

The first conference attracted just under one hundred attendees, a number that remained steady until the move to the Wyndham. Attendance has tripled. Since the founders of the Lincoln Forum consider its membership an extended family, the board has decided to cap registration at three hundred, to ensure individual attention to every enrollee.

To serve better the membership, which now exceeds one thousand, the forum publishes two bulletins a year, maintains a website, and communicates through e-mails. In addition, the Lincoln Forum Board of Advisors enthusiastically supports scholarships for teacher and student attendees at forum symposia.

The Lincoln Forum has established two annual awards: the Richard Nelson Current Award of Achievement, for individuals who contribute significantly to the study of Abraham Lincoln and the Civil War; and the Wendy Allen Award, presented to institutions that have demonstrated excellence in promoting, through publications, events, and exhibits, the Civil War era. Past recipients of the Richard Nelson Current Award are the Gettysburg College professor Gabor Boritt (1996), C-SPAN's founding chairman Brian Lamb (1997), the scholar John Hope Franklin (1998), the former U.S. senator and Lincoln scholar Paul Simon (1999), the historian David Herbert Donald (2000), the historian Garry Wills (2001), the historian James M. McPherson (2002), the actor Sam Waterston (2003), the Ulysses S. Grant Association president and documentary editor John Y. Simon (2004), the sculptor John McClarey (2005), the biographer Doris Kearns Goodwin (2006), the novelist Jeff Shaara (2007), the documentary filmmaker Ken Burns (2008), Supreme Court Associate

Justice Sandra Day O'Connor (2009), the historian Mark E. Neely Jr. (2010), the incomparable battlefield guide Ed Bearss (2011), the historian Eric Foner (2012), and the author of the screenplay for the film *Lincoln*, Tony Kushner (2013). Honorary awards went to Professor Richard Nelson Current in 2000, to Chairman Frank Williams on the tenth anniversary of the forum in 2005, and to founding Forum Treasurer Charles D. Platt in 2006. The Wendy Allen Award has been presented to the Ford's Theatre Society in Washington, D.C.; the Lincoln-Douglas Society in Freeport, Illinois; the Ulysses S. Grant Association and Presidential Library at Mississippi State University in Starkville, Mississippi; and the Lincoln Shrine of Redlands, California.

This is the fifth volume of essays in the Lincoln Forum series from Fordham University Press.

The hope remains that the Lincoln Forum will continue to make significant contributions to the study of America's greatest political leader. His leadership characterizes the promise of democracy in the world.

Frank J. Williams
Founding Chairman, the Lincoln Forum

Index

The North's Civil War
Andrew L. Slap, *series editor*

John Y. Simon and Harold Holzer, eds., *The Lincoln Forum: Rediscovering Abraham Lincoln.*

Thomas F. Curran, *Soldiers of Peace: Civil War Pacifism and the Postwar Radical Peace Movement.*

Kyle S. Sinisi, *Sacred Debts: State Civil War Claims and American Federalism, 1861–1880.*

Russell L. Johnson, *Warriors into Workers: The Civil War and the Formation of Urban-Industrial Society in a Northern City.*

Peter J. Parish, *The North and the Nation in the Era of the Civil War.* Edited by Adam L. P. Smith and Susan-Mary Grant.

Patricia Richard, *Busy Hands: Images of the Family in the Northern Civil War Effort.*

Michael S. Green, *Freedom, Union, and Power: The Mind of the Republican Party During the Civil War.*

Christian G. Samito, ed., *Fear Was Not In Him: The Civil War Letters of Major General Francis S. Barlow, U.S.A.*

John S. Collier and Bonnie B. Collier, eds., *Yours for the Union: The Civil War Letters of John W. Chase, First Massachusetts Light Artillery.*

Grace Palladino, *Another Civil War: Labor, Capital, and the State in the Anthracite Regions of Pennsylvania, 1840–1868.*

Christian B. Keller, *Chancellorsville and the Germans: Nativism, Ethnicity, and Civil War Memory.*

Sidney George Fisher, *A Philadelphia Perspective: The Civil War Diary of Sidney George Fisher.* Edited and with a new Introduction by Jonathan W. White.

Robert M. Sandow, *Deserter Country: Civil War Opposition in the Pennsylvania Appalachians.*

Craig L. Symonds, ed., *Union Combined Operations in the Civil War.*

Harold Holzer, Craig L. Symonds, and Frank L. Williams, eds., *The Lincoln Assassination: Crime and Punishment, Myth and Memory.* A Lincoln Forum Book.

Earl F. Mulderink III, *New Bedford's Civil War.*

David G. Smith, *On the Edge of Freedom: The Fugitive Slave Issue in South Central Pennsylvania, 1820–1870.*

George Washington Williams, *A History of the Negro Troops in the War of the Rebellion, 1861–1865.* Introduction by John David Smith.

Randall M. Miller, ed., *Lincoln and Leadership: Military, Political, and Religious Decision Making.*

Andrew L. Slap and Michael Thomas Smith, eds., *This Distracted and Anarchical People: New Answers for Old Questions about the Civil War–Era North.*

Paul D. Moreno and Johnathan O'Neill, eds., *Constitutionalism in the Approach and Aftermath of the Civil War.*

Steve Longenecker, *Gettysburg Religion: Refinement, Diversity, and Race in the Antebellum and Civil War Border North.*

Harold Holzer, Craig L. Symonds, and Frank L. Williams, eds., *Exploring Lincoln: Great Historians Reappraise Our Greatest President.* A Lincoln Forum Book.